FOOD PRODUCTION AND FOOD PROBLEM IN INDIA

About the Author

Ali Mohammad *(b. 1946)* is a distinguished author and teacher. An M.A. and Ph.D. from the Aligarh Muslim University, his field of specialization is economic geography. As a senior Research Fellow at the Centre of Regional Development, Jawaharlal Nehru University, he has had many opportunities for handling various research projects on the problems of the Indian agricultural development. Dr. Mohammad has to his credit numerous research papers and many books including *Situation of Agriculture Food and Nutrition in Rural India* (Concept, 1978) and *Dynamics of Agricultural Development in India* (Concept, 1979).

Currently, Dr. Ali Mohammad is a Reader, Centre for West Asian Studies, Aligarh Muslim University, Aligarh.

FOOD PRODUCTION AND FOOD PROBLEM IN INDIA

ALI MOHAMMAD

CONCEPT PUBLISHING COMPANY PVT. LTD.
NEW DELHI-110059

ISBN : 978-81-7022-269-9

Edition 2021

Published and Printed by

Concept
Since 1974

Concept Publishing Company Pvt. Ltd.
A/15-16, Commercial Block, Mohan Garden,
New Delhi-110059 (INDIA)
T : +91 11 41101460
E : publishing@conceptpub.com, *W* : www.conceptpub.com

DEDICATED

TO

TARLOK SINGH

ICS (Retd.)

(Ex-Member Planning Commission)

Acknowledgements

The present work entitled *'Food Production and Food Problem in India'* is an outcome of a scheme on various themes and problems on India sponsored and financed by the United Nations Development Programme (UNDP) and Indian Council of World Affairs for which I am extremely grateful.

I am grateful to Mr. Tarlok Singh (Hon. Chairman of the Indian Council of World Affairs) who was keenly interested to complete the present work and provided all the required assistance especially in organising a number of meetings of the experts of all the South Asian Countries to chalk-out the outlines and chapter schemes of the present work.

I am also grateful to Mr. Rajpati Ram who assisted me in various ways especially working as a Research Associate in this project.

I wish to express my gratitude to all the officials and data source agencies especially the Directorate of Economics and Statistics, New Delhi.

Reader,
Centre of West Asian Studies,
Aligarh Muslim University,
U.P.

ALI MOHAMMAD

Contents

List of Figures

List of Tables

1

Introduction

In recent years we have been made more aware of the problems of agricultural development especially the self-sufficiency in agricultural production in general and food production in particular. The achievement of self-sufficiency implies that the level of domestic production is at least adequate to meet the basic needs of the existing population. Secondly, development of agriculture is of great importance for the overall economic development of a country like India where more than 80 per cent of the people directly or indirectly engaged and dependent on agriculture as well as its largest share in national income.

But this sector of economy have different dimensions of problems, i.e., explosive growth of population and slow rate of growth of food crops production as well as regional variations in levels and growth of foodgrains production. The most aggravating and serious situation in agricultural economy is an unequal distribution of agricultural land which causes wide spread poverty and food problem among a certain group of farmers which is known as disadvantageous group in rural community. This type of result can only be known through micro-level (village level) analysis. A district or state level analysis will be insufficient to find out the actual truth and nature of food problem in India. Therefore, a macro-level study should be supplemented with a micro-level analysis. Mostly, the studies regarding food problems have been correlated with low productivity and lower growth rates not with the population pressure which is the main indicator to judge the well being of the people. For example Kerala having the higher productivity per hectare than Rajasthan but the food problem exists in Kerala not in Rajasthan in terms of per head per day share in food production, i.e., 3000 calories for Rajasthan and only 1500 calories for Kerala. Therefore, the problem of food production and to achieve food-self-sufficiency level is a complex one. Though a number of investigations have been made sponsored by the Indian Council of Agricultural Research

(ICAR), National Council of Applied Economic Research (NCAER), Planning Commission, Ford Foundation Team, Food & Agricultural Ministry and other organizations and Research Institutes but still the problem is to be solved on this food-front. The major suggestions so far made were to increase the yield level, to accelerate the growth rate, to remove the regional imbalances, to minimise the gap between the small and big operational land holdings and change the existing cropping patterns etc. But some of these major suggestions are still not applicable. But at national level to achieve more additional production following suggestions were repeated by a number of agencies –

(i) Expansion of the cultivated area,
(ii) More frequent cropping of the existing arable land,
(iii) Increasing labour input,
(iv) Substitute higher yielding crops,
(v) The adoption of more intensive systems,
(vi) Change to a new system,
(vii) Adequate farm credit,
(viii) Adequate supply of essential production needs,
(ix) Prices incentives,
(x) Marketing arrangements,
(xi) Intensive educational, technical and farm management,
(xii) Village planning for increased production; and
(xiii) A public works department.

But still our food production problem, to achieve the first and basic goal for the well-being of the people, is unsolved and our agriculture presents the following problems –

(i) Low yield level, i.e., about Rs. 973 per hectare or 459 grams per head per day while the standard requirement is about 480 grams,
(ii) Low growth rate, keeping in view the growth of population,
(iii) Low yield level in a large number of districts, i.e., about 83 districts accounting for 32 per cent of its cultivated area contribute only 16 per cent of the total output; about 70 districts accounting for 27 per cent of the cultivated area have negative growth rate,
(iv) Low growth rate in a large number of districts, i.e. about 70

districts accounting for 27 per cent of the cultivated area here registered negative growth and 62 districts accounting for 21 per cent of the cultivated area have shown only 1.5 per cent growth rate,

(v) Low level of agricultural inputs, i.e., fertilizer consumption only 15 kg. per hectare while in Netherland, Belgium, New Zealand and Japan it is about 610 kg., 520 kg., 503 kg., and 354 kg., respectively. The improved seed utilization does not cover even 25 per cent of the cultivated area. Regarding irrigation only few states and districts have assured water supply. The chief factors behind the poor level of inputs in agriculture are (a) small size of land holding, (b) primitive techniques, (c) isolated character of economic system, (d) poverty and miserable condition of most of the farmers, (e) large-scale unemployment and underemployment resulting in a very cheap labour, (f) high rate and degree of tenancy, (g) cultural backwardness of the cultivators which prevent the use of new innovations; and (h) sluggish investment pattern by the surplus producing households,

(vi) Lack of institutional facilities and other security of our agricultural performance; and

(vii) Our agricultural land presents the symptoms of over-population, i.e., farm size and sub-division, fragmentations, declining farm income, landlessness, tendency, under employment, technological retardation and subsistance type of land use characteristics.

It may, however, be noted that unlike total agricultural output where the rate of growth slackened, the growth rate of foodgrains output improved from 2.45 per cent during the period 1955–65 to a rate of growth of 2.74 per cent per annum during the period 1965–75. This growth rate barely exceeds the growth rate of population of 2.24 per cent per annum. Consequently, despite the increase in domestic production, on an average 1.71 million metric tonnes of foodgrains had to be imported every year during 1970–75. Further, the per capita daily availability of foodgrains marginally declined from 458.6 grams during 1960–65 to 450.6 grams during 1970–75, in spite of the fact that the per capita income had registered an increase of 0.98 per cent per annum during this period. It is obvious that over the years there has existed a precarious balance between demand and supply of foodgrains and very wide yearly fluctuations have tended to aggregate the situation.

The Major Objectives of this Study

One of the basic objectives of this study is to seek regional co-operation for the well-being of the people of the South Asian Countries, such as the removal of the poverty, availability of the basic needs of the population, development of the better balanced national economies and use of the resources and potential of each country, growth of the national self-reliance and greater mutual help and interchange within the region. The mutual help and interchange can only be possible unless and until we have sound economy based on this natural resources and potentials. Agricultural resources potentiality of each country is different, one country may be richer in agricultural resource than the other, other may be richer in mineral, water and energy resources.

However, keeping in view the above mentioned problems, suggestions and developments in agriculture following objectives may be more appropriate and authentic to understand and solve the problems of Indian agriculture for mutual help, interchange and regional co-operation.

1. To evaluate the production potential of the country on the basis of environmental framework of Indian agriculture.
2. To estimate the levels of production of each food crop.
3. To estimate the growth level of each food crop.
4. To attempt to examine the relationships between output and input levels and between growth and input levels.
5. To find out the per head share of foodgrains and examine the productivity relationship with the positive and negative areas of food availability.
6. To regionalize the surplus, marginal and negative areas of food production per head per day.
7. An analysis of demand and supply of foodgrains at present and in future (A.D. 2000) will be made.
8. An analysis of food availability in terms of nutrition (quantitative and qualitative) will be done.
9. An analysis will be made to see the relative increase of population and food production.

Main Issues and Methodology

Looking at the behaviour of food prices and food output in relation to the demand for food may not seem very satisfactory in view of the low levels of nutrition among many millions of India's population. Another approach to the question is to ask how far present levels of nutrition fall below minimum acceptable standards and to use this as a measure of food shortage. Food is one of the few commodities for which it might make sense to talk about human needs or requirements rather than simply ask how much will be demanded at given prices.

In this regard (food problem) India is extremely poor by world standards and food is a major bottleneck to economic development of this country. This problem can only be solved through increased output of foodgrains both in surplus marginal and negative areas of food production. The increased output of foodgrains can be achieved through: (a) extensification in agriculture, (b) intensification in agriculture, (c) mechanization in agriculture; and (d) multiple cropping and cropping pattern. The possibilities of extensification is nil in agricultural land while intensification is possible only when other infrastructure facilities are available. On the other side we have enough natural and environmental opportunities and scope for multiple cropping. The basic problem is to exploit the agricultural resources through improving the investment policies and sources. After achieving the goal of all infrastructure facilities a proper allocation priority area and cropping pattern is to be decided for a balanced regional foodgrains production in terms of social justice and well-being of the people. Lastly, the central purpose of agricultural development planning and of the methods and decisions associated with it should be to help in bringing out a steady increase in agricultural productivity.

Methodology

Methodology in any study is generally conditioned by the objectives of the study. For the present problem a number of methods and analysis techniques are available and have been used in a number of studies on similar problems. For the present problem various methods for each chapter will be used. For instance to measure the growth and levels of productivity 'per cent annual growth rate' will be used. Firstly an average of three years data for one point of time will be taken to remove the weather abnormality agricultural production. Secondly, to measure the role of 'area increase and yield increase' in total production 'principal component' method can be used based on Minhas and Vaidyanathan studies. Thirdly, to measure the role of environmental and technological determinants 'rank correlation' techniques can be used and lastly, the role played by institutional factors can be measured by 'regression analysis'.

Some emphasis can also be given to the selection of sampled villages to measure the role of micro-variables as well as to find out the actual representative picture for the region as a whole.

Data Base: Sources and Limitations

For a successful planning and analysis of various problems in the decision of agricultural policies data are essential. Agricultural development is a complex problem, therefore, collection and source of data should be reliable and up-to-date to achieve accurate conclusions for decision-making and future planning. Without the knowledge and clear understanding of the comparability of data over time as well as pitfalls and the gaps one may lead to faulty results.

The collection of agricultural statistics in India during the British period was done for the purpose of land revenue. But due to the food problem and to reach the goal of self-sufficiency the pattern of the collection of agricultural statistics was changed and a Directorate of Economics and Statistics was set up in 1947 to co-ordinate and supervise the collection of statistics in different states. But the present structure of the Indian statistical system is decentralized. The collection and compilation of statistics is shared by the Central and as well as State Governments. The Central Statistical Organisation (CSO) is a co-ordinating agency between the centre and the states. The major statistical organisations are Central Statistical Organisation (CSO), New Delhi, Directorate of National Sample Survey (NSS), Department of Statistics (Reserve Bank of India), Statistics Division (Office of the Chief Controller of Imports & Exports), Office of the Director General of Commercial Intelligence and Statistics, Directorate of Economics and Statistics, Institute of Agricultural Research Statistics (IARS), Office of the Registrar General, Agricultural Census and Indian Council of Agricultural Research (ICAR). There are some non-governmental organisations which contributed in the progress of agricultural statistics in India such as Indian Statistical Institute (ISI), National Council of Applied Economic Research (NCAER), Indian Society of Agricultural Economics and Indian Institute of Management, and so on.

For the present problem data will be collected from various sources. Due to the limitation and nature of the present problem data will be collected from secondary sources. In order to know the changing pattern both in yield level and growth data for two points of time will be collected as well as to know the annual change data of each year will be collected. Data for the climatic variation will be collected from India Meteorological Department. Due to the unavailability of comparable data for two points of time for the states like Meghalaya, Manipur, Mizoram, Nagaland, Arunachal Pradesh and Himachal Pradesh data will be collected and related with one point of time.

However, all types of data needed for the present problem are available through secondary sources and a sufficient and an accurate understanding of the existing situation and problem in Indian agriculture can be developed.

Review of Earlier Studies and Classification

Studies based on similar problem, approach and methodology have been done by a number of social scientists either at state level or district level. Only a very few studies have been conducted at smaller unit than district due to a great variations in agricultural productivity within the district. But the approaches were not interdisciplinary. On some basic grounds approaches of a single disciplined scholar were quite different to each other. Generally the sociologists and economists were not interested and aware in giving due weightage to the geographical factors responsible for the high and low growth and low yield level of agricultural productivity. Similarly, the Geographers were quite ignorant to include the socio-economic variables responsible for the present state of Indian agriculture. The studies done so far can be broadiy grouped in the following manner–

1. Agricultural land use pattern.
2. Agro-climatology.
3. Water resources.

4. Cropping pattern.
5. Agricultural production and productivity, growth level in productivity – A regional variations.
6. Various inputs and agricultural development, determinants of agricultural development.
7. Agricultural development and planning.
8. Marketing and prices.
9. Co-operatives and credit in agriculture.
10. Technological inputs.
11. Land reform policies.
12. Food demand and supply etc.
13. Nutrition problem.

The studies[1] conducted so far are valuable in terms of methodology and objectives but the coverage is either a state or district not the country as a whole. No doubt there are some studies which have been conducted for the country as a whole but it could not cover all the aspects responsible for the present problem. However, it has been planned to produce such a study on food production and food problem which may cover all the related aspects of food production for the India as a whole.

The monograph is divided into ten chapters and an attempt has been made to analyse all the Chapters at state level to cover the various problems of food production, availability and future of it. The Chapter entitled trends in area, production and yield of foodgrains deals with the growth in area and yield broadly of cereals and pulses and it was held responsible that either area or yield increase is more responsible for the growth in production. It was analysed that in this decade yield is highly responsible for the increase in production. It is concluded that growth in production can be availed only through the increase in yield mostly from those regions and states where yield level is very low because of the unavailability of infrastructure facilities needed by the crops. Therefore, to increase the production the control over the environment is needed through the factors like technology and institutions in the weaker regions.

In the next Chapter a scheme was chalked out to discuss the role of various crops and their percentage share in the total production. For this purpose all the foodgrain crops were analysed in terms of area, yield and production growth. In this chapter all India picture was calculated to find out the per cent share of area and production in each yield categories and it was recorded that in high yield the small percentage of area contributed high per cent of production to the total production of India. In low yield categories percentage share of area is very high but its production share is very low. It is evident that still there is a big scope to increase the total production by improving the yield of these low yield categories.

Various factors like environmental, technological and institutions were analysed to find out the truth behind this existing situation. All the factors were held responsible for creating such a situation at varying degree. Firstly, the environmental factors were analysed with the help of various variables like erratic and variations in rainfall and drought affecting the agriculture and the country was divided in a number of regional physical complexes and yield level was correlated with these regions. In this chapter other factors like relief and soils were held lesser responsible than rainfall in affecting the yield and uncertainty in production. Among institutional factors it was realized that tenancy, land holding, per head agricultural income and agricultural labourers are more important in affecting the agricultural productivity. No doubt tenancy is one of the major problem in agricultural development even after various programmes and policies introduced by the government. A detailed analysis of the size of land holding and yield was made to find out the degree of relation through Gini Co-efficient method and it is concluded that the small size of land holdings are more important for agricultural development. The purpose of the analysis of per head agricultural income is to find out the impact of population and variations in all the states. It will give the clue to find out the aptitude of investment on the basis of low and high income States. The study of agricultural labourers was considered as an input for agricultural development and it was considered that in some regions agricultural labourers are important for the present level of production. In those States where agriculture is considerably well developed agricultural labourers are substituted by the technological factors. The technological factors like tractors, various irrigation machineries, fertilizers etc. were analysed in relation to yield and growth level and the concentration of these inputs in each yield categories was analysed. The concentration of these inputs was analysed in terms of percentage share of each state as well as amount of these inputs on one thousand hectare of cultivated area.

The chapter on food supply and food demand deals with the supply of food based on the total production and total population of the state. In this chapter growth of population and foodgrains is related to find out the imbalances as well as per head requirement of food is related with the standard requirement. The surplus and deficit situation is calculated on this basis.

In the chapter 'food availability in terms of surplus and deficit' an attempt has been made separately on cereals and pulses availability. In this connection positive and negative states are located. Due to the variations at state level in terms of surplus and deficit a district level calculation is needed to get more reliable picture and number of districts in each state should be counted. The amount of surplus and deficit in eac i state with percentage share to the total surplus of the country is calculated. Lastly a district level result is obtained after calculating the amount of surplus and deficit in each state.

In the Chapter 'Potentials for development and perspectives for A.D. 2000', results are obtained for various crops on the basis of various projections. In the last summary, conclusions and recommendations are included briefly and some basic issues are raised for future implications and planning.

REFERENCES

1. (a) Angrish, A.C., Some Aspects of Food Problem in India, *Congress Committee Economic Review*, Vol. 18, 1966.
   (b) Agarwal, N.C., *The Food Problem of India*, Bombay, 1961.
   (c) Aykroyd, W.R., The Nutritive Value of Indian Foods and the Planning of Satisfactory Diets, *Heath Bulletin*, No. 23, 1951.
   (d) Ali Mohammad, *Food and Nutrition in India*, Rajesh Publication, New Delhi, 1977.
   (e) Ali Mohammad, *Situation of Agriculture, Food and Nutrition in Rural India*, Concept Publishing Company, New Delhi, 1978.
   (f) Ali Mohammad, *Dynamics of Agricultural Development in India*, Concept Publishing Company, New Delhi, 1978.
   (g) Bhalla, G.S., *Performance of Indian Agriculture*, Sterling Publishing Company, New Delhi, 1979.
   (h) Bhalla, Shiela, Agricultural Growth—Role of Institutional and Infra-structural Factors, *Eco. & Pols. Weekly*, Vol. III, No. 45, November, 5-12-1977.
   (i) Bhatia, B.M., *India's Food Problem and Policy Since Independence*, Bombay, 1970.
   (j) Shafi, M., *Regional Imbalances in Agricultural Productivity of Uttar Pradesh*, Concept Publishing Co., New Delhi, 1984.
   (j) Dantwala, M.L., *India's Food Problem*, Bombay, 1951.
   (k) Gopalan, C., Major Nutritional Problem of India and South-East Asia,

Proceedings of Seventh International Geographical Congress, Vol. 3, 1966.

(l) Sukhatme, P.V., The World's Hunger and Future Needs in Food Supplies, *The Journal of the Royal Statistical Society*, Vol. 124, 1961, London.

(m) Sukhatme, P.V., Protein Strategy and Agricultural Development, *31st Annual Conference of the Indian Society of Agricultural Economics*, Banaras Hindu University, 1972.

(n) Sukhatme, P.V., Food and Nutrition Situation in India, Part II, *Indian Journal of Agricultural Economics*, Vol. 16, 1962.

(o) Sukhatme, P.V., *Feeding India's Growing Millions*, Asia Publishing House, 1965.

(p) Parikh, H., Statewise Growth in Agricultural Output— An Econometric Analysis, *Arthvijnana*, Vol. 8, March, 1966.

(q) Shetty; Agricultural Production Trends and Components, *Indian Journal of Agricultural Economics*, April, 1970.

(r) Prabhachander, J., Districtwise Measurement and de-composition of the Growth of Agricultural Output in Punjab during Post-Independent Period, *Indian Economic Review*, Vol. VI.

(s) Minhas, B.S., Growth and Output in India, 1951— 54 to 1958— 61. Analysis of Component Elements, *Journal of Agricultural Statistics*, Vol. XVII, No. 2, 1965.

(t) Tarlok Singh; Agricultural Development in India: Policy and Problems, *Indian Council of World Affairs*, New Delhi.

(u) Gupta, B.D., Agrarian Change and New Technology in India, *U.N. Research Institute for Social Development*, Geneva, 1976.

(v) Minhas, B.S., Rapproteurs Report on Measurement of Agricultural Growth, *Indian Journal of Agricultural Economics*, Vol. XXI, 1966.

(w) Narula, S. & Vidyasagar, Methodology for Working Out Contribution of Area & Yield in Increase Production, *Agricultural Situation in India*, 1973.

(x) Report of the National Commission on Agriculture, 1976 (Ministry of Agriculture & Irrigation, New Delhi), Part III, Demand and Supply.

(y) *Ibid*, Part II. Policy and Strategy, Chapter 2-3.

(z) Jasbir Singh, *The Green Revolution in India: How Green it is, Postscript to an Agricultural Atlas of India*, Vishal Publication, 1974.

2

Trends in Area, Levels of Output and Productivity of Foodgrains

The performance of agricultural sector is judged primarily by its ability to expand production of food and raw materials. Increased agricultural production is of critical importance when both population and income grow in low income countries, particularly if the poorest segments of the population share in the income growth. For example the ratio of population growth and agricultural growth should not be the same, i.e., the quality of food demanded will change the pattern and volume of demand. Therefore, agricultural production in terms of quantity and quality must accelerate if future demands are to be met.

It was observed generally that the increase in agricultural production may come from three sources:

(i) Extension of agricultural land,
(ii) Increase in yield or intensification method, and
(iii) Change in cropping pattern or increasing percentage share of high yield giving crops.

These sources were largely effected by the intensification of agriculture through the increased use of fertilizers, irrigation, application of HYV and mechanization. Generally, expansion in area took place in the decade 1950–1960 and it played a vital role and held responsible for the increased production when technology and mechanization was not introduced to the effective extent. Similarly in the decade of 1960–70 it was observed that the increased production was due to the increase in area and yield both but the role of increased yield was more than the increased area particularly in the later half of this decade (1965–70) which is known as the post-Green Revolution period. During the period (1970–80) yield situation is changed due to the rapid innovation of the technology and mechanization only in some pockets of the country, therefore, yield is largely responsible for the increase in production.

A number of analysis and observations are made during the period 1950–80 and some important studies are well known to measure the role of increase in area and yield for increased production.[1] Therefore, a crop-wise analysis is necessary to find out the above mentioned truth. For the present problem we have two types of increased area, i.e. an increase in cultivated area and secondly an increase in high yield giving crops like rice and wheat. Therefore, an analysis of changing cropping pattern is necessary. Lastly, an analysis of crop-combination regions may be made to locate a particular crop in a particular region suited for the increase in agricultural production or to increase the area under a particular crop. For example during 1960–79 there was a phenomenal change and encroachment over the low yield giving crops area by high yield crops like wheat and rice. The role of various factors, i.e., environmental, technological and social will be considered to measure the present change in area and yield under each crop. Though all the major and minor crops are included in this study but particularly emphasis will be made on those crops which are occupying larger area. Therefore, the area under every crop can be divided into four zones: (i) High yield and high spread, (ii) high yield and low spread, (iii) low yield and high spread, (iv) low yield and low spread. The zone of high yield and high spread is considered to be the most efficient zone whereas the zone of low yield and low spread is the most inefficient zone of production. On this basis the most suitable crop pattern can be identified and suggested.

The present position of cereals and pulses is also considered separately because of the pulses crisis in India as well as its nutritional value in Indian diets. The predominance of foodcrops and its variations at state level will be discussed in terms of percentage share of foodcrops and non-foodcrops.

The data for this analysis relates to the year 1968-69 to 1978-79. In order to remove the environmental abnormalities an average of three years data have been used, i.e., 1968-69, 1969-70, 1970-71 as one unit and 1976-77, 1977-78, 1978-79 for another unit to find out the growth picture in area, production and yield.

The purpose of the present study is to examine the causes of non-fulfilment of targets and to assess the possibilities of increasing food production. A comparison of the performance of agriculture of other adjoining countries and well developed agricultural countries will reveal the fact that the performance of Indian agriculture is not satisfactory. Unlike the U.S.A. and Japan, India has the advantage of an accumulation of scientific knowledge for increasing productivity of land manifold. And since the gap between present and potential productivity in India is much greater than in countries like China, which had already achieved a very high level of intensity of land use and cultivation practices and land-man ratio is very low (0.13 hect. per head). The net cultivated area of China and India is more or less equal but production of China is 300 million metric tonnes while in India it is only about 150 million metric tonnes. Therefore, the trend in area growth will indicate the possibilities of expanding the area under cultivation and increase in intensity of cropping. An analysis of the trend of yield level will reveal the possibilities of the growth in future as the country is represented by a very low yield growth due to the insufficient development of technology etc.

It will be more meaningful to analyse the agricultural problems in terms of agricultural responses to population pressure in India. It will be more obvious if we say that per unit of land productivity will lead only to the levels of potential exploitation while per head share in agricultural production will reveal the actual situation and problems of agriculture and foodgrains and will be more helpful for planning in terms of need and social justice.

In traditional system of agriculture like India to bring new land has always been the quickest and easiest way of increasing the output. The expansion of the cultivated land has also been the major response to population pressure. The reason is quite obvious, i.e., traditional agricultural societies have already had the techniques which can raise crop yields rapidly except of few districts of India.

After independence the growth in agricultural production has come from three sources; expansion of acreage, increase in yield and shifts to more valuable crops. Expansion of acreage has been more important during the period 1950–60 while during the period 1960–70 increased area and yield both were responsible for the increased production. But the expansion in area was less important than the increase in yield.

Trends in Area Growth

A significant change in area took place during this period. No doubt that there has been insignificant change in cultivated area but a significant growth was recorded crop-wise. The nature of growth was from one better crop to another inferior crop. For example, rice and wheat encroached over the area of pulses and some non-high yielding crops. The Table 2.1 shows the change in area in cereals and pulses as well as foodgrains.

In cereal crops area change from 1968-69 to 1978-79 was significant due to the demand and increasing pressure of population on food demand. The pulses recorded a very slight change due to the low yield as compared to the cereal crops, therefore, the change in area was stagnant. It was also noticed that better land of pulses were encroached by wheat crop and more inferior land was captured by pulses. The area being stagnant or more or less equal but the production was recorded lesser in ratio to the increase in area in pulses.

The more significant change was recorded cropwise as it is evident from the Tables 2.2 and 2.3. During this period rice and wheat recorded maximum growth in area, i.e., about 6.0 and 27.0 per cent respectively. This growth in area is due to the nature of high yield giving crops than the other crops of the cropping season. These crops also recorded high growth in yield level as well as these crops gives better output per unit area than all the crops being grown in the season.

No doubt that there has been a little change in area in all the crops but it is so significant as it is recorded in rice and wheat area. All other crops like jowar, bajra, maize, millets ragi, barley, gram and arhar recorded a very insignificant growth in area but its share in total production was not considerable due to the low yield rate of this increased area. Everywhere the increase in rice and wheat crops was recorded on better land while other crops were shifted in inferior land.

A comparative analysis of the increase in area between cereals and pulses indicate that a considerable increase was recorded in cereal crops and a balance of requirement was maintained with the increasing pressure of population in the country. With the increase of area production also increased to a considerable extent, i.e., from 84.00 to 119.00 million metric tonnes during this period. While increase in pulses was stagnant both in area and production. The present situation of pulses is not fulfilling the growing demand of the population.

TABLE 2.1: All India: Trends of Area, Production and Yield (Cereals, Pulses and Foodgrains) 1968-69 to 1978-79

Years	CEREALS			PULSES			FOODGRAINS		
	A	P	Y	A	P	Y	A	P	Y
1968-69	99.17	83.60	843	21.26	10.42	490	120.43	94.29	783
1969-70	101.55	87.81	865	22.02	11.69	531	123.57	99.49	805
1970-71	101.39	96.19	949	22.53	11.82	525	123.92	109.41	883
1971-72	110.47	94.08	936	22.15	11.09	501	122.62	106.37	867
1972-73	98.36	87.12	886	20.92	9.91	474	119.28	97.26	815
1973-74	103.11	94.66	918	23.43	10.01	427	126.54	104.85	829
1974-75	99.12	89.71	905	22.58	10.40	461	121.69	100.95	830
1975-76	103.73	107.99	1041	22.45	13.04	533	128.18	121.00	944
1976-77	101.21	100.36	992	22.98	11.36	494	124.19	111.65	899
1977-78	103.77	114.01	1099	23.50	11.97	509	127.26	126.12	991
1978-79	104.57	119.20	1140	23.95	12.17	508	128.52	131.39	1022
	(5.45)	(42.58)	(35.23)	(12.65)	(16.79)	(3.7)	(6.72)	(39.35)	(30.52)

Note: Figures in bracket indicates % growth of 1978-79 over 1968-69 in Area, production and yield.
A = Area in Million Hectares
P = Production in Million Tonnes
Y = Yield per Hectare in kgs.

TABLE 2.2: All India: Percentage Share of Area and Production of Foodgrain Crops

Crops	1968-69		1969-70		1970-71		1971-72		1972-73	
	Area	Production	Area	Production	Area	Production	Area	Production	Area	Production
	1	2	3	4	5	6	7	8	9	10
Rice	30.69	42.29	30.49	40.63	30.21	39.30	30.79	40.95	30.76	40.45
Jowar	15.55	10.43	15.06	9.77	14.07	7.58	13.68	7.34	13.01	7.18
Bajra	10.07	4.04	10.11	5.35	10.42	7.41	9.60	5.06	9.91	4.05
Maize	4.75	6.06	4.74	5.70	4.71	6.86	4.62	4.85	4.89	6.58
Small Millets	3.94	1.92	3.83	1.74	3.88	1.73	3.65	1.59	3.58	1.60
Ragi	1.86	1.75	2.25	2.13	2.00	2.00	1.98	2.10	1.95	1.98
Wheat	13.25	19.84	13.45	20.19	14.44	21.15	15.61	25.11	16.32	25.49
Barley	2.29	2.58	2.24	2.73	2.10	2.65	2.00	2.45	2.05	2.45
Total Cereals	82.40	88.91	82.17	88.24	81.83	88.68	81.93	89.45	82.48	89.78
Gram	5.90	4.58	5.79	5.57	6.30	4.86	6.45	4.83	5.84	4.68
Arhar	2.10	1.93	2.16	1.85	2.14	1.70	1.91	1.60	2.03	1.99
Other Pulses	9.66	4.57	9.87	4.33	9.74	4.38	9.70	4.12	9.66	4.54
Total	17.66	11.08	17.82	11.75	18.18	10.94	18.06	10.55	17.53	11.21

TABLE 2.2 (*Contd.*)

Crops	1973-74		1974-75		1975-76		1976-77		1977-78		1978-79	
	Area	Production	Area	Production	Area	Production	Area	Production	Area	Production	Area	Production
	11	12	13	14	15	16	17	18	19	20	21	22
Rice	30.26	42.09	31.13	39.54	30.80	40.27	31.08	38.30	31.65	41.81	31.28	40.97
Jowar	13.21	8.69	13.30	10.40	12.55	7.85	12.70	9.31	12.82	9.88	12.55	8.80
Bajra	11.01	7.18	9.27	3.27	9.07	4.75	8.64	5.13	8.73	3.75	8.82	4.20
Maize	4.75	5.54	4.82	5.55	4.70	5.99	4.87	5.60	4.47	4.74	4.50	4.73
Small Millets	3.61	1.88	3.67	1.61	3.65	1.59	3.57	1.47	3.60	1.64	3.47	1.47
Ragi	1.86	1.98	2.08	2.03	2.05	2.31	2.04	1.95	2.04	2.27	2.04	2.31
Wheat	14.69	20.81	14.80	24.08	15.96	23.83	16.80	26.03	16.66	24.87	17.29	26.63
Barley	2.09	2.27	2.37	3.13	2.10	2.64	1.79	2.05	1.57	1.83	1.43	1.61
Total Cereals	81.48	90.44	81.44	89.61	80.88	89.23	81.49	89.84	81,54	90.79	81.38	90.72
Gram	6.13	3.92	5.79	4.04	6.49	4.86	6.33	4.80	6.27	4.29	6.12	4.44
Arhar	2.09	1.35	2.08	1.83	2.08	1.73	2.04	1.47	2.06	1.53	2.07	1.46
Other Pulses	10.29	4.30	9.68	4.52	10.51	4.81	10.14	4.20	10.92	3.68	10.44	3.36
Total Pulses	18.51	9.57	17.55	10.39	19.08	11.40	18.51	10.47	19.25	9.50	18.63	9.26

TABLE 2.3: All India: Percentage Growth in Area, Production and Yield of Foodgrain crops (1968–71 to 1976–79)

Crops	Area	Production	Yield
Rice	+6.25	+21.73	+14.63
Jowar	-11.96	+22.77	+39.53
Bajra	-11.42	-6.74	+5.47
Maize	+0.57	-1.81	-2.41
Small Millets	-5.81	+4.27	+10.85
Ragi	+3.41	+36.54	+32.03
Wheat	+27.36	+03.88	+12.68
Barley	-25.43	-15.96	+12.68
Total Cereals	+2.47	+24.66	+21.67
Gram	+7.41	+9.98	+2.49
Arhar	-0.28	-1.01	-0.71
Other Pulses	+8.34	+0.94	-6.76
Total Pulses	+7.00	+4.65	-2.14
Total Foodgrains	+3.28	+22.40	+18.41

Foodgrains Production

According to the data provided by the Ministry of Food and Agriculture, the output of foodgrains increased from 94.3 million metric tonnes during 1968-69 to 131.4 metric tonnes during 1978-79. Keeping in view the environmental abnormaly it was felt wise to get an average result of triennium, (1968–71) and (1976–79), as average foodgrain produced was 105.1 million metric tonnes and 123.03 million metric tonnes respectively in India.

The average percentage growth rate of foodgrains works out to be 22.4 during this period at the annual growth rate of 2.3 per cent. This growth rate, as one can see easily, falls short of a targeted rate of four per cent and barely exceeds the population projected growth rate of 2.1 per cent per annum. Consequently, despite the increase in domestic production we could not achieve the level of sufficiency. Furthermore, the per capita daily availability of foodgrains marginally declined from 452.0 grams during 1968–71 to 447.8 grams during 1976–79. It is obvious that over the years there has existed a precarious balance between demand and supply of foodgrains and very wide yearly fluctuations have tended to aggravate the situation.

It is interesting to note that whereas area increase contributed 3.28 per cent and yield increase 18.41 per cent during this period.

The average rate of growth hides the fact that there have been large scale year to year fluctuations in output of foodgrains in India. With a very small margin between the rate of growth of output and of population (in fact this margin was more often negative), the total foodgrains availability becomes precarious during the years of scarcity and the public distribution system is put under excessive pressure. Years of abundance as a whole have not so far been quite numerous enough as to even out the market fluctuations in supplies and prices.

Another aspect of this problem is that even though total foodgrains output has increased at an annual rate of 2.3 per cent, the increase is confined to cereals, i.e. 2.71 per cent, while the cereals output decline by 21.4 per cent during this period and 0.27 per cent per annum. In fact, the total output of pulses has increased from a level of 11.31 million metric tonnes to 11.83 million metric tonnes. On the other hand, the production of cereals as such has increased at a rate of 29.71 per cent per annum form a level of 89.2 million metric tonnes during the seventies to that of 111.2 million metric tonnes during the eighties. This imbalance has rather serious repurcussions because pulses in general are the major source of proteins for a vast majority of population in the country and the stagnation in pulse output has certainly adversely affected the total nutrient content of available foods particularly for the weaker sections of population.

It is a matter of common knowledge that there are very wide spatial variations in both the levels and growth of foodgrains output in India. Due to some limitations of the objectives of this study state-level analysis has been done and spatial analysis can only be possible through taking districts as an unit of analysis.

All the States and Union Territories have been included for the analysis. In some of the Union Territories time series data of this period could not be available, therefore, the analysis is based on only few years and change and trends have been measured.

The analysis includes the following crops - 1. Cereals – rice, wheat, jowar, bajra, maize and small millets, ragi and barley. 2. Pulses – Gram, Arhar (pigeon pea) and other pulses. It is worth noting that the Gross Cropped Area (GCA) refers to the gross area under these above crops only. Similarly, the gross output refers to the output of these crops.

Level and Growth of Foodgrains Output

According to the data foodgrains output during the period 1968–71 was 100.5 million metric tonnes and during the period 1976–79 it was 123.03 million metric tonnes. This means that food production grew by 22.4 per cent or 2.3 per cent per annum. Area under foodgrain crops increased from 122.6 million hectares to 126.6 million metric hectares that is, at an annual per cent growth of 0.41 while yield increased at a much faster rate of 2.04 per cent per annum or 820 kg. per hectare in 1970 and 971 kg. in 1980.

TABLE 2.4: Annual Growth in Area, Production and Yield

		Growth (%)		
Year	Total Production	Area	Production	Yield
1968-69	94.29	—	—	0.
1969-70	99.49	1.93	1.63	-0.28
1970-71	109.41	1.26	6.76	5.39
1971-72	106.37	2.14	8.32	6.04
1972-73	97.26	-0.76	-1.30	-0.56
1973-74	104.85	3.57	10.79	6.97
1974-75	100.95	2.49	-0.46	97.12
1975-76	121.00	-0.72	22.58	14.78
1976-77	111.65	2.91	7.61	2.97
1977-78	126.12	1.31	32.47	21.56
1978-79	131.39	1.09	35.38	24.44
1979-80	108.90	—	-16.80	—
1980-81	132.00	—	-21.10	—

In general, in all the states where agricultural output has registered a positive growth, output increases are associated with increases in both area and productivity. Regarding cereals, the only exceptions are the states of Gujarat, Karnataka, Madhya Pradesh, Rajasthan, Tamil Nadu, Delhi and Pondicherry where area decrease is not associated with the increase in output. In these states yield increase was much higher than all the states of India. Therefore, the contribution of yield increase contributed to the total output of the states. Therefore, some states like Jammu and Kashmir and Orissa where output decreased even after the increase in area due to the high decrease in yield level, i.e., about 4.00 and 11.00 per cent decrease in yield contributed for the negative growth in total output even after an increase in area by 2.00 and 5.00 per cent respectively.

An association with increase to decrease in area with increase or decrease in output and yield can be understood by making the following five categories. This situation can be explained with the understanding of geographical and environmental conditions of the area.

1. *States with decrease in area but output and yield increased* – (Gujarat, Karnataka, Kerala, Madhya Pradesh, Rajasthan, Tamil Nadu, Delhi, and Pondicherry) Kerala - area decreased, yield increased but total output decreased because of the high decrease in area and less increase in yield.
2. *State with decrease in area and decrease in output and yield*– In India not even a single state fall in this category due to the overall increase in yield.
3. *States with increase in area but decrease in yield and output* – (Jammu and Kashmir and Orissa) it happened because of the high decrease in yield level.
4. *States with increase in area and increase in yield and output* – A large number of states fall in this category - Andhra Pradesh, Assam, Bihar, Haryana, Himachal Pradesh, Maharashtra, Manipur, Nagaland, Tripura, Punjab, Uttar Pradesh, West Bengal, Dadra & Nagar Haveli, Goa Daman & Diu.
5. *States with increase in area and output but decrease in yield* – Meghalaya, Andaman & Nicobar Islands, Arunachal Pradesh.

Cereals Production

In India 80 per cent of the total area under foodgrains is devoted to cereal crops while only 20 per cent is given to pulses crops. But the percentage share in production is only 10 per cent of pulses to the total foodgrains production, it is only because of the lower yield of pulses crops than the cereal crops. For example per hectare yield of pulses is 504 kg/hect. while cereals have 1078 kg/hect. during 1976–79.

A spatial percentage share of cereal crops in the country will reveal the fact that which state have higher share in cereal crops. For the country as a whole about 81 per cent area is under cereal crops to the total foodgrain crops. This distribution is not uniform in all the states of India. In all the hill states more than 95 per cent area is devoted to cereal crops. The lowest area under cereal crops is in Rajasthan and Haryana, i.e., about 67 and 72 per cent respectively while other states are occupying about 80 per cent (Table 2.5)

TABLE 2.5: Per cent Area and Production of Cereals and Pulses

States	Cereal		Pulses	
	% Area	% Product	% Area	% Production
Andhra Pradesh	85.53	96.04	14.47	3.97
Assam	95.97	98.33	4.03	1.67
Bihar	86.03	92.90	13.97	7.10
Gujarat	89.50	95.42	10.50	4.58
Haryana	72.71	82.63	27.29	17.37
Himachal Pradesh	91.29	96.36	8.71	3.64
J & K	97.67	97.33	6.33	2.67
Karnataka	81.31	92.22	18.69	7.78
Kerala	95.68	98.73	4.32	1.27
Madhya Pradesh	72.81	81.63	27.19	18.37
Maharashtra	80.79	88.27	19.21	11.73
Manipur	97.04	99.26	2.96	0.74
Meghalaya	98.91	99.33	1.09	0.67
Nagaland	91.95	95.56	8.05	4.44
Orissa	79.74	87.79	20.26	12.21
Punjab	91.21	96.83	8.79	3.17
Rajasthan	67.51	72.51	32.49	27.49
Tamil Nadu	88.18	97.66	11.82	2.34
Tripura	98.39	99.40	1.61	0.60
U.P.	84.29	88.17	15.71	11.83
West Bengal	90.83	96.08	9.17	3.92
A & N Island	86.89	95.62	13.11	4.38
Arunachal Pradesh	100.00	100.00	—	—
Chandigarh	—	—	—	—
Dadra & N. Haveli	73.71	87.25	26.29	12.75
Delhi	93.18	97.16	6.82	2.84
Goa Dam. & Diu	100.00	100.00	—	—
Mizoram	99.40	99.76	0.60	0.24
Pondicherry	86.63	96.24	13.37	3.76
ALL INDIA	81.46	90.38	18.54	9.62

As it has already been stated earlier that cereals in comparison to pulses have higher yield level, therefore, cereals are contributing more than 90% in total foodgrain production and only 10 per cent production is shared by pulses crops. The share of cereal crops in the total foodgrain production is more than 95 per cent in the states of Andhra Pradesh, Assam, Gujarat, Himachal Pradesh, J & K, Kerala, Manipur, Meghalaya, Nagaland, Punjab, Tamil Nadu, Tripura, West Bengal and Mizoram. The states of Haryana and Rajasthan have the lowest share as the area is also low in comparison to other states of India.

TABLE 2.6: Per cent share of Area and Production of each state in India (1976-79)

Area = Million Hectares
Produ. = Million Metric Tonnes

States	1976-79		1976—79	
	Area	%	Production	%
Andhra Pradesh	7.90	7.65	8.61	7.81
Assam	2.40	2.32	2.30	2.09
Bihar	8.86	8.58	9.02	8.18
Gujarat	4.11	3.98	3.94	3.57
Haryana	3.06	2.96	4.68	4.24
Himachal Pradesh	0.75	0.73	0.99	0.90
J & K	0.76	0.74	1.05	0.95
Karnataka	5.45	5.28	6.02	5.46
Kerala	0.84	0.81	1.26	1.14
Madhya Pradesh	12.57	12.17	9.01	8.17
Maharashtra	11.45	11.09	7.58	6.88
Manipur	0.19	0.18	0.31	0.28
Meghalaya	0.14	0.14	0.15	0.14
Nagaland	0.08	0.08	0.09	0.08
Orissa	5.11	4.95	4.47	4.05
Punjab	4.14	4.01	10.07	9.13
Rajasthan	8.24	7.98	5.21	4.73
Tamil Nadu	4.55	4.41	8.28	7.51
Tripura	0.31	0.30	0.37	0.34
U.P.	16.23	15.72	18.59	16.86
West Bengal	5.74	5.55	7.75	7.03
A & N Island	0.01	0.01	0.01	0.01
Arunachal Pradesh	0.11	0.11	0.11	0.10
Chandigarh	—	—	—	—
Dadra & N. Haveli	0.01	0.01	0.02	0.02
Delhi	0.08	0.08	0.14	0.13
Goa Dam. & Diu	0.06	0.06	0.10	0.09
Mizoram	0.07	0.07	0.04	0.04
Pondicherry	0.03	0.03	0.07	0.06
INDIA	103.18	100.00	111.19	100.00

The above statements gives a peculiar picture and attract our attention about the hilly regions where pulses are grown in a negligible area. According to the existing cropping pattern the major pulses crops are absent like Arhar (pigeon pea) and gram. These two crops ecologically belongs to the rabi crops and as a whole in the hilly regions these crops cannot be grown due to climatic conditions. The other kharif pulses are occupying negligible area because rice is a high yield giving crop as compared to pulses, therefore, emphasis is more on this crop.

Increase in Area of Cereal Crops

During the period 1968–71 to 1976–79 the country experienced only 2.5 per cent growth in area though the increase in pulses was recorded 7.0 per cent. The increase in area in cereal crops are not uniform in all the states of the country. The states like Gujarat, Karnataka, Kerala, Madhya Pradesh, Rajasthan, Tamil Nadu, Delhi and Pondicherry recorded negative growth in area. Among these states Gujarat and Karnataka recorded significant negative growth. But these states recorded high growth in area under pulses crops. The highest growth in area is recorded in most of the hilly regions except of J & K and Himachal Pradesh. For example the states of Arunachal Pradesh, Tripura, Nagaland, Meghalaya and Manipur the growth was considerably very high i.e., about 75%, 61%, 45%, 21% respectively. The states like Haryana and Punjab recorded high growth in area under cereal crops because of the irrigation facility but in case of Punjab irrigation and reduction in pulses crops both are the responsible factors for such a high increase in area under cereal crops.

Increase in Production

The country as a whole recorded 24.7 per cent growth in production. Such a high growth during this period is due to the high increase in yield while the increase in area was very low. The yield per hectare increased from 886 to 1078 kg/hectare.

In all the states of the country increase in production was recorded except of J & K, Kerala and Orissa. Mostly in all the hilly states (Tripura, Arunachal Pradesh, Meghalaya, Manipur and Nagaland) the increase in production is very high except of Himachal Pradesh and Assam. In these states increase in area is more responsible for the increase in production. While in other major states increase in yield rate is responsible for the high increase in production. In the states of Punjab and Haryana increase in area was also high but increase in yield was much higher than the area, therefore, in these states both the factors are responsible equally for a high increase in production.

TABLE 2.7: Cereals Yield Level per Hectare

Yield kg./Hect.

STATES	1968—71	1976—79
Andhra Pradesh	866	1090
Assam	973	974
Bihar	875	1018
Gujarat	701	960
Haryana	1237	1527
Himachal Pradesh	1266	1319
J & K	1430	1368
Karnataka	843	1106
Kerala	1445	1509
Madhya Pradesh	647	717
Maharashtra	529	664
Manipur	1607	1615
Meghalaya	1070	1022
Nagaland	947	977
Orissa	982	875
Punjab	1921	2431
Rajasthan	534	632
Tamil Nadu	1321	1819
Tripura	856	1198
U.P.	935	1145
West Bengal	1283	1351
A & N Island	1263	1236
Arunachal Pradesh	1068	982
D & N Haveli	1126	1245
Chandigarh	—	—
Delhi	1303	1725
Goa Daman & Diu	1292	1624
Mizoram	—	624
Pondicherry	1731	2122
INDIA	886	1078

Increase in Yield

As it has already been stated earlier that yield increase is a significant factor to change the situation of agricultural production of the country. Generally in most of the states and the country as a whole increase in area is insignificant as compared to the increase in yield. The country as a whole recorded about 25 per cent growth in cereal production. But this growth is not uniform in all the states of the Country. The states of J & K, Meghalaya, Orissa, A & N Islands and Arunachal Pradesh recorded negative growth in yield. In the states of Meghalaya, A & N Islands and Arunachal Pradesh a high increase in area is responsible for the positive growth in production. While other states experienced a very high growth in yield and a very low increase in area. Among the major states of India Haryana and Punjab recorded high increase both in area and yield.

TABLE 2.8: Cereals — per cent Growth in Area, Production & Yield 1968-69, 1970-71 to 1976-1978-79

States	Percentage Growth		
	Area	Production	Yield
Andhra Pradesh	0.74	26.77	26.91
Assam	7.71	7.80	0.10
Bihar	8.01	25.57	16.34
Gujarat	-9.59	23.71	36.95
Haryana	17.38	44.94	23.44
J & K	1.57	-2.83	-4.33
Karnataka	-12.35	15.03	31.20
Kerala	-7.32	-3.20	4.43
Madhya Pradesh	-1.36	9.33	10.82
Maharashtra	5.67	32.49	25.52
Manipur	21.88	22.45	0.50
Meghalaya	27.04	21.33	-4.49
Nagaland	41.24	45.76	3.17
Orissa	4.86	-6.57	-10.90
Punjab	24.19	57.11	26.55
Rajasthan	-4.73	12.76	18.35
Tamil Nadu	-1.57	35.54	37.70
Tripura	15.27	61.39	4.00
U.P.	4.41	27.90	22.40
West Bengal	8.08	13.77	5.30
A & N Island	32.50	29.70	-2.14
Arunachal Pradesh	91.01	75.55	-8.05
Dadra & N. Haveli	28.83	42.40	10.57
Chandigarh	—	—	—
Delhi	-1.49	30.41	32.39
Goa Daman Diu	19.13	49.77	25.70
Mizoram	—	—	—
Pondicherry	-2.52	18.49	22.59
INDIA	2.47	24.66	21.67

Cereals – Yield Level

The highest yield level (> 1400 kg) category comprising the states of Haryana, Punjab, Kerala, Tamil Nadu, Manipur and other Union Territories (Delhi, D. & Diu & Pondicherry) occupying about 12.6 per cent area under cereals are contributing 22.6 per cent of the total cereal production of the country. The category (B) with the yield level 1200-1400 kg/hectare comprising the states of J & K, Himachal Pradesh, West Bengal, A & N Islands and D & N Haveli occupying only 7 per cent of the total area of India is contributing about 9 per cent of the total cereal production of the country. The medium level category between 1000 – 1200 kg/hect comprising the states of Andhra Pradesh, U.P., Bihar, Karnataka, Meghalaya and Tripura occupying about 38 per cent area is producing 39 per cent of the total production of the country. The lower categories below the national average comprising the states of Assam, Gujarat, Nagaland, Orissa, Arunachal Pradesh, Madhya Pradesh, Maharashtra, Rajasthan and Mizoram are occupying about 43 per cent of the area and contributing only 30 per cent of the total production of the country (Table 2.9).

TABLE 2.9: Cereals – Yield Level (Fig. 1)

Yield Category	Area		Production	
	Million Hects.	% to India	Million Tonnes	% to India
A. > 1400	12.96	12.56	24.90	22.60
B. 1200-1400	7.28	7.06	9.82	8.91
C. 1000-1200	38.90	37.70	42.76	38.81
D. 800-1000	11.81	11.45	10.84	9.84
E. < 800	32.23	31.23	21.85	19.84
Total	103.18	100.00	110.17	100.00

A. – Haryana, Kerala, Manipur, Punjab, Tamil Nadu, Delhi, Goa Daman & Diu, Pondicherry.
B. – Himachal Pradesh, J & K., West Bengal, A. & N. Islands, Dadra & Nagar Haveli.
C. – Andhra Pradesh, Bihar, Karnataka, Meghalaya, Tripura, Uttar Pradesh.
D. – Assam, Gujarat, Nagaland, Orissa, Arunachal Pradesh.
E. – Madhya Pradesh, Maharashtra, Rajasthan, Mizoram.

The above analysis indicates that mostly all the union territories and hilly states are also under higher yield categories. Secondly a large part of the country is under lower categories where agricultural production can be increased or if the level of yield is increased of all the lower categories to the level of high category the total production can be increased just double to the present amount of production.

Cereals – Growth Level

The growth level Table 2.10 indicates that higher growth is not associated with the higher yield giving states. As all the higher yield states are located in the medium level growth category.

TABLE 2.10: Cereals — Growth Level (Fig. 2)

Growth Category		Area		Production	
		Million Hects.	% of the total of India	Million Tonnes	% of the total of India
A.	> 30	14.19	13.75	18.38	16.69
B.	20 - 30	42.86	41.54	49.62	45.06
C.	10 - 20	29.68	28.77	23.26	21.12
D.	0 - 10	10.30	9.98	13.06	11.86
E.	0 -(-5)	0.92	0.89	1.21	1.10
F.	> (-5)	5.22	5.07	4.58	4.11
	Total	103.17	100.00	110.11	100.00

A. — Gujarat, Karnataka, Tamil Nadu, Delhi.
B. — Andhra Pradesh, Haryana, Maharashtra, Punjab, Uttar Pradesh, Goa Daman & Diu, Pondicherry.
C. — Bihar, Madhya Pradesh, Rajasthan, Dadra & Nagar Haveli.
D. — Assam, Himachal Pradesh, Kerala, Manipur, Nagaland, Tripura, West Bengal.
E. — J & K., Meghalaya, A. & N. Islands.
F. — Orissa, Arunachal Pradesh.

The highest growth, comprising the states of Gujarat, Karnataka, Tamil Nadu and Delhi, is concentrated in about 14 per cent area with about 17 per cent of the total output of the country. The states of Andhra Pradesh, Haryana, Punjab, Maharashtra, Uttar Pradesh, Goa Daman & Diu and Pondicherry recorded 20-30 per cent growth comprising an area of 41 per cent with 45 per cent production of the country. The second largest category in terms of area (29%) recorded 10-20 per cent growth in the states of Bihar, Madhya

Pradesh and Rajasthan with the 21 per cent production of the country. About 6 per cent area of the country recorded negative growth mostly in the hilly states. The table 2.10 indicate that a large part of the area is recording higher level of growth. The states of Bihar, Madhya Pradesh and Rajasthan comprising an area of about 29 per cent can be brought out under higher growth if other infrastructure facilities are made stronger.

Pulses Production

In India 18.5 per cent area of the total foodgrain is occupied by various pulses. Among them 'Arhar' (Pigeon pea) and gram is important in all the states of India. But its contribution to the total foodgrain production is very low because of the very low yield level. The states of Haryana and Rajasthan occupy the highest percentage in terms of area, i.e., 27 and 32 per cent respectively. The states of Karnataka, Maharashtra, Orissa and D & N Haveli are occupying the area above the national average while the states of Andhra Pradesh, Bihar, U.P. and Pondicherry are slightly below the national average. Other states and Union territories are far below the national average.

Because of low yield level as compared to cereals the pulses are contributing only about 9.6 per cent to the total foodgrain production of the country while it is occupying about 18.5 per cent of the total area under foodgrain production. During the period 1976–79 the per hectare yield of pulses was only 504 kg/hec. But this yield is not uniform in all the states of India. The states of Haryana, Punjab and Uttar Pradesh have much higher yield than the national average. In some of the states of India yield level is very low while percentage share in area is considerable higher such as in the states of Andhra Pradesh, Gujarat, Maharashtra and Tamil Nadu. In other states yield level is more or less on the average yield of the country.

It has already been discussed earlier that in hilly regions pulses are grown in a negligible area because of the various ecological problems for this crop.

Increase in area

During the period 1968–71 to 1976–79 the country recorded 7.0 per cent growth in area while cereals recorded only 2.5 per cent. The most striking feature of this growth structure is that generally growth in area was negative in those states which shares higher per cent area. Secondly mostly all these major states recorded negative growth in production because of this low increase in yield. Therefore, the production of pulses was not satisfactory as it recorded only 4.6 per cent growth. It is mainly because of the negative growth in yield by 2 per cent even after 7.0 per cent increase in area.

The states of Rajasthan, Tamil Nadu, Tripura and Orissa recorded a very high growth in area and yield. Both these factors combindly resulted for a very high growth in production. Generally the states of higher percentage share in area showed a negative growth in area except of Rajasthan.

The decrease in area especially in the states of Bihar, Kerala, Madhya Pradesh, Punjab, U.P. and West Bengal area due to innovation of high yield seeds for other cereals crops and, secondly, the low yield of pulses in these states.

The situation of the hill states is important where increase in production is needed keeping in view the lack of requirement of pulses. The increase seems only by increasing the area under pulses as yield level is generally to the level of yield of the country.

Increase in Production

At state level increase or decrease in production is the result of increase or decrease in yield and area. A high increase in area supplemented by high increase in yield will result to a high increase in total production. The increase in production can go down of the increase or decrease in area and yield is not achieved in a proper ratio. Regarding the pulses crops all types of situation are experienced. There are only two states (Bihar and West Bengal) where negative growth is experienced in area production and yield while other states either experiencing negative growth in area or production or yield but in different ratio.

As compared to cereals the pulses recorded a very insignificant increase both in production and yield though the area increase is more than the area increase in cereals and even after the yield recorded negative growth an increase in production by 4.6 per cent is due to the increase in area by 7 per cent. A number of complicated situation can be observed from the table 2.14 increase in production.

TABLE 2.11: Pulses — Per cent Share of the Area Production of each state in India

Area = Million Hectares
Produ = Million Metric Tonnes

States	1976–79		1976–79	
	Area	%	Production	% (Share of each state)
Andhra Pradesh	1.34	5.76	0.35	2.96
Assam	0.10	0.43	0.04	0.34
Bihar	1.44	6.19	0.69	5.83
Gujarat	0.48	2.06	0.19	1.61
Haryana	1.15	4.94	0.98	8.28
Himachal Pradesh	0.07	0.30	0.04	0.34
J & K	0.05	0.21	0.03	0.25
Karnataka	1.25	5.37	0.51	4.31
Kerala	0.04	0.17	0.02	0.17
Madhya Pradesh	4.69	20.15	2.03	17.16
Maharashtra	2.72	11.69	1.01	8.54
Manipur	0.01	0.04	—	—
Meghalaya	—	—	—	—
Nagaland	0.01	0.04	—	—
Orissa	1.30	5.59	0.62	5.24
Punjab	0.40	1.72	0.33	2.79
Rajasthan	3.96	17.02	1.98	16.74
Tamil Nadu	0.61	2.62	0.20	1.69
Tripura	0.01	0.04	—	—
U.P.	3.03	13.02	2.49	21.05
West Bengal	0.58	2.49	0.32	2.70
A & N Island	—	—	—	—
Arunachal Pradesh	—	—	—	—
D & N Haveli	0.01	0.04	—	—
Chandigarh	—	—	—	—
Delhi	0.01	0.04	—	—
Goa D. & Diu	—	—	—	—
Mizoram	—	—	—	—
Pondicherry	0.01	0.04	—	—
INDIA	23.48	100.00	11.83	100.00

Firstly, there are some states where a significant increase is recorded in area, production and yield such as Gujarat, Himachal Pradesh, Maharashtra, Rajasthan, Tamil Nadu, Tripura and D & N Haveli. Secondly, there are states where in spite of area decrease yield recorded high increase such as Kerala, Madhya Pradesh, Punjab and Delhi. Lastly there are some states where area and production both increased but yield decreased such as in Haryana and Orissa. Among all these situations the satisfactory situation exists only in those states where increase is recorded in all the sections i.e., area, production and yield and these states are Assam, Gujarat, Himachal Pradesh, Karnataka, Maharashtra, Rajasthan, Tamil Nadu, Tripura and D & N Haveli. However, growth situation in production for the country as a whole is not satisfactory or in other words the growth situation is more or less stagnant.

TABLE 2.12: Pulses — Per cent Area and Production of Pulses (1976—79)

States	% Area to the total foodgrains	% Production to the total foodgrain Production
Andhra Pradesh	14.47	3.97
Assam	4.03	1.67
Bihar	13.97	7.10
Gujarat	10.50	4.58
Haryana	27.29	17.37
Himachal Pradesh	8.71	3.64
J & K	6.33	2.67
Karnataka	18.69	7.78
Kerala	4.32	1.27
Madhya Pradesh	27.19	18.37
Maharashtra	19.21	11.73
Manipur	2.96	0.74
Meghalaya	1.09	0.67
Nagaland	8.05	4.44
Orissa	20.26	12.21
Punjab	8.79	3.17
Rajasthan	32.49	27.49
Tamil Nadu	11.82	2.34
Tripura	1.61	0.60
U.P.	15.71	11.83
West Bengal	9.17	3.92
A & N Island	13.11	4.38
Arunachal Pradesh	—	—
D & N Haveli	—	—
Chandigarh	26.29	12.75
Delhi	6.82	2.84
Goa Daman & Diu	—	—
Mizoram	0.60	0.24
Pondicherry	13.37	3.76
INDIA	18.54	9.62

TABLE 2.13: Pulses — Yield per Hectare State Level

Kg./Hectare

States	1968–71	1976–79
Andhra Pradesh	237	266
Assam	374	395
Bihar	636	479
Gujarat	330	392
Haryana	826	855
Himachal Pradesh	395	523
J & K	618	555
Karnataka	331	406
Kerala	376	431
Madhya Pradesh	363	432
Maharashtra	339	371
Manipur	—	397
Meghalaya	563	625
Nagaland	—	519
Orissa	504	479
Punjab	756	825
Rajasthan	384	498
Tamil Nadu	242	325
Tripura	387	440
U.P.	823	824
West Bengal	643	547
A & N Island	—	375
Arunachal Pradesh	—	—
Chandigarh	—	—
D & N Haveli	417	510
Delhi	667	690
Goa D & Diu	—	—
Mizoram	—	250
Pondicherry	—	538
INDIA	515	504

Increase in Yield

The country as a whole experienced negative growth by 2.14 per cent during the period 1968–71 to 1976–79 or more or less the yield situation is stagnant during these years i.e. 515 to 505 kg/hec. respectively. The highest negative growth is recorded in the state of Bihar, i.e. about 25 per cent. It is because of the innovation of HYV cereals which enchroached the better pulses area. Secondly, it is due to the much lower yield level of pulses than many other cereal crops, therefore, the emphasis shifted from pulses to other cereal crops. The state of West Bengal and J & K also recorded negative growth by 15 and 10 per cent respectively. The states like Haryana and Orissa recorded negative growth about 4 and 5 per cent. Therefore, the situation in most of the states is not satisfactory.

TABLE 2.14: Pulses — Per cent Growth in Area, Production and yield of Pulses

States	Percentage Growth		
	Area	Production	Yield
Andhra Pradesh	-1.34	10.66	12.24
Assam	10.73	16.72	5.62
Bihar	-11.54	-33.40	-24.69
Gujarat	14.09	35.41	18.79
Haryana	8.52	12.26	-3.51
Himachal Pradesh	13.63	50.60	32.41
J & K	0.19	-10.03	-10.20
Karnataka	4.46	28.04	22.66
Kerala	-8.92	4.49	14.63
Madhya Pradesh	-5.14	12.74	19.01
Maharashtra	11.02	21.49	9.44
Manipur	—	—	—
Meghalaya	0.00	11.11	11.01
Nagaland	—	—	—
Orissa	57.46	49.66	-4.96
Punjab	-8.42	-0.15	9.13
Rajasthan	22.21	58.49	29.69
Tamil Nadu	39.43	87.07	34.30
Tripura	61.29	83.33	13.70
U.P.	-22.99	-22.85	0.12
West Bengal	-19.42	-31.53	-14.93
A & N Island	—	—	—
Arunachal Pradesh	—	—	—
Chandigarh	—	—	—
D & N Haveli	32.50	80.87	22.30
Goa Daman & Diu	-50.43	-48.72	3.45
Mizoram	—	—	—
Pondicherry	—	—	—
INDIA	7.00	4.65	-2.14

The highest growth is recorded in the state of Tamil Nadu followed by Rajasthan and Himachal Pradesh where increase is more than 25 per cent. But in these states yield is lesser than the national average. An improvement in yield is the major problem which can be solved with the help of irrigation and HYV seeds.

Pulses – Yield Level

As it is evident that higher level of yield is obtained from the states of Haryana, Punjab and Uttar Pradesh which contribute about 28 per cent of the total production of the country. These states constitute about 20 per cent of the total area under pulses of the country. The yield category (300-500) below the national average comprising the states of Assam, Bihar, Gujarat, Karnataka, Kerala, Madhya Pradesh, Maharashtra, Orissa, Rajasthan and Tamil Nadu etc. contribute only 66 per cent of the total production of the country and occupying a very insignificant situation. Therefore, it is obvious that the pulses situation is very serious regarding the occupancy of land under a very low yield level.

TABLE 2.15: Pulses – Yield Level (Fig. 3)

Yield Category	Area		Production	
	Million Hectares	% to India	Million Tonnes	% to India
A. > 700	4.57	19.66	3.81	28.10
B. 500-700	0.73	3.14	0.40	2.95
C. 300-500	16.60	71.43	8.99	66.30
D. < 300	1.34	5.77	0.36	2.65
Total	23.24	100.00	13.56	100.00

A. – Haryana, Punjab, Uttar Pradesh.
B. – Himachal Pradesh, J & K., Meghalaya, Nagaland, West Bengal, Dadra & Nagar Haveli, Delhi, Pondicherry.
C. – Assam, Bihar, Gujarat, Karnataka, Kerala, Madhya Pradesh, Maharashtra, Manipur, Orissa, Rajasthan, Tamil Nadu, Tripura, A & N Islands.
D. – Andhra Pradesh, Mizoram.

Pulses – Growth Level

It is obvious from the growth level Table 2.16 that about 24 per cent production is achieved from the area of negative growth rate while in cereals only 5 per cent production is achieved from this type of category. About 53 per cent production is obtained from a very low growth categories. Therefore, on the whole the situation of pulses regarding the growth level is very unsatisfactory. Only the states of Himachal Pradesh, Tamil Nadu, Karnataka and Rajasthan fall under high level of growth but their production contribution is only 22 per cent of the total of the country.

TABLE 2.16: Pulses — Growth Level (Fig 4)

Growth Category	Area		Production	
	Million Hectares	% of the total of India	Million Tonnes	% of the total of India
A. > 30	0.68	2.93	0.24	2.03
B. 20 — 30	5.22	22.47	2.49	21.07
C. 10 — 20	6.08	26.17	2.40	20.30
D. 0 — 10	6.25	26.90	3.87	32.74
E. 0 — (10)	2.45	10.55	1.60	13.54
F. (-10) — (-20)	1.11	4.78	0.53	4.48
G. < (-20)	1.44	6.20	0.69	5.84
Total	23.23	100.00	11.82	100.00

A. — Himachal Pradesh, Tamil Nadu.
B. — Karnataka, Rajasthan, Dadra & Nagar Haveli.
C. — Andhra Pradesh, Kerala, Madhya Pradesh, Meghalaya, Tripura.
D. — Assam, Maharashtra, Punjab, Uttar Pradesh, Delhi.
E. — Haryana, Orissa.
F. — Gujarat, J & K, West Bengal.
G. — Bihar.

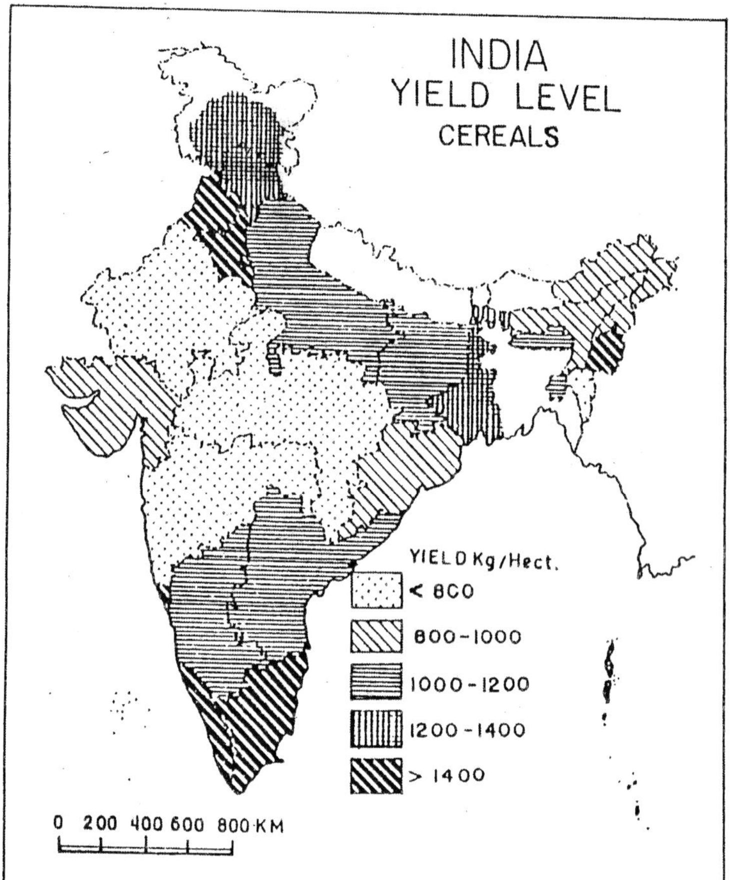
INDIA
YIELD LEVEL
CEREALS
YIELD Kg/Hect.
< 800
800-1000
1000-1200
1200-1400
> 1400
0 200 400 600 800 KM

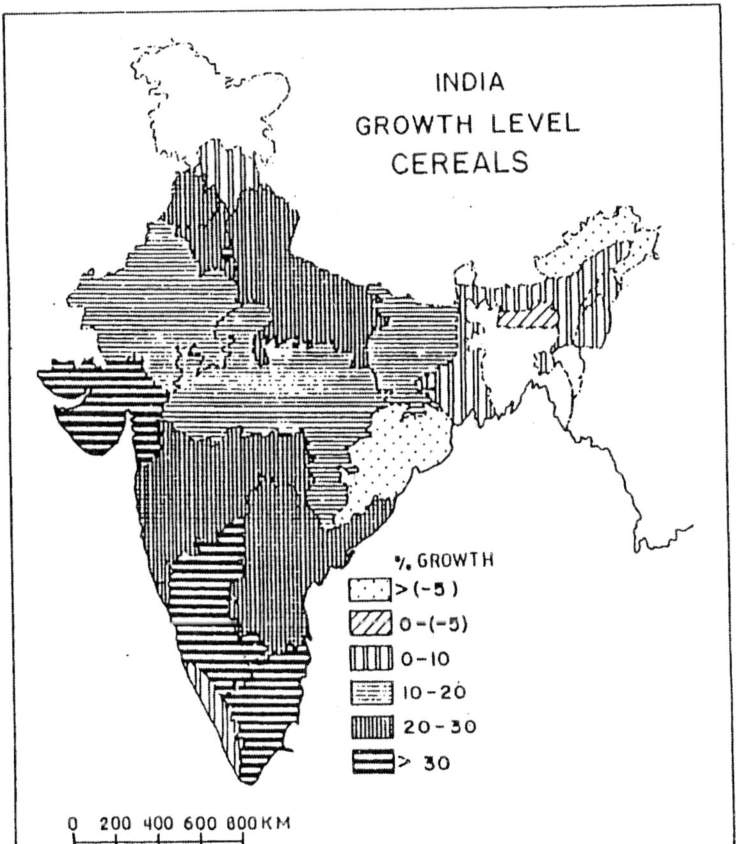
INDIA
GROWTH LEVEL
CEREALS
% GROWTH
> (-5)
0-(-5)
0-10
10-20
20-30
> 30
0 200 400 600 800 KM

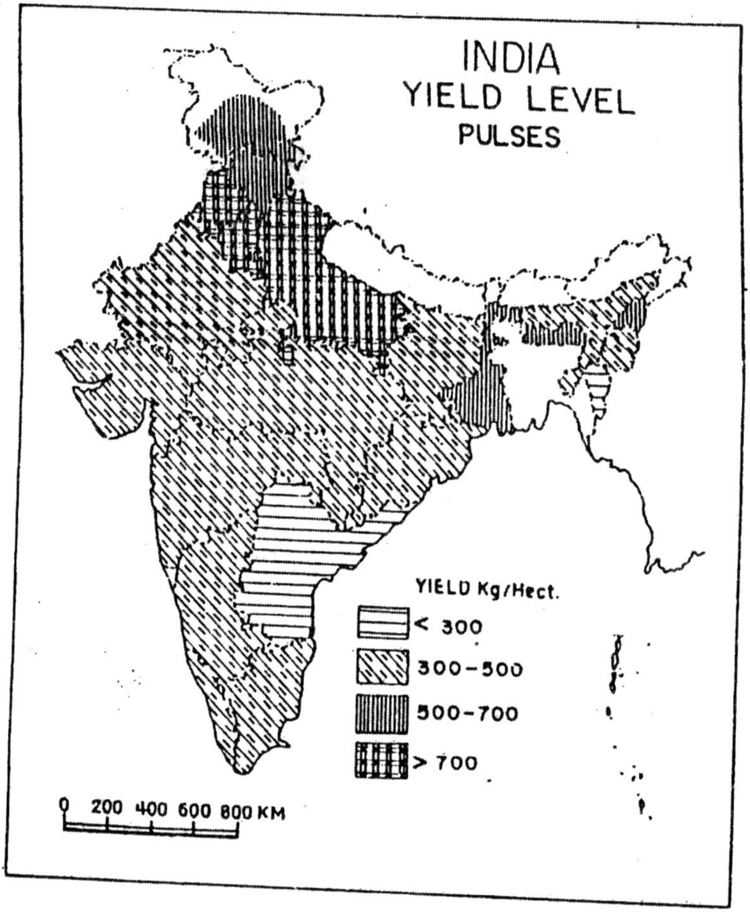
INDIA
YIELD LEVEL
PULSES
YIELD Kg/Hect.
< 300
300–500
500–700
> 700
0 200 400 600 800 KM

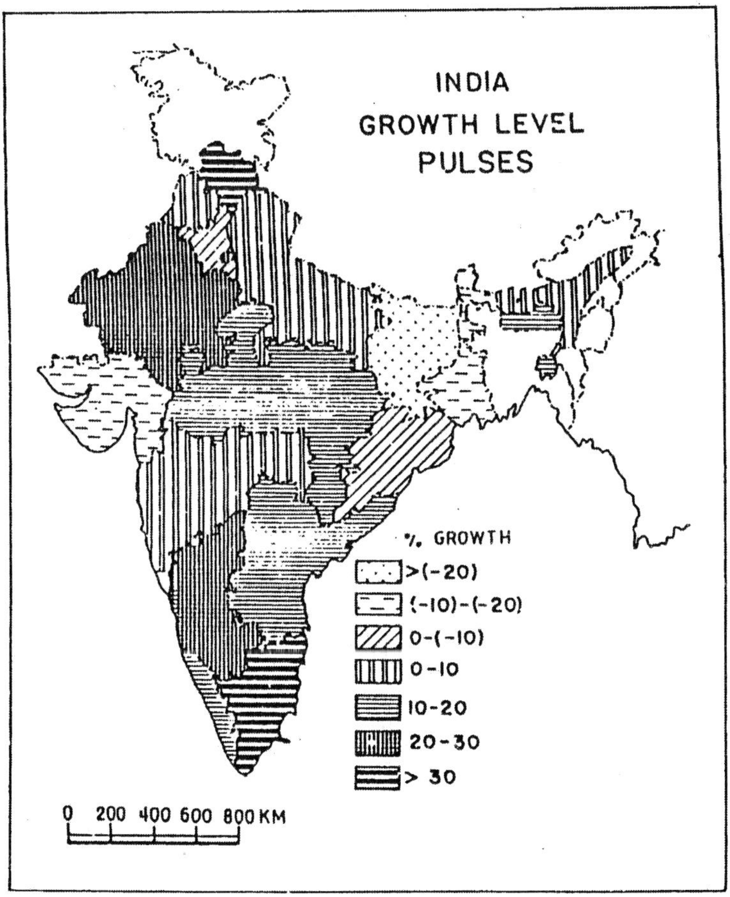
INDIA
GROWTH LEVEL
PULSES
% GROWTH
>(-20)
(-10)-(-20)
0-(-10)
0-10
10-20
20-30
> 30
0 200 400 600 800 KM

REFERENCES

1. (a) Vaidyanathan, A., Performance and prospects of crops production in India, *Economic and Political Weekly*, Vol. XII No. 33834 special No. 1977, pp. 1355-1368.

(b) Bhalla, G.S., *Performance of Agricultural Crops in India*, Sterling Publishers, 1978. New Delhi.

(c) Hanumantha Rao, C.H., Agricultural Growth and Rural Poverty – Some lessons from Past Experiences, *Economics & Pol. Weekly*, Vol. XII, No. 33-34, 1977, pp. 1369-1374.

(d) Tyagi, B.N., A Study of the Impact of Green Revolution on the Regional Development of Agriculture, *Indian Journal of Agri. Eco.*, Oct-Dec. 1974.

3

Environmental Framework of Indian Agriculture – A Regional Dimension

All the developing countries of the world have more or less the same problems of agricultural development as in India. But there are certain problems which are unique, i.e. reliance of agrarian economy on a highly erratic and unpredictable monsoon rainfall. The magnitude of crop failures and widespread economic losses depends upon the rainfall and its high or low range of variability.

In Indian context weather will continue to be as one of the major deciding factors of agricultural production. About 80 per cent of the cultivated area depends on rainfall, low precipitation and majority of these areas belong to drought prone districts. So the dominating factor limiting expansion of agriculture are the low irrigation potential utilization and unproductive nature of rainfall.

Weather is a key variable in agricultural production, and land is the residual claimant of agricultural earnings. Since our farming solely depends on rainfall which changes the whole production schedule and the entire system becomes indeterminate. This phenomena is applicable to entire region with the exception of the variability in the degrees of risk in certain regions which also create regional imbalances in farm productivity. Advancement in irrigation and flood control have been made but it has touched only the fringe of the problems and on the whole monsoon is still a powerful control to be reckoned within all calculations of agricultural planning.

Though the environmental, economic and institutional factors are all important in shaping the pattern of Indian agriculture but the environmental conditions holds the greatest influence on not only the existing pattern but even to measure the agricultural potential for future planning. Our technological development is not enough to fulfill the requirement for backward agricultural development and even the implementation of it is conditioned by the environmental or economic conditions. The various input (fertilizer, HYV and irrigation, mechanisation) for agricultural development is available meagerly which is not enough to control the environmental determinism. India being a vast country is not homogeneous in environmental factors. These regional physical variations affect the cropping pattern, extension of cultivation, intensity of cultivation and systems and nature of irrigation etc. Therefore, for the purpose of analysing the crop production potential and to lay down priorities for certain region it seems necessary to have an environmental regional framework.

The form and nature of the terrain is one of the major deciding factors of land use as well as grewth and spatial distribution of crops. Relief and structure of the land have exercised a direct influence on land use, cropping pattern and spatial diversity in crop and yield. Even in the alluvial plain, extended for Rajasthan - Punjab to Bengal, Assam, factors of climate, soils and hydrology give rise to clearly marked divisions in the agricultural land occupance. For example, bajra is a first ranking crop in arid and semi-arid environment while rice in the humid conditions in Bengal - Assam plain within the same relief region of Satluj-Gangetic plain.

Therefore, a perfect analysis is needed of the India agricultural environment to understand how a particular kind of farming systems have developed in a particular area and how they are similar to or different from the farming of other areas, how these farming systems are changing and to demarcate 'Weaker Areas' and to delimit the areas of agricultural dynamism. An agricultural geographer should organize such type of studies with reference to the agronomic, socio economic basis of farming in time and space perspective. However, on the basis of comprehensive study of land, climate and soil available, water resources, the crop distribution and yield, cropping pattern, crop status, corp combination, levels of agricultural production, delimitaticn of crop producing regions, the weaker and disadvantageous areas can be easily delineated.

Due to the spatial differences in physical environment, there is a considerable spatial differences in the trends of agricultural development. The regional variations in the distributional patterns of agricultural controls may reflect a number of agricultural circumstances. With vast areal differences in topography, climate, soils, irrigation facilities etc. the agricultural attributes would not naturally be uniform all over India. The areas having assured rainfall and developed water supply differ from the areas where rainfall is low or scanty and irrigation facilities are available only to a small proportion of the net area sown and where the possibilities of further development of irrigation are limited. In the latter, the progress in agricultural development should only be lower in the long run as compared to the farmer having assured rainfall and adequate irrigation facilities.

However, the regional distribution of crops exhibits the physical complexity of the region. The agricultural fabric of India is perhaps the best expression of its physiognomic environment in its geographical setting. Cropping pattern or cropping zones and agricultural regions of India are direct result of terrain characteristics, soils and rainfall. The diversities of morphology, lithology and climatic factors reflect in degree of intensity and diverse pattern of crops in the region.

Due to the low level of input in Indian agriculture, it is controlled by the environmental factors. These inputs have been innovated and diffused only in those areas where the natural factors are favourable and more chances to have the higher profitability.

To get an idea of the productivity of various land type, land should be classified for a rational land use planning. Selection of crops should be based on these classification to get the maximum results through the knowledge of the suitability of land for specific purpose. Therefore, through the land capability classification survey it becomes possible to devote the existing land to the most suited crops. Hence, the land use planning should largely rests upon the land of special qualities for special uses.

Relief Features and Slope Zones

Keeping in view the relief feature with agricultural relevance India can be divided into eight slope zones where cropping pattern more or less is quite different on each relief zones. These regions can further be sub-divided into many regions for agricultural relevance. For example, the alluvial plain from Rajasthan – Punjab to Bengal Assam experiences varied climate and water availability. Therefore, the agricultural development or diversity in levels of development is on account of the limitations imposed by only one factor i.e. soil moisture or soil moisture retaining capacity in these sub-regions.

Taking into consideration the relief feature of India as a whole, about 48 per cent of the total land area has an elevation of below 300 metre. This area have mostly alluvium soil and agriculture is practised extensively with minimum natural limitations as water logging, flooding, water table, soil infestations and saline efflorescence and paucity of moisture in certain parts i.e. western part of India and leeward areas of the ghats. In this region differences in relief are less important than differences in soils and variations in rainfall, therefore, spatial variations possess variable agricultural potentials throughout the area.

The relief zone between 300 to 600 metre plays an important role in the spatial distribution of crops. The total area covered by this region is about 26 per cent of the total area of India. The main appearance of the upland is that of an old, worn and rugged upland but a large portion is accessible for cultivation. 1. High mountains (over 2400 m.), mountains (1200 to 2400 m.), high hills (600-1200 m.), high plateaus (600-1200 m. in southern India), low hills (300-600), low plateau (300-600) plains (150-300 m) low plains (below 1500 m., generally affected by the water logging the flood).

On the whole physical resource base of India offers both opportunities and challenges to the agricultural endeavour. Relief as such has little effect on agriculture, for the proportion of the land which is too steep or too high to cultivate but not creating any uncertainty. Actually India has been blessed with extensive plains possessing a wealth of agriculture. The configuration of India, thus provides important opportunities for agricultural extensions and future development of irrigation and dry farming. Topographically large tracts are level which are suited to the extensive use of farm machinery in the future, provided these are well drained. In these tracts, though land has enough capability for agricultural development, yet the great limiting is the paucity of moisture created by the rainfall hazards.

Land and Soil Capability

Land use planning largely rests upon the land special qualities for special uses. With competent soil survey work and other production factors optimum farming systems can be developed. Therefore, a detailed soil survey at micro-level (suitability of soil for a particular crop) is necessary all over India which has great potentials to meet the Indian food deficit.

A land capability map is an essential tool for future agricultural planning. The only dependable way determining the capability of land is to make a careful examination of its soil cover in the field. This is done by examining and determining the soil depth, texture, permeability, available moisture capacity, inherent fertility, organic content and other characteristics that affect the use and management and treatment of the agricultural land. Soil must be classified according to agricultural capability rather than genetic classification where agricultural planning purposes are concerned.

Different structure of soil have different requirements of fertilisers both in quality and quantity. However, soils may suffer due to the climatic reasons as salinity and alkalinity, water logging deficient in chemical and biological nutrients especially in the region of semi arid and arid. Secondly, climatic factors are also responsible for the soil moisture deficiency, thirdly, problems of erosion exist especially in the areas of Chambal Catchment and in other regions of different magnitude. Anyone of the above factors may cause a depressing effects on crop yield.

. As it is clear that production capabilities of the soil differ from place to place and specific soil is suited only to specific crops. However, soil is a very complex phenomena of environment, needs a detailed micro-level survey to find out the deficiency for a particular crop.

Soils Classification is Relation to Agricultural Performance

Soil may be traditionally classified into five broad macro regions related to major regional complexes; the alluvial soils, the sandy soils the black soils, the laterite soils, the red soils lying on the metamorphic rocks for a proper correlative study of the areal pattern of crops. It is essential to gain detailed knowledge of the patterns of soil within soil macro-regions.

1. The alluvial soils possesses great natural fertility and less dependent on soil management than other soils. But in some regions due to the excessive use of the land for higher yield it has been modified. The effect of rainfall is very significant as in some parts alluvial is loose in texture on account of low rainfall and excessive evaporation and in some parts it is compact due to heavy rainfall and low lands.

This is the largest and the most important soil of India, contributing the largest share to the agricultural wealth of the country which covers about 22 per cent of the total soil cover.[1] A great deal of sub-ordinate variations in soil composition exist owing to the spatial variability in rainfall, the nature of transported materials and weathering process. Therefore, it is divided as riverine alluvium, coastal alluvium, deltaic alluvium, saline and alkaline soils, calcareous alluvial soils and brown pedocal soils. It is the most significant and fertile amongst the Indian soils, producing a wide variety of crops i.e. paddy, wheat, sugarcane, cotton, tobacco and oilseeds. The old alluvium occupying higher grounds is not subject to flooding and replenishment of fertility is not possible. Old riverine alluvium is confined mainly to north-western, northern and north-eastern parts of India occupying the plains of Punjab, Haryana, Uttar Pradesh, Bihar, West Bengal and Assam Valley. The coastal alluvium have low fertility rating and moisture holding capacity is poor due to the sandy to sandy loam texture. Coconut and paddy are the important crops being raised on this soil. The deltaic alluvium of Godavari, Krishna, Cauvery (Thanjavur distt.) are heavier and richer in plant nutrients and good crops of paddy is grown as the fertility rating of this soil is very high. Old alluvium are generally affected by salinity and alkalinity which is concentrated in western Uttar Pradesh, Punjab and Haryana plains. The fertility rating is considerably low in the districts of Pilibhit, Bijnor, Moradabad, Meerut (U.P.) and Karnal (Haryana) but due to the high level of input (irrigation and fertilizer) in some of these districts productivity level is high. A wide belt of black alluvium is found in Punjab and Haryana (Ferozpur, Bhatinda, Hissar) which is suited to Cotton and wheat cultivation.

2. Sandy soils have developed where rainfall is scanty and arid and semi-arid conditions prevails. These soils cover about 8.5 per cent of the national soil over. Due to the less moisture retaining capacity in the soil, these soils have limited capacity to face even the short period of drought and hence crops suffer. The chief characteristics of these soils are that these are very light, well drained and highly permeable which causes for poor average yield.

The scarcity of moisture prevails because this region receives only 30 cms. of rainfall. Inferior quality of food crops (millets, jowar and pulses) are grown on these soils. Due to the sandy nature of soil in eastern Rajasthan uplands and north-east in Chambal basin, the soil is fertile but very much prone to erosion due to the soft nature of soil and low cover of vegetation and, therefore, gully erosion on a very extensive area have been formed. On the whole this tract is fertile but not productive due to unfavourable conditions. This soil needs extension of irrigation systems. This soil is suitable for barley, rapeseeds and mustard cotton, as well as wheat millet, maize and pulses.

3. Black soils cover about 24 per cent of the total cover of the soil. These soils have different fertility level at different places. The deep black soil (high-fertility), medium black soil (moderate fertility), the shallow black soil (low fertiiity) and the mixed red and black soils have depressed fertility. The deep black soil is found on level topography of the Deccan plateau as well as in the river valley basin. It is spread on Maharashtra plateau along the valleys of Tapti and Purnea river, Wardha valley and plain of Nagpur. This belt is important for growing the cotton. This soil have a considerable capacity of moisture retaining, therefore, rabi crops is also successful without irrigation. The deep black soils are also found in Gujarat in the districts of Surat, Broach and Baroda. In Madhya Pradesh it covers the major parts of Narmada Valley and level plateau of Vindhya and Satpura, especially in the districts of Narsimhapur and Hoshangabad. In Mysore, black soils are found mainly in the districts of Bijapur, Gulbarga, Bidar, Belgaum, Dharwar and Raichur. Northern parts to Telengana region extending from Adilabad in the west of Khammam district in the east. These soils are characterised by their heaviness and high fertility due to the high clay content. These are intensively cultivated and particularly suitable for cotton, wheat and jowar. The medium black soil is less fertile than the deep black soil. These soils are developed on uplands and slopes and texture varies from loam to clay loam. These soils have high moisture retaining capacity, therefore, rabi crops can be successfully grown. Cotton, wheat and jowar are the major crops where irrigation facilities are available, rice and sugarcane are also grown. In Madhya Pradesh, this soil cover the largest area comprising mainly the Malwa plateau, Nimar region and extending upto Sidhi district, in Gujarat it is found in Sabarkantha and Baroda districts. The shallow black soils cover hill slopes of Maharashtra. These soils are sandy in nature and suited to the gram, cotton, wheat and jowar crops. This soil can give better production if irrigated and manured. The poor soil mixed with red and black soils are found throughout peninsular India on the rugged hills. These soils are located in Dharwar, Belgaum, Raichur and Bijapur districts of

Karnataka and in Tamil Nadu Coimbatore plateau. In Madhya Pradesh these soils are in Bundelkhand and Baghelkhand areas. These soils differ to a large extent in depth and fertility and producing large number of crops depending on climatic conditions and types of irrigation. In Uttar Pradesh these soils are found in southern upland in the districts of Jalaum, Hamirpur, Banda and Jhansi. On the whole, their fertility rating is low to medium. These soils at upper elevation are usually unsuitable for cultivation.

4. The red soils have mainly a sandy and loamy texture, such as, gravelly sands on upper slopes, sandy and deeper loams on the lower slopes, and loams and clayey loams on the valley bottoms. Their productive capacity varies on the basis of variable texture. On the whole these soils cover about 29 per cent of the total soil cover. The red soils are the deepest with highest productivity. These soils dominate in Orissa, south-eastern Madhya Pradesh, eastern Maharashtra, north and central Andhra Pradesh, the plantation districts of Shimoga, Hassan and Coorg in Mysore and eastern Kerala. They produce a large variety of crops (paddy, jowar, ragi) with irrigation. The red gravelly sandy soils occupy a considerable area in Tamil Nadu, Mysore and Andhra Pradesh. These are utilised mainly for the cultivation of inferior Kharif millets and pulses and with irrigation cotton can be grown. The red yellow loams have a widest distribution. There are dominant expanses of these soils are observed in Orissa, Madhya Pradesh and Assam. These soils have low fertility rating. They can produce a number of crops under irrigation.

The red soils differ in physical composition with a black soils. Black soils are clayey white red soils are sandy and coarser in texture and also less moisture is retained by soils. The red soils is very much drought prone, it can be proved agriculturally good when it is irrigated. In the valleys red soils are of very high productive value, when irrigated and manured they may yield two or three crops a year. Irrigation is essential over most of the red loam lands.

5. Laterite is a very porous soil with low fertility and very much prone to the drought because of less capacity to retain moisture. These are developed on the flat topped hills and gently sloping surfaces of Andhra Pradesh, Mysore, Kerala, Maharashtra, Tamil Nadu, West Bengal and Assam. It occupies about 4 per cent of the national soil cover. On lower grounds paddy is grown on this soil. On the whole this is a soil of commercial crops like coconut, coffee,

rubber and tea when it is irrigated.

6. Forest soils cover about 7 per cent of the total soil cover. On the terraces paddy is grown. This soil is largely suitable for orchards, crops, forest trees maize and wheat.

7. Tarai soils are sub-recent origin with alluvial texture. They lie in the narrow elongated region of the foothills of Himalayas. This soil is very fertile due to the high content of nitrogen. When it is reclaimed good crops of paddy sugarcane and wheat can be produced.

8. 'Khadar' is a sandy soil adjacent to the river banks which vary in texture from river to river. It contains some times undue proportion of sand and is consequently endowed with comparatively inferior quality. It is of recent origin having been deposited from the annual inundation of the river, where the silts or sandy loams are deposited it retains high fertility. The soil is liable to dry out in times of low rainfall or leached out when the rainfall is heavy. Generally poor quality grains are grown on this soil, i.e. maize, millets barley and gram etc.

Keeping in view the marked a real differences in soils and relief all agricultural lands are not of homogeneous quality. For example an ideal soil for oilseeds is not necessarily the best soil for gram crops, or the most suitable soils for wheat and rice identical since climatic conditions not the same everywhere, an alluvial soil while suffers from soil moisture deficit in the north west may have advantages in area of high rainfall in Bihar and Bengal plains. Even today a detailed soil survey is needed in the context of recommend the crop rotation, cropping patterns, crop combinations and methods of cultivation with judicious use of the surface and ground water.

Rainfall Characteristics

The spatial distribution of rainfall is not adequate everywhere. The inadequacy and uncertainty often causes partial or complete failure of crops leading to periodic scarcity or even famine conditions. In this situation farmer has to adopt dry farming methods in the areas of low and uncertain rainfall.

The striking features of the rainfall distribution are very heavy over 400 cm. over the Southern slopes of Khasi Hills, Brahmputra Valley and the Western ghats, heavy rainfall amounting to over 200 cm. over the whole of Assam and the west coast of the Peninsula and low rainfall of less than 40 cm. over west Rajasthan and a large portions of it receiving less than 20 cm. There are large pockets of central Maharashtra and Marathwada (Districts of Dhulia, Jalgaon, Ahmednagar, Sholapur, Sangli, Aurangabad and Bihar) and some pockets in south Tamil Nadu where the annual rainfall is below 75 cm. It is possible to go into greater detail and delineate and hard cores of low rainfall at micro-level (stationwise). For example, Hissar district in Punjab receives only 37 cm. and Rohtak 46 cm. Jaisalmer 16 cm and Ganganagar 25 cm. Kutch district 32 cm. Anantpur 54 cm. Billary in Mysore 57 cm and Ahmednagar district Maharashtra 58 cm. These are some pockets in West Rajasthan which receive less than 10 cm. of rain per year.

However, most of the rainfall in the country is received during south west monsoon which is about 80% of the annual rainfall. In the arid and semi-arid parts it accounts for more than 90%. In Maharashtra and north Gujarat the share is more than 95%.

In the monsoon rains of the country there can be four important variations from the normal. Firstly, the beginning of the rains may be delayed considerably over a large part of the country; secondly, there may be prolonged breaks lasting over the greater part of July and August; thirdly, the rains may end considerably earlier than usual and lastly, the rains may persist more than usual in one part of the country. The consequences of third variations are occasionally very serious and have been disastrous in the extreme in the drought prone areas.

The rainfall during the cold weather is scanty but essential and economically important for the production of wheat crops over northern India and this rain is very significant in south east Madras, also. The less the rainfall and more variability and vice-versa is a general observation of the variability of Indian rainfall in space and time. Long breaks in the monsoon and abrupt retreat of it is disastrous to crops or produces droughts followed by famines. A detailed description of the distribution and variability of rainfall in space and time is given below.

1. In the months of January and February rainfall is light. The average exceeds 5 cm. in east Assam, Bihar, north U.P. eastern and southern half of Tamil Nadu, South Kerala, North Punjab and Haryana and adjoining U.P. and J&K to the hills of U.P. where rainfall varies from 10 to 30 cm. for J & K, this account for 20% of the total annual rainfall. In north east Assam rainfall varies upto 10

cm., the average on the whole state being 6 cm. In terms of annual this rainfall accounts for only 20% of the total. In the peninsula rainfall is mainly confined to a narrow coastal belt to the south of Madras. The variability of rainfall is very high over entire country, being more than 80 to 100 per cent, except of Kashmir, and North east Assam where it is 40 to 50 per cent. The frequency of rainy days is 10 to 20 in central Southern Kashmir and 10 to 15 in North east Assam. In the plains at the foot of the Himalayas, the frequency generally exceeds 5 days.

2. In the months of March-May, about half of the country receive more than 5 cm. of rains. In the Khasi and Jaintia Hills rainfall reaches 10 cm. Similarly rainfall increases in south east direction with maximum over south Kerala. The average for the whole State being 40 cm. Another significant area is Kashmir which receives 20 to 40 cm. In this season, the average for the whole state is 24 cm. which is 23% of the annual. Although rainfall is highly variable over most of the country yet it is noteworthy that co-efficient of variations is less than 30% in north east Assam and between 40% to 50% in the southern India (excluding coastal belts). Rainy days increases in frequency to more than 40 in North East Assam, the average for the whole of Assam being 31. Sub-Himalaya West Bengal average is 20 days. The other significant areas central and southern Kashmir and adjoining Himachal Pradesh where the rainy days range between 10 to 30 and in the peninsula south of 13° N and west of long. 77° E. with 10 to 20 days. Himachal Pradesh and J & K have about the same average of 15 days and Kerala 20 days.

3. In the months of June-September 80% or more of the total annual rainfall is received throughout the country. Assam, Bengal, coastal Orissa and the peninsula South of lat. 18° N. and excluding the west-east coast, Gujarat, North Maharashtra, Kutch and adjoining Rajasthan and M.P. the season accounts for more than 90% of the annual. Orissa, Eastern M.P., Bihar, West Bengal, Assam, and west coast receive more than 100 cm. of rainfall during this period. Sub-mountain belt extending from north Bihar to Jammu also receives more than 100 cm. during this season. The lowest rainfall of the season is in the extreme south-east peninsula where it is less than 10 cm. and in the extreme west of Rajasthan the same situation prevails.

The variability of rainfall of these months is of great significant from agricultural point of view. In July, which is rainfest month over most of the country, the co-efficient of variation is 40 to 50% except of the western India and Jammu area and southern India excluding west coast. Co-efficient of variation over most of these areas exceeds 60% and reaches 80 to 100% or even more. Over a small area along the west coast and in east Assam, coefficient of variation is less than 30%. A noteworthy feature is that, over most of the peninsula east of western Ghats, the coefficient of variation is as high as 80% to 100%. Variability features for August are similar to July. Co-efficient of variation for the month of September, the month of withdrawal of the south west monsoon, show a marked change in peninsula, where it is now reduced to 60%. The main point is the very high variability over most of the country when individual months are considered. There is however a marked change when south-east monsoon season (June-September) is considered as a whole. In Assam and along the west coast, this variability is less than 20%. In east Rajasthan, Gujarat and the peninsula excluding south Tamil Nadu, seasonal coefficient of variability is 30 to 40%.

In the monsoon season the frequency of rainy days exceeds 75 along the west coast, south and north east Assam and northern portion of sub-Himalayas and Bengal. The noteworthy sub-divisional average are coastal Karnataka 92 days, Kerala 79, Konkon 84, Islands 80, Assam 68, sub-Himalayan west Bengal 70. The lowest is in the extreme western Rajasthan & South east Tamil Nadu with less than 5 days. West Rajasthan average is 14 days.

4. In the months of October to December rainfall is more than 20 cm. in the peninsula (Karnataka, South Andhra Pradesh and Southern Karnataka). A narrow east coast strip gets more than 75 cm. and in most of Kerala rainfall exceed 50 cm. Some of the significant sub-divisional averages are Kerala 55 cm., Tamil Nadu 48 cm., Coastal A.P. and Rayalseema 21 cm. In Gujarat, Rajasthan, Western M.P., Western U.P. and Jammu region, rainfall everywhere exceeded 5 cm. In Himachal Pradesh and central southern Kashmir, rainfall varies between 5 to 15 cm. The rainfall of this season accounts for more than 30% of the annual in the peninsula (southern) in the southeast of Tamil Nadu the percentage exceeds 30. In the Northeast of India the percentage varies from 5 to 10. Co-efficient of variability is 40 to 50% in the peninsula (southern) with more than 20 days of rainfall. The significant sub-divisional average are: Kerala 26, Tamil Nadu 22, Bay Islands 34. In Assam and in small areas north of Srinagar in Kashmir 7 days only.

Elsewhere in the country the frequency of rain days is small.

As most of the rainfall of the country is received during the south east monsoon period. Rainfall is generally 100 cm. in areas to the east of 70° E. (eastern Uttar Pradesh, Bihar West Bengal, Assam, Orissa and eastern part of M.P.). Rainfall exceeds 250 cm. along the entire west coast and the western ghats and over most of Assam, adjoining sub-Himalayas West Bengal. Annual totals upto 300 cm. have been noted in the western Himalayas also. West of the isohyetal line joining Porbandar to Delhi and from thence to Ferozpur, rainfall diminishes rapidly from 50 cm., to less than 15 cm. in the extreme west. The peninsula also has elongated area of less than 60 cm. with pockets of 50 cm.

In the entire area of the country excluding Kashmir, Rajasthan and Gujarat regions, coefficient of variability of rainfall generally varies between 15 to 30% only. Coefficient of variability, which is 20% covers west Bengal, Orissa Plateau and Assam over Gujarat and Rajasthan co-efficient of variability exceeds 40% variation of 20% isolines runs along the west coastal south of Bombay. It also covers almost the entire area of the country of long. 80° E. This is an important feature which shows the rainfall, though highly variable when considered in individual months is stable for the year as a whole. The annual frequency exceeds 100 days along the west coast with pockets of 125 days and eastern Assam and sub-Himalayas West Bengal. The principal sub-divisional averages are Assam 114, Sub-Himalayan West Bengal 99, Konkon 93, coastal Karnataka 112 and Kerala 126. Almost the entire country east of long. 78° E has rain on more than 50 days. The lowest frequency in the peninsula is in Maharashtra and Karnataka on the side of the Ghats, Rayalseema and extreme south east Tamil Nadu, with 40 days or less. The extreme west of Rajasthan and Kutch rain occur on less than 10 days in the year. The annual frequency of west Rajasthan is only 17 days, south Gujarat and Kutch 23 days, these are the lowest in the country.

Drought Affected Areas

Occurrence of drought is not a phenomena only in arid or semi-arid regions of India, but in other parts of the country too. (Semi-arid Tamil Nadu, Karnataka, Andhra Pradesh, Maharashtra and M.P. eastern Rajasthan, Gujarat, Western U.P. dry humid Uttar Pradesh, Bihar plain Orissa, moist-sub-humid west Bengal etc.). Severe drought occurred in 1966-67 in Bihar, eastern U.P. Orissa and Maharashtra, again in 1972 in Maharashtra, Karnataka, Rajasthan and Gujarat, in 1947 in Rajasthan in 1975 in Bihar South. Thus a major part of India is under a constant threat of drought. Almost every year drought is occurring. About 20% of the net cultivated area is vulnerable to this serious natural hazard every year. There was a 19% fall in agricultural output in 1965-66 resulting in a severe set back in the national economy. Similar situation also occurred in the year 1979-80.

The main characteristic and cause of drought is the water scarcity and this is a common feature for the people in dry area. But the seasonal drought of semi-arid and sub-humid region is much more devastating. Drought is a greatest natural hazard to agriculture. Specially due to inadequacy of moisture at critical time during the growing season of the crops and yield is affected very adversely. Therefore, in considering the drought problems and its intensity, we must know the critical growth period of the crop and the need for water at this particular stage. Therefore, the deficiency of water or moisture availability for the crops should not be considered at annual, seasonal or even monthly total of rainfall. Even a weekly rainfall for various critical crop growth periods should be analysed.

There are some critical periods of rainfall in a certain parts of India for Kharif crops, that if it fails the crops will be devastated. For example rainfall of the last week of September and first week of October (a period of 15 days) is of great significance both for kharif (for maturing the crops) as well as for rabi (sowing starts at this time) and moisture availability is needed for proper maturing of grains germination of the seeds. Though the percentage and amount of this rain [this rain many local names for example in Uttar Pradesh) it is known as *Sona* or *Sonawa* and in the eastern part (Bihar) it is known chiefly as *Hathia*] is very negligible in comparison to the rainy season and annual rainfall, but its contribution to both the crops (rabi and kharif) yield is very high. But this rainfall of the last week of September and first week of October in the cotton belt proves to be very injurious for cotton crops. However, different crops have different types of need vary in time and space. For example rainfall in the months of December and in March in the irrigated tract is damaging while in unirrigated tract rainfall is beneficial during the entire crops season. Similarly for rice crop heavy rain is useful in July but injurious and adversely affected by heavy rain in August. The Institute of Agricultural Research and Statistics has carried out a linear regression analysis with yield as the dependent variable and total rainfall during the five crop growth phases as independent variable. It was noticed that about 47% variation in wheat yield was due to variation in the rainfall during each period. In Raipur district (M.P.) the total rainfall for the months of June and August does not have much effect on rice production, the total rainfall during the month of July and September has greater influence on the crop yield. During the month of July a deficiency of the order of 16% in rainfall should have an adverse effect on crop production, while the corresponding percentage in the month of September was of the order of 13 per cent.

Variations in Environmental Determinants and Formation of Regional Physical Complex in relation to agriculture

A natural region should be a basic unit for land use planning, in which the whole environmental complex must be taken into account. The main factors of the physical environment are geology, geomorphology, climate, hydrology, Soils and Vegetation. Of these climate and soil present special problems in distributional study. Each factor varies over the country in a different manner. Therefore, a complex (unit) should be formed based on the earth's surface within which the physical environment and all environmental conditions are relatively uniform.

The physical conditions holds important place to give a varied pattern of land use as well as useful for the evaluation of land use potential. In India there is a marked variations in physical features, and on the whole, it is a dominant factor in giving a diversified pattern of crops and crop yield in different points of time in the country. As we know the characteristics of rainfall discussed earlier as well as moisture availabilities in different soil types. Surface and ground water altitudinal differences etc., they all combindly affect the agriculture. A composite picture will give a interrelationship among the different physical factors and land use, and an individual dominant factor affecting landuse can easily be marked. Keeping in view the size and location of the country, it has been divided into many regions and subregions based on L.S. Bhatt (1967) classification as he classified the country into fifteen major regions and sixty subregions.[2]

Each physical unit will be helpful in evaluating the regional potentials in crop production, priority to a particular crop, cost benefit analysis either by reclamation of the land or irrigating the land according to the need of irrigation etc. It will also be helpful in understanding the magnitude of the problems of land use integration, soil erosion and conservation, tapping of areas with extremely low or high capability for production planning as the landuse planning for agricultural purposes should largely rests upon the land of special qualities for special uses. These aspects need a thorough analysis in terms of the physical setting. Physical complex together with the crop productivity and crop association regions will help to identify regions for landuse planning and to visualize regional specialization in long terms planning. It will also help in deciding the norms of agricultural inputs in a scientific manner keeping in view the nutrients of soil and effect or intensive irrigation so that the cultivated land may be cultivated profitably for a long time. It will also help to estimate the input requirement. A micro-level study or a physical complex will be helpful in classifying the land into various capabilities classes and especially to evaluate the production potential of the physical units. However, on the basis of physical variations (temperature rainfall, relief, structure of the soil and water availability etc.), the country can be divided into many regions and sub-regions in accordance to agricultural problem.

1. **West Coast**
   A. Northern (Surat, Valsad, Thana, Kolaba, Ratnagiri, Dadar and Nagar Haveli, Daman)
   B. Central (North Kanara, S. Kanara and Goa)
   C. Southern (all districts of Kerala, Kanyakumari)

2. **Western Ghats**
   A. Northern (Dangs, Nasik, Poona, Satara, Sangli, Kolhapur, Belgaum)
   B. Southern (Shimoga, Chikmagalur, Hassan, Coorg, Nilgiri)

3. **East Coast**
   A. Northern Deltaic (Mahanadi Delta) - Cuttack, Puri.
   B. Northern Non-Deltaic (Balasore, Ganjam, Srikakulam, Vishakhapatnam)

C. Central Deltaic (Krishna-Godavari Delta); (East Godavari, W. Godavari, Krishna, Guntur)
D. Central non-Deltaic (Nellore Angola)
E. Southern Deltaic (Cauvery Delta), (Thanjavur, Karikanal)
F. Southern Non-Deltaic (Chingleput, North Arcot, S. Arcot, Ramanathapuram, Tirunelveli, Pondichery).

4. **Peninsular Plateau-South**
   A. Mysore Plateau (Kolar, Tumkur, Mandya Mysore, Bangalore)
   B. Coimbatore Plateau (Salem Tiruchirapalli, Coimbatore, Madurai, Dharmapuri)

5. **Peninsular Plateau-Central**
   A. Khandesh (Tapti Basin)-Dhulia, Jalgaon.
   B. Ajanta-Balaghat Hill & Valleys (Ahmednagar, Aurangabad, Parbhani Bhir, Nanded, Osmanabad, Bidar).
   C. Upper Krishna Basin (Sholapur, Gulbarga, Bijapur, Dharwar)
   D. Tungbhadra Canal (Raichur & Ballary)
   E. Telengana (Nizamabad, Madak, Nalgonda, Hyderabad, Mahbubnagar)
   F. Transitional Area (Anantpur, Chitradurga)
   G. Rayalseema (Kurnool, Cuddapah, Chittor).

6. **Peninsular Plateau-North**
   A. Chambal Ravines (Morena, Bhind, Gwalior, Datia, Shivpuri, Sawai Madhopur).
   B. Bundelkhand, Plateau (Jhansi, Tikamgarh, Chattarpur).
   C. Malwa Plateau (Mandsor, Ratlam, Ujjain, Indore, Dewas, Shajapur, Guna, Rajgarh, Vidisha, Sehore, Raisen, Sagar, Damoh, Kota Jhalwar.
   D. Narmada Trough (Dhar, West Nimar, East Nimar, Hoshangabad, Narsimhapur).
   E. Mahadeo Hills-Betual, Chindwara, Seoni.
   F. Vidarbha (Buldana, Akola, Amravti, Yeotmal, Wardna, Nagpur).

7. **Peninsular Plateau (North-Eastern)**
   A. Rewa Plateau (Panna, Satna, Rewa, Mirzapur)

B. Baghelkhand Plateau (Jabalpur, Sidhi, Surguja, Shahdol, Mandla, Raigarh)
C. Chotanagpur Plateau (Ranchi, Singhbhum, Palamau Hazaribagh, Dhanbad, Purulia)
D. Chattisgarh Sambalpur Area (Bhandara, Balaghat, Durg, Bilaspur, Raipur, Kalahandi, Bolangir, Sambalpur, Sundargarh)
E. Orissa Hills (Mayurbhanj Keonjhar Dhenkanal, Boudh-khondmals)
F. Bastar Hills & Forests (Koraput, Bastar, Chanda)
G. Adilabad, Karimnagar, Warangal and Khammam.

8. **North-Eastern Mountain and Valleys**
A. Brahmaputra-Tista Valley (Lakhimpur, Sibsagar, Nowgong, Darrang, Kamrup, Goalpara, Cooch-Behar, Jalpaiguri, Darjeeling)
B. Cachar-Tripura Lowlands (Cachar and Tripura)
C. Shillong Plateau (Garo Hills, J & K Hills)
D. North-eastern Folded ranges and Valleys (Mizo Hills, Arunachal Pradesh, Nagaland, Manipur)

9. **The Lower Ganges Plain**
A. Lower Ganges Plain (Gorakhpur, Deoria, Ballia, Azamgarh, Ghazipur, Champaran, Saran, Muzaffarpur, Darbhanga, Saharsa, Purnea, Bhagalpur, Santhal Paragana, Monghyr, Patna, Gaya, Shahabad, Malda, W. Dinajpur)
B. Ganges Delta (Murshidabad Birbhum, Nadia, Burdwan, Bankur, Midnapur, 24-Parganas, Hooghly, Howrah)

10. **Upper Ganges Plain**
A. Western U.P. Plain (Bulandshahr, Meerut, Saharanpur, Muzaffarnagar, Bijnor, Moradabad, Rampur, Bareily, Pilibhit, Kheri, Sitapur, Hardoi, Shahjahanpur, Badaun, Aligarh, Mathura, Agra, Etah, Mainpuri, Farukhabad, Etawah, Kanpur, Unnao, Lucknow, Bharatpur.
B. Eastern U.P. Plains (Bahraich, Gonda, Basti, Faizabad, Barabanki, Raebareilly, Sultanpur, Pratapgarh, Jaunpur, Varanasi, Allahabad, Fatehpur)
C. Bundelkhand Tract (Jalaun, Hamirpur, Banda)

11. **Punjab Plains**
   A. Shiwalik Foothills (Gurdaspur, Amritsar, Hoshiarpur, Jullundur, Kapurthala, Ludhiana, Patiala, Ambala)
   B. Central Irrigated Area (Ferozepur, Bhatinda, Sangrur, Karnal, Rohtak)
   C. Southern Area Margin (Hissar, Mahendragarh, Gurgaon, Ganganagar).

12. **North Eastern Transitional Region**
   A. Aravalli Ranges (Nagaur, Sikar, Jhunjhunu)
   B. Aravalli Mass (Mt. Abu) - (Sirohi and Udaipur)
   C. Mewar Plateau (Alwar, Jaipur, Tonk, Ajmer, Bhilwara, Bundi, Chittaurgarh.

13. **North Western Zone**
   A. Sand dunes Area (Jalore, Barmer, Jodhpur, Jaisalmer, Bikaner, Churu)
   B. Rann of Kutch (Kutch)

14. **Gujarat**
   A. Gujarat uplands (Dungarpur, Banswara, Jhabua, Banaskantha, Sabarkantha, Panchmahals)
   B. Gujarat Plains (Mehsana, Ahmedabad, Kaira, Baroda, Broach)
   C. Kathiawar (Jamnagar, Rajkot, Surendranagar, Bhavnagar, Amreli, Junagarh).

15. **Northern Mountains**
   A. Karakoram & Ladakh (Ladakh, Gilgit, Wazaret, Chilas)
   B. Kashmir Valley (Srinagar, Baramula, Anantnag)
   C. J & K Hills (Punch, Jammu, Kathua, Udhampur, Doda, Mirpur, Muzaffarbad)
   D. Hills of Punjab & Himachal Pradesh (Kangra, Lahaul & Spiti, Simla, Mahasu, Sirmur, Kinnaur)
   E. U.P. Hills (Pithoragarh, Almora, Nainital, Chamoli, Garhwal, Tehrigarhwal, Dehradun, Uttar Kashi).

16. **Islands**
   A. Andaman & Nicobar (Andaman & Nicobar Islands)
   B. Lacca Dive, Minicoy, and Amini Divi Islands.

1. These three sub-regions are situated in a longitudinal narrow belt having more or less a common characteristics. The physical characteristics (relief, rainfall, soils) on the whole have a dominant influence on the existing pattern of landuse. For example paddy and groundnut are the major crops. Both these crops are well suited to the physical characteristics of the region. For future specialization, except of paddy and groundnut, pulses and extension of horticulture can be grown very successfully. Kerala coast is characterised by its double rainfall from both the monsoon (south-west and winter rains). On this Coast landuse pattern and intensity of cultivation reflect the influence of natural environment coconut and paddy cultivation in the coastal plain & valleys, Rubber, Tea and Coffee on the hill slopes and tapioca and pepper in the foothills. The coastal Maharashtra which extends from Bombay to Ratnagiri is suited to horticulture and livestock rearing because of lateritised foothills soil. Cultivated tracts are very narrow and often interrupted by residual hills. Therefore, the extent of cultivated lands and the scope for future expansion are limited. Due to the uneven topography makes it less suitable for increasing the area under cereals and to provide irrigation to the existing cultivated land. On the whole cropped land use in this region is characterised by its intensive cereal farming with emphasis on paddy cultivation. Paddy lands are mostly unirrigated as the rainfall is above the normal requirements and is fairly well distributed from June to September.

Due to the fertile soil and reliable rainfall the productivity level of this belt is very high which ranges between Rs. 949 to Rs. 2795 per hectare. Most of the districts falls between Rs. 1600 to Rs. 2000 per hectare while the national average is Rs. 975 per hectare. This region is free from natural hazards. Intensity of cultivation can be increased with the high level of inputs (irrigation, fertilizer and mechanization).

2. This is forested and rugged terrain. Variation in topography and climate serve to distinguish two separate sub-regions, one in the north and other to the south. The northern sub-region is characterised by flat topped hills and very little forest cover as such. The gentle slopes are used extensively for poor variety millets. Cultivation mostly is dominated by spice and gardens and plantation economy has reached a high level of specialization of coffee, tea and horticulture. There is a vertical zonation of landuse from the valley floor to the crestline of the western ghats which facilitates regional

generalization. This tract is highly affected by the natural limitations. Area under cultivation produces Rs. 431 to Rs. 1345 but most of the districts are below the national average.

3. Physiographically it is a wider plain with three important deltas. There is a significant variations in rainfall, landform and northern part receives rainfall mainly from south-west monsoon. Southern part receives more annual average rainfall than the north due to the significant contribution to winter rainfall. Seasonal variation of rainfall in the seasons of cropping is significant. The cultivation of paddy and sugarcane is not very much dependent on irrigation or hardly need any irrigation. A pattern of diversified cropped landuse exist due to the Canal irrigation in the deltas and tank irrigation elsewhere, especially in coastal Tamil Nadu. Deltas have diversified landuse, with paddy sugarcane and Tobacco, as in Guntur district a variety of oilseeds and pulses are also grown. This region on the whole is an agricultural region with considerable scope for diversified landuse. The uplands of this region are potentially suited to the specialization of horticulture and livestock rearing as we find some isolated pockets of such development. The southern non-deltaic plain are divided in two parts one in north and other in south of the cauvery delta. There is a marked contrasts in topography and climate and the effect of it is clear from the present pattern of landuse. The Ramnad Coast in general is dry and sandy which imposes certain inherent limitations of land productivity. The productivity level of this tract is more or less similar to that of western coast. But there is a big difference in per hectare productivity between deltaic and non-deltaic districts. Productivity level of all the districts of this region is above the national level.

Peninsular Plateau

The peninsular region of India is distinct from the surrounding regions (Ganges plain in the north, eastern and western ghats) of India both physiographically and climatologically. This region being very vast in area from north to south and east to west, it has many climatological & physiographical differences from place to place. Due to wide inter-regional differences this mass of land can be divided into four major regions – (i) Peninsular plateau, south (ii) Peninsular Plateau, central (iii) Peninsular plateau, north (iv) Peninsular plateau north-eastern.

Peninsular Plateau South

This region is less dry in comparison with its northern part and the seasonal distribution of rainfall is also different from northern part as it also receives some rainfall from winter monsoon. Mysore plateau in an area of red soil with tanks and well irrigation. Sugarcane and rice are the important crops of Mandya district while rest of the plateau is suited for rice (a first ranking crop), ragi, groundnut and maize. Coimbatore plateau is an extensive peneplain of low altitude and elsewhere interrupted by isolated hills. This plateau has agricultural diversity due to a number of crops are grown. Paddy is the major crop throughout the plateau. Other crops groundnut, tobacco, sugarcane and cotton. On the whole this region has an intensive agriculture with diversified cropping.

The intensity of cropping in this tract is higher than the other tract of peninsular India. Fertility of the soil is also higher than the other parts of peninsular. Productivity ranges between Rs. 1074 to Rs. 1795 per hectare. All the districts of the region falls above the national average of per hectare production.

Peninsular Plateau Central

This region is located in the rain shadow of the western ghats. It is also a semi-arid zone of India which is characterised as high variability zone of rainfall. This region does not receive winter rainfall. This is driest part of the peninsular. Water deficiency marked by very low rainfall and high variability which is the decisive factor in respect of the cropping pattern. Therefore, hilly areas and unirrigated areas used as grassland economy. The Tapti basin has problems of soil erosion. The Telengana region with its boulder topography and red and sandy soils of very low fertility is the area of low productivity in intensive agriculture. On the whole possibilities of developing irrigation is very limited. This is the most backward area regarding the per hectare productivity. Rayalseema is also very dry area as well as chances of developing irrigation is very dim due to deep sub-soil water.

Due to the less reliability of rainfall both in terms of amount and distribution the productivity of this region is very low. Out of twenty two districts 19 districts falls below the average of the national productivity level. On the whole productivity ranges between 265 to

1297 per hectare. Though the soil is considerably fertile but due to the lack of irrigation facilities productivity is poor.

Peninsular Plateau North

The northern Peninsular plateau falls in the transitional zone of rainfall. Basically the chambal ravines, comprising the districts of Morena, Bhind, Gwalior, Datia, Shivpuri, Sawai Madhopur which form a part of the Malwa plateau are marked off separately on account of intensive erosion giving rise to badland topography. Problems of land reclamation and soil conservation are distinct from the rest of the area. Erosion of such a magnitude is partly due to the underlying sandstone and the sandy soil on surface. These land possesses high fertility. This vast tract of land can be made productive only on the basis of reclamation on a heavy cost. Bundel Khand receives about 40 inches rainfall and soil is of mixed red and black varieties. From the agricultural point of view it is a good quality land. Vidarbha is an area of physical homogeneity in respect of Lava land and rich black soils which make this area an important for cotton growing tract.

The productivity level is slightly better than the peninsular plateau (north) which ranges between Rs. 361 to Rs. 835 per hectare. But all the districts of this tract is below national average productivity. The rainfall in this tract is not reliable but higher than the above region. Throughout this region productivity is more than the adjacent districts of the above mentioned region.

Peninsular Plateau North-Eastern

This region is marked by humid climate, forested hills and valleys. Among the sub-region, the Chattisgarh – Sambalpur area is of agriculturally important, particularly in the cereal farming. The Rewa plateau is distinct from the rest of the plateau in terms of soils. This plateau is basically a zone of transition between the plateau proper and the Ganges plains. Both in terms of physical structure and resource structure this region as a whole is one unit.

Due to the higher rainfall than the other tracts of the peninsular productivity is higher which ranges between Rs. 556 to Rs. 1133 per hectare. Productivity decreases from east to west which follows the general pattern of rainfall as rainfall decreases from east to west.

North-Eastern Mountain and Valleys

The region comprises Brahmputra-Tista Valley, Cachar-Tripura lowlands, Shillong plateau and North-Eastern folded ranges and valleys. The region experiences hot season being shorter, low average temperature and high rainfall. Soils in this region vary along the altitude i.e. in the valley alluvial soils, lateritic soil on the basis of climate, landforms and soils. This region can be easily sub-divided into mountains and valleys whose structure of landuse and potentials are quite different from each other, for example, plantation along the slopes and cereal farming in the valley floor.

Though the productivity data is not available of the mountainous area but the level of productivity of the plain tract is high which ranges between Rs. 1005 to Rs. 1495 per hectare. All the districts falls above the national average. Rainfall reliability is the major factor for this high level of productivity.

The Lower Ganges Plain

On the basis of the landform characteristics this region possesses more or less the similar characteristics from one corner to other but the total rainfall and its seasonal distribution as well as soil types and drainage vary which is responsible to divide this region in two sub-regions, i.e. the lower Ganges plain and the delta. This plain is, to a large extent, transitional between the dry old alluvium (Bhangar) of the upper Ganges plain and humid and largely Khadar (new alluvium) of the Ganges delta. Most of the part of this region is below 150 metres and is very fertile with rich alluvium. Though the soil is poor in low organic and nitrogen matter but the soil composition is such that it favours the cultivation of each and every type of crop that can be produced in semi-tropical low lands. The Ganges delta is covered with newer alluvium and every year the whole tract is enriched by the new layer of silts. A large tract of this region is covered with stagement pools of water. Rice is the dominant crop of this region.

The productivity level of the eastern part of this tract is much higher than the western part where variation ranges between Rs. 1314 to Rs. 1982 per hectare. Eastern part have high intensity of cropping than the western due to moisture availability in the soil throughout the year for cultivation. Other human and physical factors are also responsible for this higher level of productivity. In the western part of productivity ranges between Rs. 801 to Rs. 1234 per hectare where only few districts are below the national average while all the districts of eastern part have higher productivity than the national level.

Upper Ganges Plain

This region is a transitional zone between the Punjab plain and the lower Ganges plain. Rainfall throughout the region is received by the south-west monsoon but in the western Uttar Pradesh plain winter rainfall is received in little quantity which is favourable for the unirrigated crops. The soil of this region is very fertile and capable for multiple cropping. The hill districts of Uttar Pradesh, parts of eastern U.P. and Bundelkhand have a very low yield because of landforms and soils. Fertility level to a large extent differ from one part to the other parts of this region.

All the three sub-regions of this tract have different level of productivity, for example, Bundelkhand tract falls below the national average, half of the districts of eastern parts are below the national average and all the districts of western U.P. plain are above the national average. It is all due to the higher irrigation facilities in the western part.

Punjab Plains

On the whole this region is a monotonous alluvial tract with varied climate ranging from mountain to arid which has also its strong reflection on the landuse structure. The region is surrounded by the district boundaries, i.e. to the south and south-west arid Rajasthan and to the north and north-east foothills and valleys. The northern parts of the region have steeper gradients and higher rainfall in the foothills. The southern arid margin of this plain specially the Ganganagar area presents features similar to those of the Punjab plains as a result of canal irrigation.

The productivity of this tract is dependent on irrigation facilities not on monsoonal rainfall. Productivity of the southern part is much lower than the northern part because of the sandy nature of soils in the southern districts adjacent to the Rajasthan part. The productivity of the northern part ranges between Rs. 1070 to

Rs. 2212 per hectare. Most of the districts of this tract falls between the Rs. 1500 to Rs. 2000 per hectare.

North-Western Transitional Region

This region on the whole comprises the Aravalli ranges and the foothills on either side. Its distinctiveness is more due to landform. On the whole the region is transitional between the sandy semi-desert landscape of nomadic culture and the more settled, agriculturally suitable black soil plateau developed over the Deccan Lavas. The fertility of the soil of this regions considerably capable to grow any crop but due to high aridity and less moisture retaining capacity of the soil determines the cropping pattern as well as length of the crop growing period. The development possibilities of agriculture in the prevailing climatic conditions and landform is less than the possibilities of development in the field of pasture and afforestation.

All the districts of this region have lower productivity than the national average. Eastern part of this region have higher productivity than the western part due to the less aridity in the eastern part. On the whole productivity ranges between Rs. 222 to Rs. 837 per hectare. Soil of this tract is fertile but due to the unavailability of water and low moisture retaining capacity agriculturally the region is very backward.

North-Western Arid Zone

Arid and semi-arid conditions prevail throughout the region. Water table is also very deep (about 130 metre). The tract is bare of natural vegetation except of thorny bushes. Cultivation is limited only to those areas where the irrigation facilities are available by canal. When a little or sufficient rain falls the tract can grow successfully the crop of bajra. When monsoon recedes early rabi cultivation suffer and without irrigation successful rabi cultivation becomes impossible. Soil to a large extent is fertile enough to produce rabi as well as kharif crops but due to the very low moisture retaining capacity in the soil even the survival of kharif crops becomes impossible.

The productivity in this region is lowest in the country which ranges between Rs. 54 to Rs. 683 per hectare. This is due to high arid condition and no irrigation facilities. This region can grow only one crop i.e. kharif even with great risk.

Gujarat

This region is distinct from the surrounding area because of its extensive alluvial plains and maritime influences along with increasing rainfall towards the coast. Gujarat uplands mark the pediment region of the Aravallis and are clearly identifiable from the coastal plain and the Malwa plateau. This part of Gujarat plains are important as extensive arable lands where the emphasis is on cereal and cash crop farming water logging and saline encrustation are the main problems in a large part of the plain.

This region on the whole have higher productivity than the surrounding regions. Productivity per hectare ranges between Rs. 508 to Rs. 1308 per hectare with the exception of Kheda districts where productivity is 1830 due to the Intensive Agricultural District Programme. On the whole productivity ranges above and below marginally of the national average of the whole region.

Northern Mountains

This is a vast complex of mountain system. The region has great regional diversity regarding climate of altitude. Altitude varies from 1500 metres to 7500 metres, and soils from a vast tract of alluvium to glaciated soils. On these basis the region has been divided into many sub-divisions. The region on the whole has vast potentials for agricultural development. Ladakh is totally a arid region cultivation can only be based on irrigation facilities and wheat is the major crop. Kashmir valley is the heart of this region. A major part of the Valley is available for cultivation. Rice, wheat and maize are the main crops. In this tract abundance of water resource is available as well as alluvial soil with short duration of weather to grow only the rice crop. On the whole the cultivation in this tract is limited above 3500 m. and generally rabi crops affected badly between the altitude of 2500 m. to 3500m. In the Himachal Pradesh and U.P. Himalayas climate favours both for kharif and rabi crops. Sometimes occurrence of frosts damage the crops.

Per hectare productivity varies to a large extent due to the cropping pattern where rice is a dominant crop productivity is much higher i.e., Kashmir Valley. Only Kashmir Valley region is above the national average, rest of the part of this vast tract falls below the national average. In some of the parts temperature control is the main limiting factor for rabi crops.

The islands of Andaman Nicobar and Laccadive groups are remarkable and physically different from each other. The Andaman group receives more than 100 inches of rainfall which have given rise to thick forest cover. The agricultural lands occur mostly along the coast and the river valleys. The Laccadive islands are less important agriculturally. In all these Islands rice is a dominating crop with some commercial crop like coconut etc.

References

1. Singh, Jasbir, *Agricultural Atlas of India,* Kurukshertra University Press, 1971, Kurukshetrra (India).
2. Bhatt, L.S., (1967), *Regional Physical complexes,* mimeo, Indian Statistical Institute, New Delhi.

4

Institutional Factors in Indian Agriculture

LAND TENURE AND AGRICULTURAL DEVELOPMENT

The term "land tenure" is used to express legal and traditional relations between persons, groups and classes that regulate the right to the use of land, transfer thereof and enjoyment of the products and the duties that go with those rights. In other words, land tenure means the manner in which the land is held. It can, therefore, be considered as a reflection of the power relations between persons and groups in the use of land.

In India, the principal source of the people's livelihood is agriculture, where feudal and semi-feudal land relations have helped to perpetuate agricultural backwardness, where landlordism still arrests the economic development in the country side. Land is the stronghold of our people. Seventy per cent of the people of this country earn their living directly from the lands and the progress of the country depends upon the progress of agriculture as about 45 per cent national income is received from this single sector of economy.

Land tenure relations are reflected in the internal productive and social organization of farms, and in the relations of the farmers with other individuals, groups, and institutions. As most statistics on Indian agriculture refer to 'agricultural units', and call this agricultural unit or 'operating unit' as the census unit, it is useful to consider it as the basic unit for purpose of tenure studies.

The study of land tenure problems has been taken partly in response to the increasing discontentment of the peasants. Successful peasant supported revolutions have taken place in India. Not only are the peasant becoming more articulate, their vociferous supporters are also to be found among intellectuals, professionals, businessmen, bureaucrats, urban workers, and many other groups that are growing in number and influence. The peasants are demanding greater participation in the society which, in their views, has been denied to them and, as a result, the traditional land owning elite has monopolised a disproportionate share of wealth, prestige, status and political power in the society.

That the traditional land tenure systems should be singled out as being particularly unjust, is natural enough in view of the deteriorating social and economic conditions in the countryside. The majority of the peasants live in utter poverty and insecurity, in stark contrast to the affluent landowners and other privileged groups in our society.

There are ample grounds for concern about Indian economy since population has been increasing faster than agricultural production. Indian agriculture has not been able to provide so far the necessary surplus to feed to the over growing urban population, thereby contributing to inflationary food price increase and the drain on valuable foreign exchange due to import of foodgrains.

To be sure, the problems of unrest, injustice and stagnation for which land reform, is so often offered as a panacea, are closely interrelated. The slow economic growth obviously contribute to social unrest, while social unrest itself may lead to social injustice and discourage investment, thus perpetuating economic backwardness. Toynbee emphasizes that economic productivity depends upon the training and employment of human ability which, he say, "in the final analysis is mankind's sole capital asset". He concludes that "economic efficiency and social justice ultimately go hand in hand".

On the other hand, economists commonly emphasizes the competitive nature of two goals of efficiency and justice. They frequently say that policy makers must choose between the greater social justice through land reform and the greater economic efficiency by means of development policies.

It is, therefore, necessary to investigate the relationship between the existing system of land tenure and economic development. We have to ask that to what extent the prevailing Indian land tenure systems act as a constraint to economic development? Would land tenure reform result in greater political tranquillity, social justice and economic growth?

Land System of India–A Historical Retrospect

During the Hindu period in Indian history the peasants were having no property right in land, except the right to a share of produce. The king's customary share was equal to 1/6th to 1/4th of the produce, which was known as customary pargana rate.

Below the king were the cultivators, having the actual ownership of the land which is today broadly described as permanent land heritable occupancy right.

As in the Hindu period so also in the Mohammedan period, the king's customary share was equal to 1/4th to 1/3rd (½) as, for instance, in Aurangzeb's time. A complex system of land tenure and land rights existed at the beginning of the British rule. These may be described province by province.

During 1756–1763 in North Bengal the position was State-Zamindars-Raiyats. According to Grand, the zamindar had supreme proprietary rights in land but it was a limited right. The permanent settlement of land (Cornwallis, 1793) gave all the zamindars perpetual hereditary proprietary rights in the soil, subject to the payment of revenue to the Government and limited by the existing customary rights of the Rayats.

The permanent settlement system was extended to the area around Banaras in 1795, and a few years later, the directors of the British East India Company asked the Madras Government to enter into permanent of engagement with the zamindars in Madras. Except in north and extreme south of the Presidency, where the zamindars happened to be representatives of the ancient lines of powerful chiefs, the experiment proved a disastrous failure. Meanwhile, Sir Thomas Munro had introduced in certain parts of the province a system of direct settlements with the cultivators themselves, and after a long controversy he was able to convince the directors of the superiority of his system, especially in tracts where there were no enterprising intermediaries. The system was established in the greater portion of the Madras Presidency and subsequently it was also introduced in the Bombay Presidency and Burma. The system is commonly known as Raiyatwari system.

In the area which used to be called the north-east provinces or United Provinces (U.P.), British administrators found a somewhat different system of land tenure in existence at the time of annexation. In South there were many petty "routes" who had been allowed to contact for a sum of revenue and given the name of Taluqdars (Talukadars) but over the rest of the province there were many proprietary bodies who claiming descent from ancient chiefs or other notables, were in possession of the village area. The British merely recognized the proprietary rights of these individuals and made them jointly or severally liable for the revenue to be paid, a system which was subsequently adopted in the Punjab, but on a slightly different plan.

The proprietary bodies, usually village communities as in the U.P. and the Punjab have been thus described by John Stuart Mill, "The peasant proprietors compound with the state for the fixed period. The proprietors do not engage individually with the government but by village. The village through its headman undertakes to pay so much for so many years themselves as signing to each man his quota. Primarily each man cultivates and pays for himself but ultimately he is responsible for his co-villagers and they for him, they are ultimately bound together by a joint responsibility. If one of them is compelled to sell his rights to meet demand upon him the others have a right to pre-emption.

In the Central Provinces (M.P.) under the Maharashtra administration the revenues of the villages has been farmed out to individuals, who in course of time had required a quasi-proprietary position. Their status was formally recognised by the British who made them responsible for payment of the revenue. In these provinces, however, the mistake committed in Bengal of making the assessments unalterable for aver, was not repeated. These settlements known as temporary settlements are subject to revision.

Types of Land Tenure

"The system of land tenures in India exhibits almost every conceivable variations from immense estates, containing thousands of tenants to minute holdings of well under an acre in size. It is nevertheless possible to classify the holdings into certain fairly well defined groups". There are, in the main three types of land tenure.

(a) Landlord tenure which is called the zamindari system. In this case, as in West and East Bengal, one person or a few joint owners are made responsible for a single sum of land revenue assessed on the whole estate and payable to the government.

(b) Joint village or village community tenure which is known as Mahalwari system. In this case as in U.P. and the East and West Punjab, smaller estates were held collectively by co-sharing bodies of village communities, where the members are held jointly and severally responsible for land revenue.

(c) Independent single tenure which is described as Raiyatwari system. In this case, as in Madras, Bombay, Sind and Berar land is held individually owned and cultivated separate holding and individual responsibility for its payment is ensured. These separate cultivators and owners in the aggregate constitute a Raiyatwari village.

The type of land tenure, such as described above, determines the form of settlement of the land revenue, the gradations of interest and rights in land, their recognition and inter-relation and the nature of their assessment.

Settlement

The term "settlement" refers to the settlement of land revenue which technically consists in the determination of (a) the revenue that is, the rental or the produce which the state may claim, (b) the party or parties liable for payment, and (c) the record of all the private interests. Rights in land, therefore, imply a cadestral record, assessment of the revenue and the means of collection. The collateral record is prepared by a field-to-field survey. Along with this survey, a record is prepared showing the rights of land. These are kept up-to-date. Land revenue is usually collected in instalments to suit the convenience of those who pay.

From the point of duration, there are two types of revenue settlement (a) permanently settled estate system; and (b) temporary settled estate system. The former type where the share of the state is fixed perpetuity prevails as in Bengal (East and West), Bihar, Orissa (about half), Madras (about one third) and a smaller proportion of Assam and Banaras districts of U.P.

The later (period) type where the share of the state is fixed for a temporary period, prevails in the U.P., the Punjab (East, West), in nearly the whole of central provinces (M.P.) and about one-fourth of Orissa and in some areas of permanently settled provinces.

The second way of classifying settlements is on the basis of the three tenure systems stated above and may be shown in the tabular form thus:

Tenure (landlord)	Varieties of Joint village tenure	Varieties of independent single tenure
1. Parmanent settlement (Zamindars of East and West Bengal)	1. U.P. Mahalwari settlement except Oudh Talukadar	1. Madras Raiyatwari
2. Temporary settlement (remaining zamindars of East and West Bengal)	2. Punjab Mahalwari	2. Bombay and Berar Raiyatwari
3. Temporary settlement (Oudh)	3. Madhya Pradesh Malguzari	3. Special system of Assam and Coorg

In India, until 1947, the land system was far from being helpful to the farmers. About half of the land was held by the zamindars who formed only four per cent of the rural population. The three-fourth of the rural people hold only sixteen per cent of the land consisting mostly of small farms. A large number had no land of their own and worked as tenants or farm labourers.

During the British days in India, the Government found it difficult to collect rent (revenue) from individual farmers. So it appointed agents (zamindars) to collect revenue. Though the Government collected revenue at the fixed rate from the agents, it was common for agents, from time to time, to increase the rent they obtained from the tenants.

As population increased, rent changed by the agents rose higher and the value of land increased. In some areas, the tenants had to pay a rent which was as much as the value of the two thirds of the land. The landlord or agent spent none of this money for land improvement.

While the landlords grew rich due to exorbitant land revenue the tenant remained poor getting but a small share in return for his labour. Nor had he any security of tenure. The landlord could send him away at any time and appoint another farmer in his place. A tenant had very little interest in the land he tilted under such circumstances. As hardship of the tenant increased, the production from the land decreased. There were also landless farm labourers. The figures are given below:

The Rise in the Agricultural Labourers

Census Years

Years	1882	1921	1931	1933	1944	1947	
Labours (Lakhs)	7.5	21.5	33	35	68	50	Estimates

The figures given by R. Palme Dutt on class differentiation in Madras (per thousand of agricultural population) are as:

Years	1901	1911	1921	1931
Labourers	385	340	317	429

For the majority of the growing class of landless labourers social security is lacking, employment is uncertain and seasonal migration specially in harvesting season is a common enough feature. Usually in the cultivating and harvesting seasons, the demand for, and wages of agricultural labourers rise high. In recent years the intensity of competitive demand for labour has increased but it will be noticed that the living condition of the unfortunate farm labourers has in no way improved.

With regard to the wages of these agricultural labourers the following table is given.

(daily wages in annas)	Year	1842	1852	1862	1872	1911	1922
	Filed labourers without food	1.5	2	3	4	4	to 6
	Price of rice (seers per rupee)	40	30	27	23	15	5

We have to discuss the reasons why agriculture did not develop under the tenant farming. Our discussion will be affective if we examine the available data on this empirical question. Reliable data on tenancy are rare (relatively). We have used two sources, viz., Census of India 1961 and the National Sample Survey. The farmer gives an exhaustive collection of data, but unfortunately stops after classifying area into three broad categories, viz., owned holding (including leases from the state), tenanted holdings and mixed holding. On the other hand, the N.S.S. (8th round) gives a much finer classification though its coverage is limited, and relates to an early date viz., 1953-54 (1960 in appendix). We have used here both the sources.

From the 1961 census we find that of the total area, the aggregate proportion of purely tenanted holding and mixed holding, which we call here "tenancy infested holdings" is 23% for rural area and 21.8% for the urban area. In particular, we would except that the relatively drier land.

We have estimated the proportion of tenancy infested area in the region of assured rainfall (1150 mm. a year) and in region with exhaustive irrigation (with 50% or more of gross sown area irrigated).

It is to be noted that prevalence of tenancy is significantly higher in the wet areas (including irrigated land) than in the dry areas. In the areas with assured rainfall, the area covered by tenancy infested holdings totals 27.6% and for areas with extensive irrigation it amounts to 35 per cent. This indicates that the importance of the tenancy question is greater than the all-India figures suggest.

The tenancy infested land, however, includes mixed holdings and the census 1961 figures relate to a period about seven years later than the N.S.S. Survey. So there is no noticeable inconsistency in the two sets of information, although the data are not incomparable categories to allow us to make any statement about the trend of change over these years.

Table 4.1 gives the breakdown of the tenancy land into different modes of owner cultivator relationship. We have found it more meaningful to aggregate the categories in a somewhat different way from that used in the N.S.S. presentation. There are four categories of rent – (a) formally fixed rent; (b) rent formally or informally (c) fixed as a proportion of output; and (d) other types and unspecified of this only (d) is share-cropping and it has been defined rigidly. But as has been noted by Thoner and Legginsky and others the line is difficult to draw between the share croppers of tenants with oral bases. With informal leases, the landlord may be able to charge a higher rent when the yield goes up, thereby making it rather similar to share-cropping from an economic point of view. Thus, a better idea of the extent of de facto share-cropping can be obtained by aggregating (b) and (c). It is very likely that the category (d) also falls within the general coverage of share-cropping but in the absence of more definite information, we leave it out from our calculation.

The table shows that for India as a whole, the percentage of share-cropping in tenancy areas is 36.6 per cent, and the de facto share-cropping areas comes to 56.6 per cent. Furthermore, 22.7 per cent of the tenancy area comes under the unspecified group. In fact only 20.8 per cent of the tenancy area is under formal contract with fixed rent. Beyond this figure we cannot be sure whether the rest of the land is free from share-cropping. Roughly out of 50 per cent of the tenancy under the de facto share-cropping only 20 per cent is definitely free from it. But the data is not available to calculate this type of table for dry and wet area.

We may, therefore, say that the tenant has relatively little interest in undertaking long run improvement in the land he cultivates, for he does not own the land and may not be able to enjoy the fruits of his efforts and investment. This applies to all types of tenant farming except those with security of tenure at fixed rents. In the case of share-cropper receives, say, 50 per cent of the gross produce than the use of current input, e.g. fertilizer costing Rs. 10 is worthwhile for the tenant only if the marginal increase in output as a result is at least Rs. 20. In fact, with interest cost the value of output increases has to exceed Rs. 20 by an amount depending on the level of the interest rate.

TABLE 4.1: Breakdown of Tenancy by Types

Population Zone	Formally fixed rent (a)	Informally fixed rent (b)	Rent fixed as proportion of output (c)	Other types and unspecified (d)
North India	27.90	13.13	27.65	31.32
East India	24.64	13.08	49.58	12.70
South India	29.06	20.00	26.03	24.91
West India	23.95	18.35	32.70	25.00
Central India	18.42	22.72	37.73	20.51
North-west India	11.18	25.02	37.97	25.83
All India	20.79	19.95	36.56	22.70

Source: N.S.S. (5).

Both the points are simple enough and have been discussed sufficiently in the past to require no elaboration here. An illustration of the second on the basis of an empirical calculation may, however, be interesting from the point of view of magnitude. We take it from a study of the intensive agricultural district programme at Thanjavur district? The rates of return to the package of improved practices are calculated for an owner cultivator (or tenant with fixed rent) and for a tenant receiving 40 per cent share of the crop. Two alternative response rates are assumed, the price of paddy being Rs. 17 per bag. The results are given in Table 4.2.

If this indicates the magnitudes correctly, then with moderate response, the share-croppers may have little incentive to apply the second one-third of the package and none at all to apply the last third. The owner cultivator or the fixed rent tenant is in a quite different position. With exercise of this kind, it is shown why the share-cropper may be very reluctant to adopt new practices or (more generally) to invest.

One limitation of the particular illustration given here is the lumping of improved practices in the package. This makes it difficult to comment on the acceptability of some specific inputs, e.g., fertilizers. In so far as I.A.D.P. practice includes using such packages, this is a relevant calculation, even though these figures of return on specific inputs in different tenurial conditions, which are being discussed extensively these days (e.g. Minhas and Srinivasan).

TABLE 4.2: Rate of Return on Investment in the Package Practices

Type of tenure	Response rate	Rate of return in percentage		
		First	Second	Third
Owner Cultivator	"High"	186	186	91
Fixed rent tenant	"Moderate"	91	72	15
40% share cropper	High	72	72	11
	Moderate	15	3	–

Source: Intensive Agricultural District Programme, Farm Management Study, Thanjavur Distt, 1964.

However, the illustration brings out the point about a significantly lower rate of return to investment of share cropped farms, a point which cannot be controverted. Reasonably sophisticated arguments have been used to show why tenancy may not have much effect on efficiency of agricultural development given certain other facts. Of these counter-arguments, the following arguments appear to us to be most important.

(1) It can be shown that if the inputs are shared in the same proportion as the returns, then the marginal rate of return will be the same for the share cropper as for the owner cultivator.

(2) While the rate of return is scaled down by crop-sharing tenancy, the return on modern inputs is often so high, that even after the scaling down, the net return is sufficiently lucrative to permit as wide a use of these inputs as the supply conditions permit. Perhaps the most satisfactory presentation of this argument in the context of fertilizers is to be found in the discussion of Minhas and Srinivasan.

There were some dismissals and some evictions on account of social pressures or offers of monetary and other gains. There were some so-called resumptions of land by land-owners with no real motive of self-cultivation but aimed at the deprivation of the tenant's rights followed by subsequent underground lease of land on crop-sharing basis. The new tenant passed as a wage labour with no legal right to land, even though he contributed fixed and working capital to the farm as well as his labour. By tying up land census figures with those of the population the census suggests even around 1961, a quarter of land was under tenant cultivation and about half of this quarter was under unrecognized, highly exploitative tenancy, paying rents as high as 40 to 60 per cent of the produce.

The effect of this on agricultural productivity is obvious. Unrecognized tenants, apart from feeling insecure and not investing in land, get neither credit nor subsidies from governmental and other agencies. The new programme of intensive agricultural development (I.A.D.P.) will obviously not pay attention to them. A farm operated by an owner farmer and a tenant farmer, both use the same kind of inputs on the same number of acres of similar quality. While in the case of the owner farmer marginal product equals (or average) marginal cost of input in the case of the tenant the situation is different. He is assumed to pay rent(at) or as a fixed percentage of produce and so he concentrates on the marginal net product (net rent) which he brings at par with the marginal (or average) cost of input. Under these circumstances, it is virtually certain that the owner farmers will use the new package of inputs whose additional returns are greater than additional cost and give him higher profit than before, but the tenant will not accept the new package as its additional returns. Often the rent deducted is less than the additional cost which, in fact reduces his profit.

Here, then, is one of the reasons for slow agricultural revolution did not come because, among other things, the real tenant who provides capital as well as labour to the farm was not identified in many cases.

Much of this could have been avoided with a little more thought. Land surrendered by tenants, of any, could have been made returnable only to government and not to the land-owners.

Conclusion

The hypothesis of this study is that the estabilished patterns of land tenure are major obstances to agricultural development of India. This is because traditional land tenure patterns impede the introduction of new technology and economically rational and labour use. Consequently the pattern of income distribution and consumption expenditure and investment that emerges restrict the growth of new industries besides fortifying a rigid social structure in which opportunities for improvement of one's social status are rare.

The existing land tenure system encourages low level of aspiration among the poor peasants. As a result there is concentration of power in the hands of those who control the land resulting in a social order in which those who work on the land have no effective representation, rendering the institutions of local government practically powerless to discharge the functions of public service.

Land legislation in the post-independence period and its implementation shows that it could not appreciably improve the condition of the tenants. The main objectives of the reforms during the post-independence period were (a) providing security to the tenants, (b) regulation of rent, (c) confirment of ownership rights, and (d) ensuring socio-economic justice through land redistribution.

The important objective of the post-independence reform legislation was the abolition of the intermediaries. The aim was to settle land in the name of the actual tiller. It was assumed that the confirment of such rights would bring a significant change in the level and volume in agricultural production. When the security of property is ensured the cultivator would naturally utilize the potentialities of his land. A full proprietary right to the peasant gives more incentive of the better utilization of labour force and increase agricultural production. But the cultivator now knows that the major portion of the fruit of his labour cannot be enjoyed by him but by the intermediary who rarely contributes anything to its actual production. It was also felt that the abolition of the intermediary interest would bring an end to the strained relationship between the landlord and the tenant. It would also result in a major redistribution of the rural income "to the advantages of those who work in the fields and to the disadvantages of who do not. With such an end in view the tenancy reform laws were enacted in the post-independence period in order to abolish the intermediary interest. No doubt that land legislation and other land reform acts (Zamindari abolition) and the abolition of intermediary interest was a complex problem.

II

Pattern of Land Ownership and Agricultural Productivity

Land ownership in India is a major drawback in our agricultural economic scene. On the basis of various research analysis and data availability it is evident that land ownership is not uniform in any region of the country and even in a single village the pattern and distribution of land is unequally distributed even to the level of insufficiency of land to give needed and required food production for a household. It is also obvious that the trend is towards the creating more inequality and posing a very complex problem in Indian agricultural scene. The existing inequality in the pattern of land ownership in India affect adversely her agricultural development and her effort to generate food surplus at the district level. The pattern of higher concentration of land ownership in a few hands does not help to augment agricultural productivity and growth rates in a developing economy. No doubt that smaller land holdings are higher yield giving units but the present characteristic of the concentration of smaller land holdings are not economic holding to generate surpluses for further investments. These crucial points cry out for an answer before any inquiry into population, malnutrition and agricultural productivity of India can ever be considered complete.

The nature of the data base for this study is rather unsatisfactory to provide proper answers and analysis to understand the actual problem. This study would have been more authentic and reliable if we had a reliable record at district level of the size of land on operational holdings actually cultivated. The major source of the data availability is NSS which give us this information with a certain degree of reliability collected from a large blocks of the country and even not at district level. The village record keeper's data is so biased and undependable that we had to discard the information on operational landholdings provided by the Agricultural Census of India. As for many areas land record keepers are not holding this type of information. Though a number of studies have already been done on the land ownership pattern and agricultural characteristics like area irrigated, fertilizers used, agricultural growth rate, agricultural productivity, food surplus or deficit etc., but the results are different for different regions which did not yield conclusive results. The census of land holdings conducted by the Registrar General in Agricultural Census of India, 1971 is the base for the present analysis.

A general distribution of operational holdings can be seen from the following table to understand the ownership in each size class of holdings.

TABLE 4.3: Distribution of Operational Holdings (1976-77)

Size Class	No. Holdings		Area	
	Million	%	Million hectare	%
<1 hectare (Marginal)	44.53	54.6	17.50	10.7
1-2 hectare (Small)	14.70	18.0	20.86	12.8
2–4 hectare (Semi-medium)	11.64	14.3	32.36	19.8
4–10 hectare (medium)	8.21	10.1	49.60	30.4
>10 hectare (Large)	2.44	3.0	42.82	26.3
	81.52	100.0	163.14	100.0

Keeping in view a number of limitations and factors an attempt has been made to assess by a number of aggregated arrangements of the data by Gini class ranges whether or not high or low degrees of inequality in land ownership pattern affect the agricultural growth and development. An attempt has been made in this analysis at two levels of aggregation and disaggregation, i.e., at six levels of agricultural productivity and at district level which will be able to reveal that inequalities in land ownership is responsible for the present state of mal-and undernutrition.

Concentration of Land Ownership and Levels of Agricultural Productivity

The Table 4.4 reveals in Gini concentrations ratio of land ownership at six levels. Higher inequality in land ownership occurs in both the highest and in the medium levels of productivity. On the other hand, lowest inequality in land ownership emerges in both high level of agricultural productivity and the lowest level of agricultural productivity. Therefore, there is hardly an statistical hierarchical relationship between the two. At first it appears that high concentration or high inequality in land ownership occurs in the very high agricultural productivity level and low inequality appears in the low agricultural productivity level, but the picture soon gets modified as both high and low inequality emerge in both high and low agricultural productivity level. A clear, unequivocal conclusion could not be drawn from this type of data. Due to the absence of any positive or negative relationship between acute inequality in land ownership pattern might mean that high agricultural productivity might occur in spite of present day inequitous distribution of land ownership. It is also considered that a more minute level of data either at district or taluka may give some different results or Gini ratio itself is an inadequate method for our purpose. The table 4.4 further reveals the fact that high productivity which occurs in level I, in spite of unjust land distribution, owes its success to the fact that all the major agricultural investments and inputs (fertilizers, tractors, irrigation rate, HYV) are being used by big land holders which helps to maintain a high level of agricultural productivity despite inequality in land ownership pattern. On the other hand high inequality in land ownership also emerges in 5th or the lowest order of agricultural productivity which occupies about more than one-third of the total districts under study. In this case we recognise a totally different case as the larger number of districts are falling in this category where inequality is very high but the productivity is very low. This may mean that a very little of agricultural inputs have gone to the category. Largely these districts are located in eastern part of Madhya Pradesh, Bihar, South Rajasthan and north Andhra Pradesh where the input levels are very low.

TABLE 4.4: Gini Concentration Ratio

Yield level	Gini concentration Ratio of land ownership	No. of Districts	% to the total Districts	Yield Categories
>-1400	0.7231	43	15.52	I
1200—1400	0.5583	20	7.22	II
1000—1200	0.7464	24	8.66	III
800—1000	0.7185	43	15.52	IV
600—800	0.6942	95	34.30	V
<-600	0.4913	52	18.78	VI

A District Level Distribution of Gini Ratio in India

The concentration of land ownership have been shown in the Table 4.5. In this table a statewise distribution of districts of all the inequality levels and total number of districts in each state and in each inequality level can be seen such as districts of high inequality (above 0.600), medium inequality (0.400 to 0.600), low inequality (0.401 to 0.500) and very low inequality (less than 0.400). It is clear from this table that about 16 per cent districts belongs to very high inequality in land ownership, 56 per cent districts show medium inequality and 28 per cent belong to the less inequality in land ownership. High level of inequality are concentrated in Bihar, Madhya Pradesh, Andhra Pradesh, Uttar Pradesh and Rajasthan. Medium inequality in land ownership occur in more than half of the total district mainly concentrated in Uttar Pradesh, Madhya Pradesh, Karnataka, Rajasthan, Andhra Pradesh, Punjab and Maharashtra. The lower categories combindly occupy 28 per cent district of India mainly concentrated in West Bengal, Gujarat, Orissa, Maharashtra and Karnataka.

On the basis of Table 4.5 it can be clearly stated that high inequality in land ownership occurs in Bihar, Madhya Pradesh which are low productivity zones, but low inequality also emerges in those districts which are low productivity zones such as West Bengal, Kerala, Karnataka and Gujarat but the level of productivity is considerably higher than the states of high inequality and low productivity like Bihar, M.P. and due to the lesser use of input as compared to the states of Punjab and Haryana the region is unaffected by a single factor of inequality in land ownership for agricultural levels of productivity. Therefore, to a large extent the hypothesis of high inequality and low productivity is proved if it is not affected by the high input levels.

TABLE 4.5: Distribution of 'GINI' Ratio at District Level

	>0.600	0.500-0.600	0.400-0.500	0.200-0.400	Total in Each State
Andhra Pradesh	6	11	—	—	17
Assam	2	4	1	—	7
Bihar	10	4	—	—	14
Gujarat	1	2	12	3	18
Haryana	—	7	—	—	7
Himachal Pradesh	—	—	—	—	—
Jammu & Kashmir	—	1	1	—	2
Karnataka	1	10	8	—	19
Kerala	1	3	2	—	6
Madhya Pradesh	9	28	6	—	43
Maharashtra	3	9	12	—	24
Orissa	—	3	6	1	10
Punjab	1	8	1	1	11
Rajasthan	4	15	7	—	26
Tamil Nadu	1	7	2	1	11
U.P.	5	41	1	1	48
West Bengal	—	3	10	1	14
Total No. of Districts	44 (277)	156 (15.88%)	69 (56.32%)	8 (24.91%)	(2.89%)

This picture will be more clear if we analyse the problem at micro-level on the basis of the availability of data and other factors may give more authentic picture such as effect of various agricultural institutions, green revolution, small and marginal farmers development programme, credit services and loans for the farmers etc. As these factors have profound effect on productivity and management of agriculture. A proper investigation of these effective factors will give proper and convincing answers to the questions like to what extent such new agricultural institutions and innovations are inducing changes in the existing inequitous distribution of land ownership. Whether or not these innovations are affecting and bringing changes upon agricultural management and productivity at the lowest level of ownership or do they further aggravate the problem of land inequality and enhance agricultural productivity.

If we analyse the Table 4.6 it is revealed that within the second and fifth Gini levels two clear cut cluster of districts emerges – (i) about 23 districts are more endowed with favourable endowed with favourable terrain, fertile, soil, easily available water and adequate rainfall (ii) about 34 less physically endowed districts in terms of rocky and undulating land, infertile soil, inaccessible water and inadequate rainfall. Within the same Gini ranges agricultural growth rates differ. These 57 districts of these low concentration of land ownership have the characteristics of low growth rate, low productivity and low availability of foodgrains per head per day. Within this Gini ratio 23 districts out of 57 districts show higher yield because these districts are enjoying better geophysical conditions than those districts which are less favourable geophysically. The most significant observation emerging from this Table 4.6 is that of growth rate where inverse relationship occur between agricultural growth rate and Gini concentration ratio of land ownership. But these are the problematic districts, as mentioned before. In general, it appears that agricultural growth rate seems to thrive on less land inequality and suffer from the present state of more concentration of land ownership in a few hands, with few exceptions. This result is an argument in favour of implementation of land reform and lowering of land ceiling to reduce land inequality as the highest growth and yield occur in lowest Gini ratio of the concentration of land ownership (Table 4.6, category 1). Only five districts fall in this category (0.360-0.385) and holding 1.80 per cent of the total country's population with 4.19 per cent growth rate and 1272 kg./hectare productivity have the highest and impressive recorded growth yield level in the country in low concentration of holding.

In this category (0.386-0.460) where sudden fall in growth rate and productivity is recorded belong to three Gini levels with marked similarity in their characteristics. These are the problem districts lying in twenty six districts of Maharashtra, Madhya Pradesh, Orissa and Bihar. The geophysical conditions are not conducive (sub-soil thin, untapped water, variable and inadequate rainfall, mountainous and undulating terrain) for a better survival and growth of crops.

TABLE 4.6: The Levels of Concentration of Land Ownership and Agricultural Characteristics

Gini Level	No. of Distt.	Population as % of total pop. of the Distt. (All)	Average agricultural growth rate	Average Agricultural Productivity	Foodgrain product as % of total production	Per head per day share in production	Gross cropped area % to total area	Average Fertilizer use % to Total	% Area irrigated
0.360-0.385	4	1.80	4.19	1272	2.15	603	2.25	3.60	3.85
0.386-0.410	5	0.83	0.53	605	0.70	400	1.44	1.24	0.41
0.411-0.435	9	2.65	-2.17	570	2.19	411	4.12	1.98	1.36
0.436-0.460	12	3.50	-0.56	809	3.14	447	4.02	1.85	1.74
0.461-0.485	33	12.81	0.78	1011	11.00	430	13.21	10.23	8.71
0.486-0.510	38	12.29	2.48	1001	14.28	578	13.93	15.73	15.63
0.511-0.535	39	12.96	2.53	903	16.05	614	14.93	14.45	16.12
0.536-0.560	46	15.38	2.36	1007	16.59	540	15.25	16.12	16.90
0.561-0.585	34	15.48	1.53	1088	15.23	485	13.68	20.70	18.43
0.586-0.610	30	10.92	1.41	1093	10.00	460	9.39	9.76	10.63
0.611-0.635	15	7.48	1.21	984	5.38	359	4.70	4.60	4.25
0.636-0.660	10	3.90	0.49	907	3.29	411	3.08	1.74	2.04
	275	100.00	1.60	938	100.00	478	100.00	100.00	100.00

As a result growth is negative, productivity among the lowest in India. The region is providing only about 6 per cent of the country's total production and holding about 10 per cent of the total gross cultivated area. This is also mainly due to the geophysical factors as well as only 5 per cent of the total chemical fertilizers and 3.5 per cent of the total irrigated area. The region also suffer from less amount of irrigated area in the country which is a crucial factor of today India's agriculture.

Within the range of Gini ratio of 0.461 to 0.485 about 33 districts fall in which agricultural growth is much less than the first category and produces about 11.0% of the total production for 13 per cent of the total production, but productivity is one of the highest among other Gini categories. These clusters of districts have 13 per cent of the gross cropped area, 10 per cent of the total fertilizer and about 8 per cent of the total irrigated area. But the performance of these districts after having sizeable amount of inputs etc. are not producing in the ratio of these inputs in terms of per head per day share in food production which is one of the lowest (44 gram per head per day) in the country. It is because of the one-third districts of it suffer from geophysical limitations and low growth rate.

In the middle Gini level category the situation is more or less balanced in about 38 districts of the country where fertilizer input and irrigation rate is considerably higher. Similar type of trend exists in seventh and eighth category as there is no marked change in the pattern. In the next category (9) the nothing is very remarkable and noticeable as overall pattern is followed like the seventh and eighth categories except of a low growth level.

In the categories (0.586 to 0.660) of the last three which belongs to the very high Gini level attracts our attention for analysis. These categories on the whole show clearcut declining trends in both agricultural growth rate and yield level as the degree of land inequality increases. It is because of the decline in irrigation rate and fertilizer input as the land holders are not able to manage and provide these basic inputs to all of his holdings. These 55 districts along with the 34 districts if ninth category or as a total of 89 districts (32% of the total districts of India) are the main problem areas in India. These districts demand an improvement in growth rate and yield level but a thorough rigorous implementation of land reform measures can bring down the proportion of land concentration in a few land holding families.

These districts are as follows:

State	Name of the districts
1. Uttar Pradesh	Lucknow, Unnao, Barabanki, Raebarelli, Sitapur, Gorakhpur, Basti, Banda, Allahabad, Mirzapur, Ghazipur, Ballia, Saharanpur, Fatehpur, Varanasi, Jaunpur, Azamgarh Sultanpur, Faizabad, Pratapgarh, Deoria.
2. Madhya Pradesh	Rewa, Sidhi, Satna, Jabalpur, Shahdol, Bilaspur, Raigarh, Raipur, Gwalior, Surguja, Panna, Damoh, Mandla.
3. Bihar	Champaran, Muzzaffarpur, Monghyr, Saharsa, Purnea, Bhagalpur, Hazaribagh, Dhanbad, Gaya, Palamau, Ranchi, Singhbhum, Darbhanga, Patna.
4. Rajasthan	Ajmer, Pali, Udaipur, Alwar, Bhilware, Bundi, Tonk, Sawai Madhopur.
5. Maharashtra	Thana, Kolaba, Ratnagiri.
6. Andhra Pradesh	Nizamabad, Medak, Karimnagar, Warangal, East Godavari, West Godavari.
7. Punjab	Hoshiarpur.
8. Gujarat	Ahmedabad.
9. Kerala	Cannanore.
10. Tamil Nadu	Tirunelveli.
11. Assam	Sibsagar, Cachar.

Therefore, keeping in view the total production and per head per day share of foodgrains in each Gini ratio (Table 4.6) lowest share is provided by the high concentration of land category on the basis of total production while in the middle categories the situation in all respect is balancing. Only the problem is lying in upper and lowest category which can be removed by removing the concentration of land in high Gini ratio area as well as by removing the concentration of marginal lands (holdings) in the lowest Gini ratio's area, i.e., category 2 and 3.

III

Agricultural Labourers and Agricultural Productivity

The census of India defines an agricultural labourers as an employees of a cultivator, whose business merely is to perform physical labour in the manner required by the cultivator. The census of 1961 distinguished between a cultivator and an agricultural labourer in the following words:

In brief any person was to be treated as cultivators if he or she was engaged either as employer, single worker or family worker in cultivation of land or supervision or direction of cultivation of land. . . . An agricultural labourer was defined as a person who worked in another persons land for wages in money, kind or share. He must have no right or lease or contract on land on which he worked.

The definition of agricultural labourer adopted in 1971 by the census of India is not similar to the census adopted in 1961.

An agricultural labourer is defined a person who worked in another persons land for wages in money kind or share was regarded as an agricultural labourer. He has no risk in the cultivation but merely worked in another persons land for wages. (C.I. Monograph No. I, 1971, *Indian Census in Perspective,* p. 170).

Such a definition of agricultural labourer is obviously narrow. It fails to distinguish between a landless agricultural labourer and a worker who derives his livelihood from both cultivation and agricultural labour. It is likely, therefore, that the latter are generally included in the category of cultivators. The dwarf-holding marginal farmers generally augment their earnings by accepting agricultural wages employment. Beside, a part of the other rural workers (artisans, Craftman) many of whom belong to lower castes, are obliged to work as agricultural labourers in order to make both ends meet. It may be worth noting that in Uttar Pradesh 73 per cent of the cultivators and 16 per cent of workers in household industry reported agricultural labour as secondary work in 1961.

We may, therefore, define agricultural labourers as those who derive the major portion of their income from agricultural labour irrespective of whether they own land or not, derive income in cash or in kind, are employed as attached or casual labourers and get work regularly or seasonally.

Growth of Agricultural Labour in India

Agricultural labour system was the outgrowth of commercialization of agriculture introduced during the British period; its size continued to grow during the post-independence period also. In 1981, there were about 75 lakh agricultural labourers, the number increased to 280 lakh in 1951 and further to 480 lakh in 1971. The proportion of agricultural labour to the total workforce of the country has been increasing. This proportion stood at 16.9 per cent in 1901, 17.4 per cent in 1921, 19.7 per cent in 1951, 16.71 per cent in 1961 and 26.0 per cent in 1971 (Table 4.7).

The share of agricultural labourers to the total agrarian working force increased 16 per cent to 26 per cent during 1961–71. Thus, in relative terms the rate of growth of agricultural labourers has been abnormally high due to the definitional change also. Some economists and demographers disputed about the reliability of the comparisons made on the basis of census data of 1961 and 1971. The concept of 'workers' was itself changed in the 1971 census and it appears that this also has reduced the feasibility of making a reliable comparison.

Due to rapid transformation of the traditional agrarian economy of India more than one fourth of the rural population is composed of landless agricultural labourers who have nothing to sell their own except of their labour power. It is generally observed that an increasing number of peasants are thrown into the ranks of agricultural labourers.

The high proportion and the high rate of growth today are also accounted for by the fact that the pace of industrial development has been too slow to create employment opportunities for the rapidly growing labour force. During this decade (1971) the decline of small scale industries (in terms of employment) has been more rapid than the growth of employment in industries. This non-compensating industrial growth has pushed a vast majority of the surplus workers into the ranks of landless agricultural labourers. During the decade 1961–71, new agricultural practices have been introduced in varying degrees in many parts of the country. Tractorization has generally increased the demand for hired labour. In some areas of the country, this demand generating factor, along with a slight increase in real wages has been more significant and has resulted into polerisation of the farm population.

However, in some of the regions of India the present increase of agricultural labourers has resulted from the pauperization of the peasantry. The dwarf-holding farmers have been pauperised and bonded by an indissoluble debt burden. The artisans have been pauperised by a rapid decline of traditional industry without a compensating industrial growth.

The agricultural labourers are economically one of the weakest section of the agricultural classes or they are the most dis-advantageous of the agricultural society. They are mostly landless belonging to the lower castes. In a very few cases they have holding of their own, which are extremely small in size, or get land to cultivate on sublease. They get work only seasonally and not regularly. The wages are often inadequate and their payment frequently irregular and unsatisfactory. In short they are the exploited class. The minimum wage rate regulations have been in force but have seldom been enforced strictly. The proportion of agricultural labourers is very high, for example, in the eastern part of India and in other parts which are much backward and poverty stricken as compared to the western part of India. On the other extreme the proportion of agricultural labourers is the lowest in the Himalayan hill districts, which again have very low development indices. In this region the employment of wages labour is low because of natural difficulties and irrigation, and primitive agricultural practices.

The proportion of agricultural labourers varies very widely from district to district. The proportion is generally very high in the eastern part of U.P., Bihar, Madhya Pradesh, Andhra Pradesh and Orissa and extremely low in northern hill district of U.P., Haryana, Punjab, N.E. Hill states, West Bengal and union territories. During the decade 1961–71 the employment of wage labour has steadily increased in some of the high yield level regions of India and today they rank very high in the employment of wage labour. Similarly the growth of agricultural labourers during the decade 1961–71 varies widely from district to district. It has been very rapid in high yield level districts of India, though there are some noteworthy exceptions.

In the present study an attempt is being made to make a comparison of 1961–71 census data on cultivators and agricultural labourers. On the basis we shall try to locate the regions where the proportion of agricultural labourer is higher as compared to others, and also the region where the growth of agricultural labourers during the decade 1961–71 has been relatively high. An analysis of these regional variations should provide useful guidelines in drawing a development programme for the country which reaches the relatively backward regions, districts and groups. As Gunner Myrdal[1] points out, '. . . . the proportion of social and economic equality is a pre-condition for attaining substantial long term increase in production. Lastly, the concentration of agricultural labourers may be correlated with the high yield level areas as well as high yield regions which have more wage rate than the low yield regions.

Employment, Wages and Agricultural Labourer in Relation to Agricultural Productivity

In India seasonal employment is a characteristics of agricultural labourers. The first Agricultural Labour Enquiry (1950-51) revealed that male agricultural labourers found employment on an average for 189 days on wages in cultivating jobs, and for 29 days in non-cultivating jobs, i.e. 218 days in all. On the remaining days, they were either unemployed or were employed in their own tiny holdings. Largely agricultural labourer has seasonal source of employment because of abundant labour supply, the wage rates are very low. The first Enquiry revealed that the average annual income of agricultural labour households from all sources was Rs. 447 in 1950-51; the Second Enquiry revealed a fall to Rs. 437 in 1956-57. The Rural Labour Enquiry estimated the average annual income of an agricultural labour household at Rs. 660. If we put this rise in income against the rise in prices during the period, we find that the real income of the agricultural households did not change significantly. In the post HYV period, according to an 'National Commission on Agriculture' the average annual income has gone up but not in the ratio of price rise of the foodgrain crops. At regional level the wage rate has increased with the increase in agricultural productivity. For instance the difference in the wage rate between Punjab and eastern U.P. is about three times due to the higher yield level in Punjab than the eastern Uttar Pradesh.

TABLE 4.7: Concentration of Agricultural Labourer

	% worker to the total population	Cultivator % to the total worker	Agricultural Labourer	
			% to the total worker	location quotient (L.Q)
1. Andhra Pradesh	41.4	32.2	37.9	1.44
2. Assam	28.3	56.8	9.6	0.36
3. Bihar	31.0	43.3	38.9	1.48
4. Gujarat	31.4	43.1	22.5	0.85
5. Haryana	26.4	49.1	16.2	0.62
6. Himachal Pradesh	36.9	70.6	4.2	0.16
7. Jammu & Kashmir	29.8	64.8	3.1	0.12
8. Karnataka	34.8	40.0	26.7	1.01
9. Kerala	29.1	17.8	30.7	1.17
10. Madhya Pradesh	36.8	52.9	26.7	1.01
11. Maharashtra	36.4	35.5	29.3	1.11
12. Manipur	34.6	94.0	3.6	0.14
13. Meghalaya	44.2	69.1	9.9	0.38
14. Nagaland	50.8	77.7	1.4	0.05
15. Orissa	31.2	49.2	28.3	1.07
16. Punjab	28.9	42.6	20.1	0.76
17. Rajasthan	31.2	64.9	9.3	0.35
18. Tamil Nadu	35.8	31.3	30.5	1.16
19. Tripura	27.8	55.4	20.0	0.76
20. Uttar Pradesh	30.0	57.4	20.0	0.76
21. West Bengal	27.9	32.0	2.6	0.10
22. Mizoram	45.6	83.5	0.3	0.01
23. Delhi	30.2	2.6	1.2	0.05
24. Arunachal Pradesh	56.4	78.3	1.9	0.07
25. Andaman & Nicobar	39.5	13.6	4.6	0.18
26. Pondicherry	29.9	11.8	11.5	0.44
27. Goa, Daman & Diu	31.7	24.0	15.0	0.57
28. Chandigarh	33.3	2.9	1.4	0.05
29. Dadra & Nagar Haveli	47.1	72.9	16.9	0.64
INDIA	35.15	47.22	26.3	1.00

Concentration of Agricultural Labourers and Agricultural Productivity

Agricultural labour is one of the major input in India's traditional and subsistence level of agriculture. Though the origin of agricultural labour is related with the inception of the commercialization of agriculture but due to the intensive system of farming on non-commercialized agricultural land its importance has increased due to also the low level and poor distribution of technology.

A concentration map on the basis of location quotient is prepared which can be correlated with the levels of agricultural productivity, either the concentration of high and low level is being followed by agricultural productivity or not can easily be understood and importance of various factors can be determined. On the basis of each category and variations total number as well as per cent districts can be seen from the Table 4.8.

TABLE 4.8: Concentration of Agricultural Labour in each Category

Category No.	Variations	No of districts	% of the total districts of India
I	> 1.25	75	21.99
II	1.0-1.25	56	16.42
III	0.75-1.00	55	16.13
IV	0.50-0.75	52	15.25
V	< 0.50	103	30.21
		341	100.00

The concentration and per cent distribution of agricultural labourers can be seen at state level from the Table 4.7. In India as a whole 26.3 per cent of the total workers are engaged as an agricultural labourer. This national average is not uniform in all the states of the country. Somewhere it is 1.4 per cent in other state it is 30 per cent. In all the union territories and hill states the percentage share is far below the national average, i.e. in Himachal Pradesh it is 4.2%, Jammu and Kashmir 3.1%, Manipur 3.6%, Meghalaya 9.9%, Nagaland 1.4%, Mizoram 0.3% and in Delhi, Arunachal Pradesh, Andaman and Nicobar, Pondicherry and Chandigarh it is 1.2, 1.9, 4.6, 11.5 and 1.4 respectively. The percentage of agricultural labourers are also very low in Rajasthan, i.e., 9.3% due to the extensive system of cropping

TABLE 4.9: Frequency Distribution (Concentration of Labour - District Level)

States	< 0.50	No. of Districts in Each State and Categories				
		0.50-0.75	0.75-1.00	1.00-1.25	< 1.25	Total
Andhra Pradesh	1	1	1	2	16	21
Assam	7	1	1	—	—	9
Bihar	1	1	2	1	12	17
Gujarat	2	5	7	3	2	19
Haryana	2	4	—	—	—	6
Himachal Pradesh	9	—	—	—	—	9
Jammu & Kashmir	10	—	—	—	—	10
Karnataka	2	2	7	2	6	19
Kerala	—	—	3	3	4	10
Madhya Pradesh	5	6	12	13	7	43
Maharashtra	3	4	2	4	12	26
Manipur	5	—	—	—	—	5
Meghalaya	3	—	—	—	—	3
Nagaland	3	—	—	—	—	3
Orissa	0	1	2	9	1	13
Punjab	—	6	5	—	—	11
Rajasthan	20	4	2	—	—	26
Tamil Nadu	3	0	1	5	5	14
Tripura	3	—	—	—	—	3
Uttar Pradesh	20	13	8	9	4	54
West Bengal	3	2	1	5	5	16
- Mizoram	1	—	—	—	—	1
- Delhi	1	—	—	—	—	1
- Andaman Nicobar	1	—	—	—	—	1
- Pondicherry	1	—	—	—	—	1
- Goa Daman & Diu	0	1	—	—	—	1
- Chandigarh	1	—	—	—	—	1
- Dadra Nagar Haveli	1	—	—	—	—	1

pattern, low yield level, and less requirement of outside labour than the family labour though the operational holdings are higher than those regions where the holdings are smaller but concentration of agricultural labour is high. On the basis of location quotient and concentration of agricultural labourers out of 29 units (States) only eight states are above the national average (Andhra Pradesh, Bihar, Karnataka, Kerala, Madhya Pradesh, Maharashtra, Orissa and Tamil Nadu). In Andhra Pradesh out of 21 districts 16 districts belong to the highest level of concentration where the concentration is highest in India. In the adjoining districts of Maharashtra, Madhya Pradesh, Karnataka and Tamil Nadu the concentration is also very high and it is the single belt of higher concentration of this segment of population. Second highest concentration is located in Bihar where out of 17 districts 12 belong to the high level of concentration Table 4.9. If we see the levels of agricultural productivity these belts belong to the medium level of agricultural productivity of India. But this is not the single factor which is determining the concentration of high level. For example in eastern Maharashtra and northern part of Karnataka Cotton is a major commercial crop which requires labour at peak hours. Secondly in coastal Andhra Pradesh and Bihar rice is a major crop which requires intensive seasonal labour though the size of land holding is smaller than Rajasthan. While in Rajasthan and western part of Madhya Pradesh crops like jowar, bajra and maize are less labour requiring crops which enables the lowest concentration of labour. In Punjab and Haryana wheat is a major crop which requires more labour starting from ploughing, sowing and harvesting but the substitute of labourers are available in the form of mechanization, therefore, a major part of Punjab is under medium level of concentration of agricultural labourers. Hence, the high level of agricultural productivity in Punjab is determined or related with both the factors like mechanization and agricultural labourers.

IV

. er Capita Agricultural Income in India and Agricultural Productivity

The per capita agricultural income has been analysed both at state as well as at district level. The time periods chosen are trieniums of 1968–71 and 1976–79. There are three main objectives of the study, viz., (i) to estimate per capita agricultural income at the district level, since such data would be of vital use in identifying districts with very low or high per capita income, (ii) to study the behaviour of district wise per capita incomes over time, particularly in reference to the periods chosen, to measure the impact of growth rates on the regional patterns of income distribution, and (iii) lastly, to study the behaviour of level of inequality both at relatively aggregated level of the states and in more details of the districts. The need of the study can hardly be emphasized. Although, there have been studies regarding time trend behaviours of levels of spatial disparity in

India,[2] both at state and district levels, even at further disaggregated levels of regional units, there has never been any study to evaluate the behaviour of spatial disparities in terms of income criteria at district levels simply because of the limitations of availability of data. Moreover, there have been fragmented studies of the Green revolution, which suggests high level of unequal distribution of benefits, whether inter-personal or inter-regional.[3] But, there have been little systematic study to provide complete and comparable picture.

In recent years many studies appeared on the problems of regional disparities. Many of them related with the cross-sectional (at one point of time)[4] or being limited to regional level, or studying only a limited area of the country and therefore, proving inadequacy in terms of any non-Indian study of the process of regional disparity. Cross-sectional studies are useful in identifying relative areas of backwardness of advancement, but would fail to ascertain spatial inequality as a process. On the contrary, in inter-temporal studies, the time interval should be sufficiently large enough to allow for identification of the process of spatial inequality, as in the case of Sampert.[5] In the present study, the choice of time, has been to compare the levels of per capita income, changes thereof, and changes in levels of regional inequality during this period. Again the fluctuations of agricultural output in India is severely dependent on environmental factors and the fluctuations are so wide that choosing a single year may prove to be either a peak or a trough period. Therefore, agricultural statistics used are in terms of moving averages of the trieniums.

As it has been pointed out earlier, the major objectives of the present study is to estimate the per capita income at district level. Such, estimates are not available.[6] It is also not possible to estimate gross or net income statistics for districts for all commodities, due to lack of systematic informations of non-agricultural sectors, either in terms of manufacturing industries or services. But agricultural statistics at district level are available with sufficient reliability as well as over a sufficient length of time.[7] But, the estimates of districtwise income on the basis of agricultural sector alone may not be solely reflective of the entire economy. But, there are reasons to use this with sufficient reliability to reflect the extent of productiveness, therefore, advancement of a district or the vice-versa. India, the agricultural sector contributes in the range of

45% to the national income directly and another 20% indirectly. On the other hand, about 70% of the population depend on agriculture and about a similar share of the total population lives in rural areas where the chief occupation is agriculture. Therefore, for all practical purposes, national income in rural India is to a greater extent agriculture dependent. So, using agricultural statistics to estimate incomes of rural population would not be a serious limitation of the study.[8] The possibilities thus, left are of estimating gross output figures in terms of value and the summing up for each district. Data on prices have been used are of All India whole sale Prices to make the gross output figures for both the periods comparable overtime. Admittedly, there are large variations in even wholesale prices of agricultural commodities inter-regionally, under restrictive commodity movement conditions, at least operating during the periods of study. But, estimation of prices, regionally, would again be far beyond the scope of the present study, and therefore, All India Wholesale prices have been used. Lastly, census of India provides for decadal districtwise population figures of rural and urban population but for the present point of time, the rural population estimates have been suitably projected into mid-points of the trieniums with compound growth rate methods.

Agricultural Income

Statewise agricultural income figures show that the per capita incomes vary from Rs. 92.0 in Kerala to Rs. 480 in Punjab with the average income of the country being Rs. 285, with the coefficient of variation at a level of 35%. Classifying statewise incomes with the help frequencies of less than Rs. 100; Rs. 201 to Rs. 300 and between Rs. 301 to Rs. 500 etc., puts the incomes in three categories, low (I) in one state only (Kerala), medium (II) in 7 states (U.P., Rajasthan, Haryana, Himachal Pradesh, J & K, Bihar and Assam) and the rest of 9 States in the high category (III).

But during this period per capita gross agricultural incomes seen at vary appreciably from Rs. 92 in Kerala to Rs. 807 in Punjab with a national average of Rs. 391. As in the case of the earlier period, only one state (Kerala) belongs to the very low category, states of Assam, Orissa, Bihar, U.P., Andhra Pradesh, Maharashtra, Rajasthan, Himachal Pradesh, Jammu and Kashmir being in the second category a down gradation of the states of Orissa, Maharashtra and

Andhra Pradesh; the states of Gujarat, Madhya Pradesh, Karnataka and Tamil Nadu in the medium group (III), Haryana in the high group (IV) and Punjab is the only state in the very high group. It seems, all the states in the latter 3 categories have performed appreciably well during this decade.

Estimates of annual compound growth rates of the per capita gross agricultural income in these years of study show that out of the total (16) states under study there has been positive growth rates in only 8 states, while the rest 8 states suffer from a negative trend in the incomes, with a marginally positive growth rate of +0.39 for the nation as a whole (total output growing at the rate of +2.15 and rural population by 1.76. The growth rates have been as low as -5.68% in case of Maharashtra to a marginal position of 0.04% in case of West Bengal and to as high as +6.71% in case of Punjab. A regionwise classification, shows that the major part of the positive growth rates of the per capita income are in Northern India with very high in Punjab, Haryana and Jammu and Kashmir (latter due to low based figures) followed by U.P., Rajasthan and Assam in the North-East. The only exception in the South in the State of Tamil Nadu, with a marginally positive growth rate. Among the negative growth rates notable are the States of Gujarat (with higher base year figures), Maharashtra and Orissa.

An assessment of the situation provides a hypothesis that, during the period appreciable positive changes in rural agricultural incomes have only been noticed in the northern half of the country, while negative trends have been clear in larger parts of the country, marginally affecting the per capita income of the nation as a whole.

A districtwise estimates of per capita income for this period (two points of time) gives all details such as percentage annual compound growth rates thereof, compound growth rates of population (rural and total income gross). During the base year triennium, the per capita income was as low as Rs. 28 (at the prices of 1976–79 triennium) in Ladakh district of the State of Jammu and Kashmir, too as high as Rs. 747 in Bhatinda district of Punjab. A classification of districts into frequency groups shows that out of the 284 districts total of 9 districts fall in the lowest group (less than Rs. 100 per capita income) 151 districts in the low group (II) with income between Rs. 101 to 300, 106 districts in the medium and high groups (III & IV) with income between Rs. 500 to 700 and only two districts in the highest category (V), with income more than Rs. 700. The maximum concentration of districts are in the II & III categories, implying 257 districts out of 284 had a per capita agricultural income between Rs. 100 to 500 at 1976–79 prices.

However, a statewise break-up shows, interestingly enough, that most of the districts of the lowest group are concentrated in the states of Kerala (4), Rajasthan (2), Tamil Nadu (2) and Jammu & Kashmir (1) while the second group is concentrated in U.P. (33 out of 48), Rajasthan (17 out of 28), Orissa (6 out of 11), M.P. (15 out of 43), Andhra Pradesh (9 out of 17) and both Bihar and Assam entirely, with 15 and 8 regional units respectively. On the other hand, States of Assam, Bihar, J.&K., Kerala, Maharashtra, Orissa, Rajasthan, Tamil Nadu, U.P. and West Bengal have no districts in either the high (IV) and very high categories (V).

The picture becomes even clearer in the cartographic representation that the low agricultural income (I & II) form a clear regional pattern in (a) East & North-East in Assam, West Bengal (except North Bengal), Coastal Orissa and Bihar, (b) in whole of U.P. (except small parts of North-Eastern U.P., and North Central M.P.) (c) in Rajasthan, North-Western U.P., and North-Western Gujarat, (d) in Telengana area and (e) South Western coast and part of Northern plain area. The medium income districts (III) form regional patterns in (a) North-Western India (parts of Punjab, Haryana and U.P.), (b) North-Central India (parts of Eastern Rajasthan, North-Western M.P. and Gujarat, (c) Maharashtra-Karnataka transitional zones (d) Southern Coastal plains and the high income district (IV & V). Concentrating in (a) Punjab and Haryana plains and (b) isolated pockets in Gujarat, coastal Andhra Pradesh (west Godavari and Nizamabad) and districts of Madhya Pradesh and Bellary of Karnataka.

The situation in the triennium (1976–79) shows cardinal changes in the low income districts (both I & II) concentration largely in (a) larger parts of N. Central and N. Eastern U.P., whole of Bihar, South Western Bengal and larger parts of Orissa and plains of Brahamputra, (b) medium income districts (III) in Chattisgarh area (Low population areas) coastal Andhra and Tamil Nadu, parts of North-Western Bengal, parts of plain Karnataka and Southern Maharashtra, larger parts of Gujarat, Eastern Rajasthan and Western Madhya Pradesh and the development peripheries of the Punjab Haryana agricultural belt extended into U.P. and the (c) high agricultural districts (IV & V) concentrating largely in the Punjab and Haryana plains, (the central and South-Western parts, with the districts of Ganganagar in Rajasthan), the Kathiawar peninsula, Thanjavur district of Tamil Nadu and districts of Shimoga, Raichur and Bellary of Karnataka.

There is a considerable diffusion of the number of districts from the medium categories (II & III) towards both the ends, either into I to IV, and V, while in the period of '68-71, 257 districts of 284 fell into III and IV categories, in 1976–79, 245 fell into the above categories. More so, about the medium category is that (III) the number of districts getting reduced from 106 to 89, a reduction by 15%, the districts being distributed to high or low classes. The number of district with per capita agricultural income less than Rs. 100 (I) increasing from 9 to 11, between Rs. 101 to 300 from 151 to 156 and above Rs. 700 from 2 to 11, a more than 500% increase. Secondly, on the other hand, most of the low income districts (I & II) are concentrated in few states, i.e. 13 out of 17 in Andhra Pradesh, all 15 of Bihar, 7 out of 8 in Assam, 10 out of 15 in Karnataka, all 7 in Kerala, 20 out of 43 in Madhya Pradesh, 23 out of 25 in Maharashtra, 8 out of 11 in Orissa, 17 out of 26 in Rajasthan and 30 out of 48 in Uttar Pradesh, with 11 districts each in Orissa and Punjab have the uniqueness of the former being 8 in the lowest (I) and the later 9 in the highest (V) groups. All the districts in the (V) class (above Rs. 700) are concentrated in one region of Punjab (6), Haryana (4) and Rajasthan (1).

Changes in per Capita Income (Agricultural)

Changes in per capita agricultural incomes have been estimated in terms of annual compound growth rates in percentages. The growth rates range between - 10.97% in Bhir, - 10.80% in Aurangabad, 9.9% in Sholapur, -9.23% in Osmanabad etc. in Maharashtra to +10.50% at Sangrur, +9.50% at Hoshiarpur of Punjab to +8.90% at Ambala of Haryana. Out of 284 districts, which are being classified into 5 classes of growth rates, the first two (I and II) in negative and last three in positive changes, show that 151 districts (more than half) have changed negatively with 108 districts suffering high negative growth rates in terms of per capita agricultural income. Only 88 districts show significant positive compound growth rates. But, the pattern of this distribution is also markedly uneven i.e. states like Orissa, have all the 11 units (all 13 districts) in high negative growth categories (I) and Punjab with all the 11 districts in highest positive growth rate category (V). States like Maharashtra, M.P., Andhra Pradesh, part of Rajasthan, Karnataka and Gujarat are the casualties of negative growth rates. The spatial pattern makes it clear, that significant negative growth rates were being concentrated in states of Bihar. Virtually, the whole of central India (peninsular part) including Orissa, larger parts of M.P., Maharashtra, Telengana areas of Andhra Pradesh and Northern Karnataka. Area of highest positive growth rates being concentrated in two divergent areas, (a) the north-western plains of Punjab, Haryana, Western U.P. and Jammu region of J & K, parts of Southern Rajasthan and Northern Gujarat, (b) the other region being coastal Tamil Nadu, the isolated pockets in Karnataka, West Bengal and Assam.

TABLE 4.10: Per Capita Agricultural Incomes (Compound Growth Rates of Incomes Rural Population)

	PCAI (Rs.) 60's (1968–71)	PCAI (Rs.) 70's (1976–79)	CGR %	CGR of Rural Population %
1. Andhra Pradesh	338	295	-1.71	1.68
2. Assam	226	265	2.03	0.50
3. Bihar	179	163	-1.22	1.78
4. Gujarat	406	396	-0.33	2.28
5. Haryana	461	602	3.40	2.27
6. J & K	194	265	3.98	1.63
7. Karnataka	361	323	-1.39	1.82
8. Kerala	92	81	-0.20	2.23
9. Madhya Pradesh	327	305	-0.88	2.29
10. Maharashtra	325	204	-5.68	2.03
11. Orissa	315	262	-2.28	2.03
12. Punjab	480	807	6.71	1.12
13. Rajasthan	235	291	2.72	2.32
14. Tamil Nadu	330	355	0.94	1.53
15. Uttar Pradesh	263	295	1.52	1.41
16. West Bengal	270	271	0.04	2.38
INDIA	285	391	0.39	1.84

PCAI — Per capita Agricultural income (Food crops only).
CGR — Compound Growth Rate.
Rur. Pop. — Rural Population.

Areas of marginal increase or decrease are on the fringes of these two divergent regions as in the case of larger parts of U.P., West Bengal, Karnataka, Tamil Nadu and Rajasthan. The statewise changes in agricultural income shows that 8 out of 16 states have suffered from negative growth rates, the lowest being- 5.68 per cent annually in Maharashtra, to maximum positive growth rate of +6.71 per cent in Punjab and 3.39 per cent in Haryana and 3.98 per cent in J & K, (because of the low base figures). States of medium and marginal positive growth rates are Assam, Himachal Pradesh, Rajasthan, Tamil Nadu, U.P., and West Bengal. Followed by Maharashtra, Orissa has the growth rate of -2.28 per cent followed by Andhra Pradesh (-1.71%), Bihar (-1.22%) and Karnataka (-1.39%). Here, also, the regional pattern of change in per capita agricultural income is quite clear, the North Western India enjoying from marginally to high positive growth rates, the Central Indian States with high negative growth rates and South India with either marginal positive or negative growth rates. At the eastern most, West Bengal, and Assam enjoy marginal to relatively high positive growth rates respectively.

The above study can be summarised which have achieved the following findings:

(1) That, in spite of the growth of various inputs in the period of green revolution and its impact over the whole economy, still the pockets highly effected in the beginning are still have higher income than the districts which were on the previous position. In spite of this the per capita income from agricultural sector seems to have declined in larger parts of the country (53% of the districts), while significant increase has been observed in slightly over 15 per cent of the total number of districts. However, the growth was steady and followed the old pattern.

(2) The study reveals that there is a regional concentration of districts where either faster agricultural diversification has taken place. All the districts of the highest income class (Rs. 700) are concentrated in one region, i.e. North-Western India (Punjab and Haryana). A very large part of the next higher class districts are also concentrated around these districts and so, it gives way to, in a pattern of rings, as in a gravitational fixed to the lowest income areas. Only, a very few districts in

west Bengal, Tamil Nadu, Karnataka and Gujarat are better of in isolated manner.

(3) Thirdly, concentration of districts, where higher positive growth rates of income are observed regionally, as in the case of North-Western India, relating to former and eastern to central and western India (Bihar to Maharashtra, part of Telengana and Karnataka).

TABLE 4.11: Frequency Distribution (per Capita AGR. Income) (A Distt.-Level Study) 70's

S. N.	States	No. of Districts in each Income Group					
		100	100-299	300-499	500-699	700	Total
1.	Andhra Pradesh	0	11	6	0	07	17
2.	Assam	0	7	1	0	0	8
3.	Bihar	1	14	0	0	0	15
4.	Gujarat	0	4	8	5	0	17
5.	Haryana	0	0	2	3	2	7
6.	J & K	1	1	1	0	0	3
7.	Karnataka	0	10	6	3	0	19
8.	Kerala	4	3	0	0	0	7
9.	Madhya Pradesh	0	21	22	0	0	43
10.	Maharashtra	0	24	1	0	0	25
11.	Orissa	0	8	3	0	0	11
12.	Punjab	0	0	2	3	6	11
13.	Rajasthan	3	14	8	0	1	26
14.	Tamil Nadu	1	4	6	1	0	12
15.	Uttar Pradesh	0	30	16	2	0	48
16.	West Bengal	0	6	9	1	0	15
	ALL INDIA	10	156	91	18	16	284

TABLE 4.12: **Frequency Distribution of Growth Rates of per Capita Income Compound Growth Rates**

S. No.	States	-1.0%	-1.0-00	0.0-1.00	1.01-3.0	3.01+	Total no. of distt.
1.	Andhra-Pradesh	12	3	1	1	—	17
2.	Assam	2	4	-	1	1	8
3.	Bihar	8	2	3	2	—	15
4.	Gujarat	7	2	2	4	2	17
5.	Haryana	—	—	2	1	4	7
6.	J & K	1	—	—	—	2	3
7.	Karnataka	9	3	1	4	2	19
8.	Kerala	3	2	1	1	—	7
9.	Madhya Pradesh	21	10	9	3	—	43
10.	Maharashtra	21	1	3	—	—	25
11.	Orissa	11	—	—	—	—	11
12.	Punjab	—	—	—	—	11	11
13.	Rajasthan	7	2	1	7	9	26
14.	Tamil Nadu	—	5	3	1	3	12
15.	Uttar Pradesh	6	8	16	12	6	48
16.	West Bengal	—	1	3	7	4	15
	INDIA	108	43	45	44	44	284

References

1. Gunnar Myrdal (1968), Asian Drama, — An Enquiry into the Poverty of Nations, New York, *20th Century Fund,* Vol. II, p. 1369.
2. Ashok Mitra (1967), Levels of Regional Development in India, census of India, 1961 [Vol. I, Pt. I-A (i)]: B. Dasgupta (1972), Economic classification of Districts in India, *Economic & Political Weekly;* M. N. Pal (1975). Regional Disparity in levels of Regional Development. Indian Journal of Regional Science (*IJRS.*) Vol. VII. No. 1, pp. 22-42; K. L. Sharma (1976), Inter-regional Disparities in Rajasthan (1961—67) IJRS. Vol. VIII. R.I.K. Sampert (1977), Inter-regional Inequality in India (1951—71). *IJRS.* Vol. IX No. 1; J.K. Gogoi (1977), Inter-regional variations in levels of Development in N. E. Region of India (1961—67) *IJRS,* Vol. IX. No. 1; A.C. Mahapatra (1978), An Alternative Models of Measuring Divergence-Convergence Hypothesis: A Study of Regional per Capita Incomes in India (1960-61) to 1973-74), *IJRS,* Vol. X. No. 2. pp. 39-50; K. R. G. Nair (1971). Interstate income disparities in India. *IJRS.* Vol. III. No.2. pp. 46-58; S. K. Rao (1973). Notes on measuring distance between regions India. *Economic & Political Weekly.* Vol. 5. pp. 793-4.
3. N. Krishnaji (1975), Inter-regional Disparity in per capita production and productivity of foodgrains, *EPW* (SN). pp. 737-85; C.H. Hanumanth Rao (1976). *Technological change and Distributions of gains in Indian Agriculture;*

P. Patnaik and B. K. Rao (1975). Some Aspects of Agricultural Development of Post-Independence India (unpublished). A.C. Mahapatra (1978). Some aspects of Green Revolution and Concentration of output: Regionwise, Cropwise and Classwise in India. *North-East Eco-Rev.* pp. 194-262.

4. Ashok Mitra (1967), *Op.cit;* B. Dasgupta (1972), *Op.cit.*, M.N. Pal (1976). *Op. cit.*
5. R. K. Sampert (1977). *Op.cit.*
6. NCAER (1963), Inter-District and Inter-State Income Differentials 1955-56. occasional paper No. 6. New Delhi.
7. Govt. of India, Ministry of Agriculture; Estimates of Area, Production and yield of Principal crops, New Delhi.
8. Use of total agricultural income of a district to find per capita income by dividing it by total population of a district would be less accurate, due to inclusion of non-agricultural population i.e. the non-rural population.

5

Technological Factors in Agricultural Productivity

Agricultural Productivity – Technological Factors

Technology in agriculture in its simplest sense means the use of power operator machines to do various farm jobs. The basic purpose of the study of Technology is to measure the agricultural efficiency created by the innovation of technology at various levels, because all the states are not mechanized equally and agriculture is not free from the environmental control. As compared to other advanced countries of the world Indian agriculture is partially mechanised and we have no such region even today to call it fully or completely mechanized. Because of this we have a major portion of agricultural land without intensive agriculture, multiple cropping and timely operations which results in poor yield per unit of land. Therefore, it is quite obvious that Indian agriculture largely depends on environmental control. This phenomenon plays both the positive and negative role in various aspects of agriculture. Even in the most positive regions the transformation of traditional agriculture can be brought to bring better results.

Agricultural Technology is unevenly distributed throughout India. In other words in 10 per cent area of India about 25 per cent mechanization is concentrated where technological development has removed the impact of environmental constraint over agriculture, and due to this fact this small area is contributing about 20 per cent of the total foodgrains production of the country. Therefore, the agricultural development depends largely on large scale distribution of technological means wanted by each region as the expansion of agricultural land through the reclamation of cultivable wasteland will not be of much help to cope with the present problem. The gains of the agricultural technology can easily be seen in the states of Haryana, Punjab and few districts of the country where surplus food situation is created due to this achievement not by cultivating all the cultivable wastelands. Therefore, the priority should be given to bring more and more technology in agriculture rather than to increase the net cultivated area for more production and agricultural technology to the level of Haryana and Punjab should be introduced in other states of the country to face the increasing challenge of population growth.

The problem of agricultural technology at regional level should be considered on top priority basis not only to increase the productivity but also to remove the regional imbalances in yield per unit area and growth in yield as it is observed that the area of high agricultural technological concentration have higher yield as well as growth with the exception of few rice dominating area of the country like Kashmir valley, Bengal and Assam etc. The regions of common geophysical conditions have varying levels of yield because of the uneven distribution of technology.

There are some regions which require different type of technology. In unirrigated regions only the irrigation can bring a phenomenal change both in yield and growth particularly in the states of Rajasthan, Maharashtra and Madhya Pradesh. There are regions where irrigation facilities are available but other technology like better seeds, fertilizers and tractors are not available, it is mostly in the eastern U.P., Bihar, West Bengal and Assam etc. There are some regions where neither the irrigation is adequately available nor the other technological facilities are available. These regions are very critical and have a very low yield. In some of the regions (Kashmir valley, hilly regions and coastal areas) technology shall be made available of different types than the plain areas. However, in order to remove the regional imbalances and increase the yield level an uniform diffusion of technology is needed required by each region.

Distribution of Tractors

The distribution of tractors is not uniform in all the States of India. The states of Haryana, Punjab and Western U.P. consisting of about 20 per cent of the net cultivated area of India have 55 per cent tractors of the country as a whole which resulted a very high level of yield than other parts of the country. Other states have an insignificant share in terms of percentage share of tractors. But this type of distribution is not very meaningful as compared to number of tractors per 1000 hectare land in each state. The Table 5.1 will reveal the number of tractors per 1000 hectare of cultivated area in relation to yield level.

TABLE 5.1: Tractors—Percentage Share of Tractors in all the States and number of Tractors per 1000 hectare of cultivated area

	States	% to the total of India	Tractors per 1000 hectare of cultivated land (number)
1.	Andhra Pradesh	3.73	0.68
2.	Assam	0.36	0.24
3.	Bihar	3.87	0.63
4.	Gujarat	5.64	1.88
5.	Haryana	11.83	4.85
6.	Jammu & Kashmir	0.34	0.51
7.	Karnataka	3.99	0.98
8.	Kerala	1.45	2.86
9.	Madhya Pradesh	3.84	0.30
10.	Maharashtra	3.55	0.44
11.	Orissa	0.93	0.23
12.	Punjab	24.44	8.23
13.	Rajasthan	6.16	0.86
14.	Tamil Nadu	3.78	1.36
15.	Uttar Pradesh	23.28	2.05
16.	West Bengal	0.36	0.09
	INDIA	100.0	1.60

The concentration of tractors per 1000 hectare of cultivated area is very high in the states of Punjab and Haryana, i.e. 8 and 5 in number respectively. For Punjab it is about one tractor cultivating 125 hectares of land while for Haryana 200 hectares land is being ploughed by one tractor. There are various factors responsible for it. Firstly the income level of the farmers is much higher than other states of India to afford tractors. Secondly, the size of the land holding is large for the proper use of tractors. Lastly, the cropping is such that it needs more ploughing than the rice dominated area as wheat requires more ploughing than rice cropped land. The States of Uttar Pradesh, Kerala and Gujarat have more than two tractors on per 1000 hectares of land. Other states have less than two tractors on per 1000 hectare of cultivated area. A very critical situation is posed by the States of Madhya Pradesh, Orissa, Assam, Bihar, Andhra Pradesh, Rajasthan and Maharashtra where number of tractors is about one on each 3000 hectare of cultivated area.

High yield level is related with the high concentration of agricultural technology with the exception of those states where rice is a dominating crop. About 80 per cent tractors are concentrated in the regions above the national average of yield. In other words 50 per cent area which is above the national average contributing 70 per cent of the total production are occupying 80 per cent tractors of the country. The contribution of tractors will be more clear if we say that 50 per cent tractors of the country is concentrated only in 15 per cent cultivated area and contributing about 30 per cent of the total national foodgrains production.

The need of tractor is felt more accute in those area where rainfall is insufficient and the soil moisture retaining capacity is very poor. The State of Rajasthan is one of the best example where monsoon recedes very early and moisture retaining capacity is very poor to plough and cover the land holding for the rabi crops. As a result a considerable percentage of cultivated and cultivable area is left without sowing due to the traditional system of ploughing. If tractor is provided in these regions at least the percentage of cultivated area can be increased to get more production. Therefore, the priority to introduce more tractors should be considered on the following grounds:

1. Nature of the cropping pattern.
2. To introduce better crops which is not being introduced in the region due to the lack of rapid plough system.
3. Size of the landholdings.
4. Income level of the farmers and financial help.
5. Regional need and profitability.

Irrigation Machinery (Electric Pump sets & Oil Engines)

Water is the most important and crucial factor in agricultural operations. It increases the intensity of cropping, it brings more and more culturable waste lands under cultivation. Without irrigation and water availability it is impossible to introduce and use high yielding variety seeds and fertilizers and without these a better survival of agriculture is not possible. Lastly, it increases the yield and render the region in high growth of yield. An analysis of water availability through rainfall indicates that region above 50 inches of rainfall is less sufferer than the region between the rainfall 20 to 50 inches. In this region cropping without irrigation is not possible at least in the rabi season. A major portion of our cultivated area is occupied by this range of rainfall area. The regions below 20 inches of rainfall have different problems like variations of rainfall in time and some times an erratic nature of rainfall occurs in this region. A high percentage of drought prone area occurs in this zone of rainfall. In this region duration of rainfall is very low. Therefore, keeping in view the chances of suffering of the crops the first priority should be given to provide irrigation facilities in these regions.

On the basis of natural factors and sources of water availability various means and measures have been adopted for irrigation purposes. The most important among them are electric pump sets and oil engines. Though its distribution is based on the sources of water availability and mechanization of irrigation started on this basis.

Distribution of electric pump sets is very unique as it is highly concentrated in the state of Tamil Nadu, Maharashtra, Andhra Pradesh and Karnataka. It is because of the lack of the canal irrigation as in the topography of these states don't permit for the canal irrigation. The Table 5.2 will reveal the total picture of the distribution of electric pump sets in all the States of India.

TABLE 5.2: Distribution of Electric Pumpsets in India and number per 1000 hectare of cultivated land

States	% share of each state	Number of Elect. Pumpsets per 1000 hectare
Andhra Pradesh	8.99	14.19
Assam	0.01	0.02
Bihar	3.28	46.16
Gujarat	2.99	8.57
Haryana	4.01	15.11
J & K	0.01	0.07
Karnataka	9.83	20.63
Kerala	0.61	10.39
Madhya Pradesh	3.74	3.22
Maharashtra	10.50	11.18
Orissa	0.02	0.05
Punjab	4.89	14.27
Rajasthan	2.21	26.74
Tamil Nadu	42.16	130.49
Uttar Pradesh	6.56	4.97
West Bengal	0.12	0.20

It is evident from the Table 5.2 that the state of Tamil Nadu, Bihar and Rajasthan are well facilitated with pumpsets irrigation machinery while other states have insignificant position even Bihar and Rajasthan are not well placed regarding this facility except of Tamil Nadu.

About 40 per cent irrigation pumpsets of the country are located in the highest yield category, i.e. above 1500 kg./hect. mostly lying in the state of Tamil Nadu. Other states like Rajasthan and Karnataka and Bihar have high concentration but yield level is not considerably high it is because of the lack of irrigation facilities and these measures are inadequate to irrigate the cultivated area.

The second major source of irrigation machinery is the oil engines but its availability is not adequate for irrigation purposes. Its distribution (per 1000 hectare of cultivated area) in terms of per cent share to the total of the country at state level indicate that the high concentration is found in the state of Gujarat, Punjab and Tamil Nadu comprising about 45 per cent of the country. Its contribution in terms of total volume of irrigation is very low due to the low capacity of irrigation, though there seems to be a very high number of it on per 1000 hectare of cultivated land as it is evident from the Table 5.3.

TABLE 5.3: Per cent Share of oil engines and number per 1000 hectare cultivated area

States	% Share of each state	Number per 1000 hectare
Andhra Pradesh	6.96	22.71
Assam	0.02	2.85
Bihar	2.63	3.68
Gujarat	23.12	31.07
Haryana	3.14	19.17
J & K	0.02	10.03
Karnataka	2.50	37.37
Kerala	1.09	68.24
Madhya Pradesh	3.39	13.68
Maharashtra	10.84	6.08
Orissa	0.35	6.21
Punjab	15.59	48.77
Rajasthan	2.26	4.21
Tamil Nadu	14.78	58.12
U.P.	12.97	21.33
West Bengal	0.32	10.30

Consumption of Fertilizers

The state level consumption of fertilizers in terms of percentage share of each state will not reveal any convincing fact because of the different size of the states. However, the following table indicate the per cent share of each state to the total of the country. The Table 5.4 reveals the amount of fertilizers used per hectare of cultivated area. In the state of Punjab, Kerala and Tamil Nadu the use of fertilizer is highest while the states like Karnataka, Gujarat, U.P. and Andhra Pradesh are slightly above the national average of the consumption of fertilizers. Other states have a very insignificant use of fertilizers. Mostly the rice growing states, as compared to wheat growing states, are the lowest in the use of fertilizers.

TABLE 5.4: Percentage Share of each State in the use of Fertilizers and its Use per Hectare

States	% Share of each state	Fertilizer use kg./hect.
Andhra Pradesh	9.96	22.71
Assam	0.34	2.85
Bihar	1.78	3.68
Gujarat	7.51	31.10
Haryana	3.52	19.17
J & K	0.38	10.03
Karnataka	12.33	37.37
Kerala	2.80	68.24
Madhya Pradesh	4.88	6.08
Maharashtra	8.89	13.68
Orissa	1.98	6.21
Punjab	11.57	48.77
Rajasthan	2.42	4.21
Tamil Nadu	13.00	58.12
U.P.	19.62	21.33
West Bengal	3.24	10.30

Yield Level and Mechanization

The Table 5.5 will reveal the actual situation of technological inputs in relation to agricultural productivity. It will also indicate the per cent area under each yield level and its contribution to the total production of the country as well as the per cent share of these yield categories in terms of output, fertilizers, tractors, irrigation machinery and per cent gross area irrigated.

TABLE 5.5: Yield Level and Percentage Share of Area, Output and Various Inputs in each Yield Category

Yield level	% Area	% Production	% Fertilizers	% Tractors	% Irrigation machinery	% Gross irrigated area
(A) >2000	6.45	12.68	13.38	16.85	16.10	12.94
(B) 1500—2000	11.32	18.76	25.24	28.95	26.00	22.14
(C) 1000—1500	36.78	41.32	38.61	34.27	28.05	42.00
(D) 500—1000	32.08	23.85	20.03	16.01	22.73	19.30
(E) <500	13.38	3.39	2.74	3.92	7.12	3.62
	100.00	100.00	100.00	100.00	100.00	100.00

The Table 5.5 indicate that only 6 per cent area of the country occupied by 'A' category of yield is producing about 12 per cent of the total production of the country. It is because of the high concentration of all inputs in this area (Punjab, Haryana and some scattered districts in the states of U.P., Tamil Nadu and Karnataka). While the lowest yield category 'E' is occupying about 13 per cent of the area but contributing only 3 per cent of the total production of the country and have a very low level of technology. In all the yield categories the relationship with various input level is clearly maintained. If we convert the total cultivated area of the country to the level of 'A' category the total production will be just double on the level of mechanised area under 'A' category.

Growth Level and Mechanization

The Table 5.6 will reveal the various facts of production growth in relation to mechanization.

TABLE 5.6: Production Growth and level of Mechanization

	Production C. Growth (%)	% Area	% Production	% Fertilizers	% Tractors	% Irrigation machinery	Gross irrigated area
(A)	> 6	10.43	12.45	16.39	37.37	13.81	19.26
(B)	3—6	19.08	23.66	22.69	31.16	20.87	26.27
(C)	1—3	43.63	45.18	43.63	23.08	46.18	38.55
(D)	(-) 1—3	17.63	14.71	11.06	6.58	10.33	12.54
(E)	> 3(-)	9.15	3.99	6.32	2.63	8.82	3.37

It is clear from the Table 5.6 that a very high growth is received only in 10 per cent area but all items of mechanization is received at a very high level and a major contribution can be cited to high level of fertilizers and rate of irrigation. In other categories with the decrease of growth other inputs are also decreasing. In negative growth rate categories there is a large decline of inputs.

6

Cropwise Area, Yield and Productivity

Rice

Rice is a most dominant crop of India which occupy 39.7 million hectares or 31.34 per cent of the gross cultivated area. In terms of production of foodgrains it shares 40.45 per cent of the total foodgrains production of the country. Not only area and production is dominant but per hectare productivity, i.e., 1254 kg./hect. is also higher than all the foodgrains crop except of wheat (1484 kg. per hect.).

A spatial variation in the spread of rice is also a very interesting phenomena in this country. Though rice being a wet crop, therefore, water is every crucial factor for a successful growth and better results for this crop as it is largely being grown not only where intensity of rainfall is higher but the development of means of irrigation has created a very favourable situation for the cultivation of this crop. On the basis of environmental and artificial irrigation facilities India can be divided into four parts keeping in view the spread and yield level of this crop, i.e., high spread and high yield, high spread and low yield, low spread and low yield. Still in India a large area is under high spread and low yield which is a most potential area to increase the total production of rice, if assured water supply is made available. In low spread and high yield level regions possibilities of expansion of this crop in terms of area is not possible to a large extent. In low spread and low yield region the removal of environmental factors can help to increase the area and yield level both. Therefore, keeping in view the potentiality of the extension of this crop in India a detailed analysis of areas, production productivity will be of great use.

The spatial variation of rice crop is largely controlled by the intensity of rainfall as well as number of long and short dry spells. In the states of Assam, Meghalaya, Manipur, Mizoram, Tripura, Kerala, West Bengal, and the Union Territories of Andaman &

Nicobar, Goa, Daman & Diu more than 80 per cent area under foodgrain crops is devoted to rice (1979). It varies from 1.51 per cent (Rajasthan where only 59 cms. annual rainfall is recorded) to 97 per cent in Tripura which record 250 cms. rainfall. The areas which cover less than 15 per cent are Gujarat, Haryana, Himachal Pradesh, Maharashtra, Rajasthan and Delhi. In the states of Bihar, Nagaland, Orissa, Tamil Nadu, Arunachal Pradesh and Pondicherry more than 50 per cent area is occupied by this crop.

Increase in Area

During the period 1968–71 to 1976–79 the country experienced 6.25 per cent increase in rice cultivated area while increase in area under cereals and pulses recorded only 2.47 and 7.00 per cent respectively. A state level analysis shows that, there is a large variations in the increase which is very high, i.e., 1.30, 59 and 52 per cent respectively because of the large scale introduction of irrigation facilities as well as rice is a higher yield giving crop among the rabi season crops. Therefore, the low yield giving crops like Jowar, Bajra, and maize were given less importance and the area of this crop was encroached by the rice crop. But in terms of percentage share in area in these states to the total area of India is very low and insignificant. Other states like Assam, Andhra Pradesh, Bihar, J & K, Kerala, Manipur, Meghalaya, Nagaland, West Bengal, U.P. and other union territories recorded an increase in area below 20 per cent. In many of the states decrease in area was recorded which is below 6 per cent. This decrease is more noticable in Kerala (-7%), Karnataka (-7%), Himachal Pradesh (-8%). Other states like Tamil Nadu, Orissa, Gujarat recorded a very insignificant decrease. In Kerala during this period an overall decrease in the cultivated area in cereals was recorded, i.e., -7.23% due to the increase in the horticultural crops.

A state level analysis of the cereal crops reveal the fact that Gujarat (-9.59), Karnataka (-12.35), Kerala (-7.32), Madhya Pradesh (-1.36), Rajasthan (-4.73), Tamil Nadu (-1.57), Delhi (-1.49) and Pondicherry (-2.52) recorded negative growth. A significant growth in area was recorded in the states of Haryana, Punjab, Meghalaya, Manipur, Nagaland, Tripura, Arunachal Pradesh due to the increased demand of foodgrains and irrigation facilities while only 2.5 per cent increase in area was under cereals recorded for the country as a whole.

The increase of area under rice is largely controlled by the availability of water and at present due to the high yield giving nature of crop all possible area has been acquired for this crop. A further increase is possible if assured irrigation facilities are made available. As it has been noticed that wherever irrigation facilities are increased area under this crop has also increased. The increase in wheat by 27 per cent and in rice by 6 per cent seems to be a wide gap in increase but if we see the increase in total volume the difference is in the ratio of 1:2 respectively in rice & wheat, i.e. an addition of 22 lakh hectares in rice 46 lakh hectares in wheat as rice is occupying just double area as compared to the wheat area.

Increase in Production

As compared to area increase in India under this crop the increase in production attracts our attention for analysis. In India as a whole only 6.25 per cent area increased during this period while production increased by 21.7 per cent due to the yield increase from 1094 kg. to 1254 kg. per hectare or about 15 per cent increase in yield level. However, it is evident that the role of area increase is less important than the increase in yield per unit of rice cultivated area.

The country produced 49.76 million metric tonnes of rice in 1976–79 and 40.9 million metric tonnes in the year 1968–71. In terms of percentage share in foodgrains there is a very slight decline in the share, i.e., 40.45 per cent in 1976–79 and 40.67 per cent in 1968–71. The monoculture states of rice producing like Assam, Kerala, Manipur, Tripura and union territories of A & N Islands of Goa, Daman and Diu share about 90 per cent of their total production of foodgrains. Other important rice producing states are Meghalaya, Nagaland, Orissa, Tamil Nadu, West Bengal, Mizoram and Pondicherry where production of rice varies between 75 to 90 per cent of their foodgrains production. In terms of percentage share in foodgrains as well as share in area these states are important but in terms of volume of production other states like Andhra Pradesh, Uttar Pradesh, Bihar, Tamil Nadu, West Bengal are important and provide more than 5 million metric tonnes of rice because of the size of the states.

Rice production recorded an average growth of 2.41 per cent per annum during this period. But this growth is not uniform or equal in all the states of India. The states like Himachal Pradesh, Karnataka,

Kerala, Orissa and Delhi recorded negative growth in production due to considerable decline in area and yield per hectare. In the states of Himachal Pradesh, Karnataka and Kerala area decrease is important though yield increased while in the states of Orissa and Delhi both the factors are responsible. The states like Andhra Pradesh, Gujarat, Haryana, Maharashtra, Nagaland, Punjab, Rajasthan, Tamil Nadu, Tripura, Uttar Pradesh, A & N Islands, Dadra and Nagar Haveli, and Goa, Daman and Diu recorded more than the national average growth in rice production, or 35 per cent area under rice in India recorded more than the national average or about 83 per cent area under rice recorded positive growth rate in production in India as a whole, only 18 per cent area recorded negative growth rate. In terms of production about 14 per cent area falls under negative growth rate (Table 6.1). If we analyse the Table 6.1 of various growth category the picture of growth in area and production in each category will give authentic situation of growth characteristics in India. In the states of Gujarat, Haryana, Punjab, Rajasthan and Uttar Pradesh highest growth in production has been recorded or as a whole these states occupy about 7 per cent of the total rice cultivated area of India and sharing about 19 per cent of the total production of India. The area between the categories 0–20 growth rates occupy about 54 per cent and producing about 51 per cent of the total production of rice of India. In other words, larger areas are occupied by the low growth rate category as it is evident that the area between 20–40 growth category occupies about 11 per cent of the total area under rice and producing about 15 per cent of the total production of India. Therefore, it is obvious that higher growth can be achieved in low growth categories (54 per cent of the total rice area) and production can be increased to a large extent. The negative growth areas of the states of Assam, A & N Islands, Delhi, J & K, Meghalaya, Orissa and Arunachal Pradesh occupies about 18 per cent area of India and producing 14 per cent of the total rice production of India which can be brought to the level of higher growth rate categories if assured irrigation facilities with HYV & fertilizers are provided (Table 6.1).

During this period India 1968–71 to 1976–79 experienced about 22 per cent growth in production with an increase of 6.3 per cent in area. It is obvious that increase in production is much higher than the increase in area, it is because of the high increase in per hectare productivity (yield), i.e., about 15 per cent. Therefore, the contribution of area increase is less significant than the yield increase in achieving higher increase in production in this crop. On the whole India received 21.7 per cent growth in production in rice and 24.7 per cent growth in cereal crops as a whole in this period.

TABLE 6.1: Rice—Growth Level (Fig. 5)

Growth category		Area		Production	
		Million Hectares	% of India	Million Tonnes	% of India
A.	>40	6.78	17.10	9.40	18.92
B.	30—40	1.85	4.67	2.59	5.21
C.	20—20	2.62	6.60	5.62	11.31
D.	10—30	9.27	23.39	11.30	22.97
E.	0—10	12.00	30.27	13.90	27.97
F.	0—(-5)	2.27	5.73	2.22	4.47
G.	<(-5)—(-10)	4.85	12.24	4.66	9.38
Total		39.64	100.00	49.69	100.00

A. — Gujarat, Haryana, Punjab, Rajasthan, Uttar Pradesh.
B. — Maharashtra, Tripura, Goa Daman & Diu.
C. — Tamil Nadu, Dadra & Nagar Haveli.
D. — Andhra Pradesh, Bihar, Pondicherry.
E. — Himachal Pradesh, Karnataka, Kerala, Madhya Pradesh, Manipur, Nagaland, West Bengal.
F. — Assam, A & N Islands, Delhi.
G. — J & K, Meghalaya, Orissa, Arunachal Pradesh.

Increase in Yield

During this period 1968–71 to 1976– 79 the country experienced 14.63 per cent growth in yield while it is 21.7 per cent for cereal crops and 2.14 per cent for pulses crop. The increase in yield for this crop is much lower than the cereal crop as a whole because many other crops received higher growth in yield than the rice crop, i.e., Jowar, Ragi and Wheat. For the country as a whole per hectare yield is 1254 kg. while it was only 1094 kg. in the years 1968–71.

The yield level is not uniform in all the states of India. The lowest yield is recorded, i.e. 613 kg./hect. in Mizoram while it is 2857 kg./hect. in Punjab followed by Haryana, i.e., 2595 kg. per hect. There are only few states which records higher yield than the national average like states of Andhra Pradesh, Gujarat, Haryana, J & K, Karnataka, Kerala, Maharashtra, Manipur, Punjab, Tamil

Nadu, West Bengal and union territories of Pondicherry, Goa, Daman & Diu and Dadra & Nagar Haveli. The highest yield is found only in those areas where irrigation facilities are available to meet the standard requirement of water for this crop. It is also evident and not a very satisfactory scene because high yield is located only in 9.7 per cent of the cultivated area of India under rice located in Punjab, Haryana and Tamil Nadu under the yield level of about 2000 kg./hect. About 45 per cent area is occupied by the yield category of 1000–2000 kg./hect. Similarly, about 42.5 per cent area is occupied by the lowest yield level. The analysis indicate that higher amount of area is concentrated in low yield level and higher yield giving areas of India are not much prone for a large scale expansion of this crop, therefore, the basic factors responsible for the higher yield can be adopted in low yield level regions to increase the total production (Table 6.2).

TABLE 6.2: Rice-Yield Level (Fig. 6)

Yield category	Area		Production	
	Million Hectares	% to India	Million Tonnes	% to India
A. > 2500	2.24	3.12	3.44	6.91
B. 2000–2500	2.64	6.65	5.67	11.39
C. 1500–2000	6.14	15.46	10.11	20.32
D. 1000–1500	12.81	32.26	15.48	31.11
E. < 1000	16.88	42.51	15.06	30.27
Total	39.71	100.00	49.76	100.00

A. – Haryana, Punjab
B. – Tamil Nadu, Pondicherry
C. – Andhra Pradesh, J & K, Karnataka, Kerala, Manipur, Goa, Daman & Diu.
D. – Gujarat, Himachal Pradesh, Maharashtra, Meghalaya, Nagaland, Rajasthan, Tripura, Uttar Pradesh, W. Bengal, A & N Islands, Arunachal Pradesh, Dadra & Nagar Haveli, Delhi.
E. – Assam, Bihar, Madhva Pradesh, Orissa, Mizoram.

It is also evident from the Table 6.2 that only 3.12 per cent area of high yield level contributes about 7 per cent in total production of rice in India and these states are Haryana and Punjab. While 75 per cent area under rice contributes only 61 per cent of the total production. No doubt that the lower yield is in those states where rice is a predominant crop and most suitable crop in the geophysical conditions of the region. The introduction of the factors responsible for Haryana and Punjab can increase the yield level of these states.

TABLE 6.3: Rice — Growth in Area, Production and Yield (1968-69 to 1970-71 - 1976—79)

States	Percentage Growth			Yield kg./hect.
	Area	Production	Yield	
Andhra Pradesh	15.24	31.01	13.68	1596
Assam	5.19	4.62	- 0.61	976
Bihar	2.13	14.72	13.95	956
Gujarat	- 4.63	38.92	45.65	1257
Haryana	59.34	178.37	74.75	2595
Himachal Pradesh	- 7.85	- 0.36	8.07	1219
J & K	11.14	3.73	- 6.69	1814
Karnataka	- 7.34	- 2.87	4.82	1892
Kerala	- 6.81	- 2.80	4.26	1516
Madhya Pradesh	7.58	9.15	1.46	766
Maharashtra	8.76	46.72	34.90	1461
Manipur	18.76	21.07	1.95	1619
Meghalaya	25.53	12.10	- 8.27	1054
Nagaland	12.36	22.54	9.08	1033
Orissa	- 1.61	- 10.89	- 9.48	907
Punjab	130.15	327.11	86.37	2857
Rajasthan	51.85	135.23	54.89	1236
Tamil Nadu	- 1.36	22.06	23.73	2143
Tripura	13.62	57.21	38.32	1184
U.P.	7.78	51.28	40.37	1050
West Bengal	3.08	5.24	2.06	1290
A & N Islands	32.50	29.70	- 2.14	1236
Arunachal Pradesh	27.62	19.63	- 6.27	1001
Chandigarh	—	—	—	—
D & N Haveli	12.79	40.40	24.50	1433
Delhi	00.00	- 3.45	- 3.48	1000
Goa D & Diu	6.11	40.46	32.35	1710
Mizoram	—	—	—	613
Pondicherry	- 2.94	12.93	16.39	2088
INDIA	6.25	21.73	14.63	1254

Wheat

Next to rice wheat is an important food crop both in terms of total volume of production and increasing trend in area production and yield. It occupies about 17 per cent of the gross cultivated area under foodgrain and shares about 26 per cent of the total production of foodgrains in the country. It is the highest per hectare yield giving rabi season foodgrain crop, i.e., 1484 kg./hectare, therefore, this single factor is quite enough to give answers to the increasing trend of wheat in terms of area in the country and all the possible rabi crop lands have been encroached by the wheat crop.

A spatial expansion and variation of this crop is a most interesting phenomena after the innovation of green revolution technology. The expansion of this crop for a meaningful analysis can be done in the two ways, firstly, the expansion in those states where this crop is a major occupying area since the beginning, secondly, the introduction of it in those states where this crop was not in existence and still it is occupying an insignificant area. The rate of increase in some states are considerably high because of the poor base year. Therefore, these types of states and increase in area is not very significant because the geophysical conditions will not allow for a large scale expansion. For example wheat was introduced in West Bengal, Assam and in many other hill areas and shows a very rapid growth rate in area. Similar is the case for rice and it was introduced in Haryana, Punjab and in many other irrigation based states but the increase and total amount of area is very small. For example wheat occupied only 0.01 million hectare in Assam in 1960's and in 1970's it occupied about 0.7 million hectare and 416 per cent increase was recorded. In terms of total volume of area this increase is insignificant and contributing nothing at the state or national level. An analysis of the expansion of the base states for this crop is more meaningful. In all the states of India the growth in wheat is considerably higher than the rice crop in terms of area, production and yield. The expansion of area under this crop is largely controlled by the irrigation facilities not by intensity of rainfall. With the increase in irrigation facilities wheat has captured the low yield giving crops area in all the states of India. Therefore, the increase is recorded in all the states except of Himachal Pradesh and Jammu & Kashmir states due to the short growing period and poor performance.

Increase in Area

During the period 1968–71 to 1976–79 the country experienced 27.4 per cent increase in area, while an increase of 2.47 and per cent was recorded in cereals and pulses respectively, the increase in area under this crop which is much higher than all other crop of the country attracts our attention for analysis and to find out more potential area for its future expansion as it is the highest yield giving foodgrains crop as well as the contribution in the increase of area for the country is due to this single crop as most of the crops recorded negative growth in area. A state level analysis shows that there is a vast variation in the growth of area under wheat. The states of Karnataka, Madhya Pradesh, Punjab and Uttar Pradesh recorded less than the national average. Therefore, it is clear that the highest increase is not concentrated in the states where wheat is already a major or native crop. This increase is very high (Andhra Pradesh, Assam, Bihar, Maharashtra, Meghalaya, Orissa, Tamil Nadu, West Bengal) either in rice or jowar growing states of India and even these states altogether are not occupying more than 8 per cent of the total cropped area under wheat. The growth of 20 per cent was recorded in 53 per cent of the wheat cultivated area lying in Haryana, Punjab and Uttar Pradesh. About 38 per cent area falls between 20–40 per cent growth level consisting of Bihar, Gujarat and Himachal Pradesh states. In the states of J & K and Himachal Pradesh negative growth was recorded but these states occupy only a negligible area under this crop as rice is a major substitute crop with the availability of required supply of water. In the state of Tamil Nadu increase in area was considerably high but yield increase was negative it shows that the expansion is not possible due to the poor performance of this crop. The analysis of future potentiality for the expansion of this crop can be explained with the Table 6.6 through per cent growth in area and per cent growth in yield level. It can be seen from this table that high increase in area with low increase in yield will not be considered a potential area of state for future expansion. These states are Assam, J & K, Meghalaya, Tamil Nadu and West Bengal which have less potentiality for future expansion of this crop. It is because of the availability of water in abundance, rice as a major and substitute crop and short growing season. There are few states where area increase is very high with the support of high proportion of yield increase like Bihar, Andhra Pradesh, Gujarat, Karnataka, Madhya Pradesh, Maharashtra, Rajasthan and Uttar Pradesh can be considered most potential area if irrigation and other inputs are made available.

Increase in Production

As compared to production increases cereals and pulses for the country as a whole, i.e., 25 and 5 per cent respectively, the increase in wheat production attracts our attention for a proper and thorough analysis. The increase in production was highest of all the foodgrain crops. About 54 per cent increase was recorded in production during 1968–71 and 1976–79 while rice, barley, gram, tur, jowar, bajra, maize, millets and ragi recorded only (-16), 10, (-1), 23, (-7) (-2), 4 and 37 per cent respectively. This increase in production is also supported by higher increase in yield.

But this tremendous increase in terms of percentage is not uniform in all the states of India. Where wheat was not a traditional crop like in Meghalaya, West Bengal, Orissa and Assam total increase in production is abruptly very high as 837 and 1150 per cent increase in Assam and Meghalaya respectively. Secondly, the states where production increased with the availability of water and other inputs and wheat was not a suitable or more traditional crop recorded a very high growth in production Table 6.6. These states are Andhra Pradesh, Bihar, Gujarat, Maharashtra, Orissa and Rajasthan. Lastly, in the traditional states like Punjab, Haryana and Uttar Pradesh the growth followed the national level pattern. Therefore, for the potential measurement increase in production in relation to area increase will help to find out more suitable area for future development of this crop in terms of national interest as this is a second largest crop in terms of area and production as well as highest yield giving crop of India. Secondly, as compared to rice which requires more water than wheat cannot be spread largely on the basis of irrigation facilities only.

The traditional states like Punjab, Haryana, Uttar Pradesh which recorded growth in production at about national level occupy about 50 per cent of the total area under wheat in the country. The states (Bihar, Madhya Pradesh, Gujarat, Maharashtra, Rajasthan) where wheat area has increased more than the above mentioned states with the help of irrigation occupy about 45 per cent of the total cultivated area of wheat of the country. Only 5 per cent area is occupied by the states where future increase is also not possible.

Increase in Yield

During the 1976–79 the country experienced about 21 per cent growth in yield while it was 21.7 per cent for cereals crop. A large variation exists at state level. In the traditional states of Punjab,

Haryana, Madhya Pradesh and Uttar Pradesh the growth in yield is quite close to the national average except of Haryana where growth is more or less half to the national average. While in non-traditional states yield growth recorded even upto 170 per cent in Andhra Pradesh, 81 per cent in Assam, 97 per cent in Meghalaya and 63 per cent in Kerala because of the poor base level of 60's and use of the Green Revolution components in 70's. While low growth in traditional states is related with the rich base level because it was a post-green revolution for these states, though yield level per hectare is still much lower in non-traditional states except of Tripura and West Bengal where yield is quite closer to Punjab, which is the highest yield giving state of India. In all the states of India yield increased except of J&K and Tamil Nadu where negative yield increase is recorded by -21 and -67 per cent respectively. The case of Tamil Nadu is most striking where yield per hectare during 1976–79 is recorded only 1222 kg. per hectare while it was 674 kg. during 1968–71 though increase in area is about 24 per cent. It shows that in Tamil Nadu with the availability of all types of green revolution components the crop survived well.

It is evident from Table 6.5 that only 25 per cent area of the country recorded yield above the national average in the states of Gujarat, Haryana, Orissa, Punjab and West Bengal while about 75 per cent area recorded yield level below the national average in the state of 'D' categories (Table 6.5). This table further indicates that the contribution in total production of high yield category is about 35 per cent of the country while medium category is contributing only 4 per cent of the nation. The yield level below the national average is contributing about 61 per cent in the total production of the country. The states of low and lowest categories are not using high yield giving inputs or in other words larger areas are not using the components of green revolution in such an important crop of the country.

It is clear from Table 6.4 that highest growth in yield is recorde only in 7.65 per cent area of the country which contributed only 4 pe cent of the national production. This high growth is concentrated in the states of Andhra Pradesh, Assam, Meghalaya, Karnataka and Maharashtra. In other words these 7.65 and 4 per cent contribution in terms of area and production falls above the national average. About 92 per cent area and 96 per cent production is received for the yield growth below the national average. It indicates that there is a tremendous scope to improve the yield level of these states (**Bihar, Gujarat, Himachal Pradesh, Madhya Pradesh, Orissa, Rajasthan, Haryana, Punjab and Uttar Pradesh**) falling below the growth of national average.

TABLE 6.4: Wheat — Growth Level (Fig. 7)

Growth category (yield)	Area		Production	
	Million Hectares	% to India	Million Tonnes	% to India
A. > 80	0.10	0.47	0.09	0.28
B. 60—80	1.55	7.24	1.19	3.75
C. 40—60	nil	nil	nil	nil
D. 20—40	8.18	38.19	9.66	30.40
E. 0—20	11.41	53.27	20.67	65.04
F. 0—(-40)	0.18	0.83	0.17	0.53
G. < (-40)	(negligible area and production)			
Total	21.42	100.00	31.78	100.00

A — Andhra Pradesh. Assam, Meghalaya.
B — Karnataka, Maharashtra.
C — Nil
D — Bihar, Gujarat, Himachal Pradesh, Madhya Pradesh, Orissa. Rajasthan. Delhi.
E — Haryana, Punjab, Uttar Pradesh. West Bengal.
F — J & K.
G — Tamil Nadu.

TABLE 6.5: Wheat — Yeild Level

Yield category	Area		Production	
	Million Hectare	% to India	Million Tonnes	% to India
A. > 2000	4.63	21.64	10.99	34.58
B. 1500—2000	0.74	3.46	1.27	4.00
C. 1000—1500	11.00	51.40	15.33	48.24
D. < 1000	5.03	23.50	4.19	13.18
Total	21.40	100.00	21.78	100.00

A — Haryana, Punjab, Tripura, West Bengal, Delhi.
B — Gujarat, Manipur, Orissa.
C — Assam, Bihar, Himachal Pradesh, Meghalaya, Rajasthan, Uttar Pradesh. Arunachal Pradesh. Dadra & Nagar Haveli.
D — J & K. Karnataka, Madhya Pradesh, Maharashtra, Tamil Nadu.

TABLE 6.6: Wheat — Growth in Area, Production and Yield (1968—71 to 1976—79)

States	Percentage Growth			Yield kg./hect.
	Area	Production	Yield	
Andhra Pradesh	69.93	359.46	170.25	654
Assam	415.79	837.50	81.56	1093
Bihar	66.04	104.03	23.79	1306
Gujarat	34.26	61.98	21.70	1716
Haryana	38.78	50.87	9.55	2146
Himachal Pradesh	- 1.97	21.12	23.54	1097
J & K	- 10.93	- 30.04	- 21.26	900
Karnataka	13.44	84.89	63.53	677
Kerala	—	—	—	—
Madhya Pradesh	3.25	25.97	22.27	862
Maharashtra	36.99	124.57	64.05	794
Manipur	—	—	—	1500
Meghalaya	533.33	1150.00	97.30	1316
Nagaland	—	—	—	—
Orissa	325.69	462.77	32.26	1726
Punjab	22.78	43.02	16.49	2564
Rajasthan	34.09	76.78	23.88	1385
Tamil Nadu	125.00	- 25.00	- 67.06	1222
U.P.	24.41	47.73	19.06	1437
West Bengal	125.52	131.18	2.48	2021
A & N Island	—	—	—	—
Arunachal Pradesh	—	—	—	1286
Chandigarh	—	—	—	—
D & N Haveli	—	—	—	1333
Delhi	24.77	59.69	27.97	2251
Goa, D & Diu	—	—	—	—
Mizoram	—	—	—	—
Pondicherry	—	—	—	—
INDIA	27.36	53.88	20.85	1484

Bajra

After rice, wheat and jowar, bajra occupies the fourth position in terms of area in the country. It occupies about 8.7 per cent of the gross cropped area of the country but percentage share in terms of production is only 4.3 of the total foodgrain production of India. The most striking feature of this crop is the low ratio of production in terms of area occupancy. As the ratio between area and production of the above discussed crops (rice, wheat, jowar) is well maintained and higher than this crop. It is because of the low yield level per hectare, i.e., 482 kg./hect. while for wheat, rice and jowar it is 1484,

1254, 706 kg./hect.

Like jowar it is also an area specialised crop of few states and a clear cut regions can be formed on the basis of ranks occupied by each crop in each state. In Gujarat it is first ranking crop occupying about 32 per cent of the gross cultivated area followed by jowar (22%), wheat (15%) and rice (10%). In Rajasthan it occupies 23 per cent of the Gross Cultivated Area and holds first rank. Other crops like wheat and gram occupies second and third rank but falls far below in the area occupancy. These two major states of bajra producing occupy equal amount of per cent share but the most striking feature is the relation between area occupancy and production shares as Gujarat is occupying 32 per cent area and providing 31% production for the state while Rajasthan on the equal amount of share is producing only 15% of the state total production. It is because of the amount and variability of rainfall as well as difference in the rate of irrigation. All these three factors are suitably available in the state of Gujarat, while in Rajasthan lesser amount of rainfall and high variability as well as unirrigated jowar creates so much difference in productivity.

In the states of Haryana and Tamil Nadu bajra is a third ranking crop occupying each 21% and 8% respectively. In both the states there exist a wide difference in yield level, i.e., Tamil Nadu (887 kg./hect.) and Haryana (448 kg./hect). The difference in yield is associated with the amount and variability of rainfall in these states. The state of Maharashtra occupies about 12 per cent of the GCA with a very low yield and occupies second rank in terms of area and fourth rank in terms of production. The low yield is associated with the high level of dependence on rainfall. In Delhi it is also a second ranking crop after wheat with an area occupancy by 14 per cent with a very low yield level. In Maharashtra it is a fourth ranking crop occupying about 9 per cent of the GCA with a low level of yield. In Pondicherry, Goa, Daman & Diu the yield is abnormally high and even per hectare yield is higher than the rice yield but the per cent share in area is very low especially in Pondicherry. In both the states yield level is more than two times higher than Gujarat and seven times to Rajasthan, these are the states of core region for this crop. It is because of the assured rainfall and needful supply of water with HYV in hundred per cent area. In the state of Rajasthan, which occupy the highest percentage share in the state, a well marked annual variations in yield exist for example in the year 1970-71 the state recorded 521 kg./hect. while in the year 1974-75 the yield was as low as 101 kg./hect. It is all because of the amount and distribution of rainfall and this single factor is responsible for an increase in yield by five times. The crop can record high yield if the environmental factors are supplemented by the assured supply of water as on this single factor use of fertilizers and HYV also depends.

Increase in Area

On the whole the country recorded about 11.4 per cent decrease in area. All the major states of bajra producing (Rajasthan, Gujarat, Maharashtra) experienced negative growth in area except of Haryana where only 13.5 per cent increase is recorded which is negligible. In West Bengal and Orissa a very high level of growth is noticed but from area and contribution point of view it is negligible. In Pondicherry where yield level is as high as seven times to all India average the area declined by 21 per cent during this period. In Karnataka where bajra occupies about 9 per cent of the GCA experienced considerable amount of increase (13.2%) is worth mentioning. On the whole the country recorded a significant decrease in this crop due to the emphasis given on high yielding kharif crops like maize, ragi and rice, as in these crops area increased specially in those states where decrease is recorded.

Increase in Production

The country as a whole experienced 6.7 per cent decrease in production with 11.4 per cent decrease in area. It indicates that decrease in production is not at the rate of the decrease in area due to the increase in yield by 5.5 per cent. The pattern of growth is not uniform throughout the country. Generally the decrease in production is related with the yield level of the states, i.e., where the yield is low decrease in production is indicated. These states are Haryana, Bihar, Maharashtra, Rajasthan and Delhi with an exception of Punjab where yield level is very high but this state also recorded negative growth due to the decrease in area and yield level both. A special mention may be given to the core area of this crop (Gujarat, Haryana and Rajasthan). In Gujarat state production increased due to the high increase in yield while the area decreased considerably. The case of Haryana is reverse to it where area increased but due to the marked decrease in yield, production recorded 26 per cent decrease. The situation of Maharashtra is different to these states where area and production both recorded negative growth even with the increase in yield level. The situation of Rajasthan is more interesting being a first ranking crop of the state where area, production and yield decreased at different rates. In this state higher decrease in area and low decrease in yield both contributed higher rate of decrease in production. In Delhi the crop occupies the second rank after wheat where decrease in area, production and yield is more pronounced than all the states of India, i.e., -43.4%, -70.49%, -47.86% growth is recorded respectively. Both area and yield reduced to half which resulted to three times lower production.

Increase in Yield

As it has already been discussed earlier that the country experienced higher decrease in area than the decrease of production. It is because of the overall increase in yield per unit of land. Among all the kharif crops bajra experienced a very low level of yield increase and this level could not cover the loss of production when the decrease in area is very low. The country as a whole received only 5.5 per cent increase in yield. If we see this pattern at states level the situation of core bajra area is more frustrating. The states of Rajasthan, Haryana, Delhi recorded negative yield growth. Orissa, Punjab, Bihar which are the peripheral region for this crop also experienced negative growth rate. Andhra Pradesh, Maharashtra, Karnataka, J&K, others insignificant states recorded positive growth rate. In Pondicherry the highest growth in yield by 159 per cent recorded followed by Tamil Nadu, J&K, West Bengal and Andhra Pradesh but the area under this crop in these states is very low which could not affect the national growth of production. (Table 6.9)

Area and Production Share in Different Yield Growth Categories

It is clear from the Table 6.7 that about 85 per cent of the gross cropped area is occupied by the negative growth rate level or about 47 per cent area of it is concentrated in -10.0 yield growth level. Only 45 per cent area is occupied by the positive growth level. These two categories producing about 43% and 57% respectively of the total production of the country. The category of -10 growth rate with the share of 47% of the GCA is producing only 35 per cent of the total production while a share of about 4 per cent area in highest growth category is producing about 8 per cent of the total production. The name of each states falling in any category can be seen with the production and area share from the Table 6.7.

TABLE 6.7: Bajra – Growth Level (Fig. 9)

	Area		Production	
Growth category	Million Hectares	% to India	Million Tonnes	% to India
A. < 30	0.45	4.07	0.40	7.50
B. 20–30	2.03	18.35	1.61	30.21
C. 10–20	0.78	7.05	0.40	7.50
D. 0–10	1.70	15.37	0.62	11.63
E. 0–(-10)	5.16	46.65	1.88	35.27
F. (-10)–(-20)	nil	nil	nil	nil
G. > -20	0.94	8.51	0.42	7.89
Total	11.06	100.00	5.33	100.00

A. – J & K, Tamil Nadu, West Bengal, Pondicherry.
B. – Andhra Pradesh, Gujarat.
C. – Karnataka, Madhya Pradesh.
D. – Maharashtra
E. – Punjab, Rajasthan, Uttar Pradesh.
F. – Nil
G. – Bihar, Haryana, Orissa, Delhi.

Area and Production Share in each Yield Level

It is evident from the Table 6.8 that about 66 per cent or two third area of the country under bajra is occupied by the lowest yield level and contributing only 46 per cent of the total bajra production of the country. The highest yield level category is occupying only 18 per cent area of the total bajra cropped area and contributing about 34 per cent of the total bajra production of the country. The medium category (500–700 kg./hect.) is occupying only 16 per cent bajra area and contributing about 21 per cent of the total bajra production. The states covered by each category of yield level can be seen from the Table 6.8.

TABLE 6.8: **Bajra — Yield Level** (Fig. 10)

Yield category	Area: Million Hectares	Area: % to India	Production: Million Tonnes	Production: % to India
A. > 750	2.01	18.17	1.78	33.46
B. 500-750	1.74	15.73	1.11	20.86
C. < 500	7.31	66.10	2.43	45.68
Total	11.06	100.00	5.32	100.00

A. - Gujarat, Punjab, Tamil Nadu, Goa, Daman & Diu, Pondicherry.
B. - Andhra Pradesh, J & K., Madhya Pradesh, Uttar Pradesh, West Bengal.
C. - Bihar, Haryana, Karnataka, Maharashtra, Orissa, Rajasthan, Delhi.

Jowar

After rice and wheat jowar is a third important crop in terms of area and production. As we have already discussed that rice (31.34%) and wheat (16.92%) together occupy about 50 per cent of the gross cropped area of the country and contribute two third (66.30%) of the total foodgrains production of the country. If we see the yield per hectare of only these two crops (Rice & Wheat) it will come to 2140 kg. per hectare while average yield of foodgrains in 1976–79 is only 1023 kg./hectare. This statement clearly indicates that the remaining food crops including jowar also are having a very low yield level or in other words only one-third of the total production of the country is received by the inferior crops which altogether occupying about 50% of the gross cropped area of the country. Therefore, a detailed and separate study is needed for the expansion of area in rice and wheat and their possible encroachment on inferior crops area which will boost the foodgrain crops production. In this regard irrigation facility can be held responsible as these two crops belonging to two different crop seasons which cannot be grown without the help of water must attract the attention of the researcher for their possible expansion. As it is evident that in a larger area rice is being grown with the help of irrigation facility with high level of yield in Punjab and Haryana and on the other hand wheat has shown a tremendous encroachment on inferior crops area but with the limitation of water availability in both the crops. Hence, water is a crucial factor for the expansion of these two crops. Still in India about two-third of the gross cultivated area is occupied by the kharif crops (depending on

TABLE 6.9 : Bajra — Growth in area, production and yield (1968–71 to 1976–79)

States	Percentage Growth			Yield kg./hect.
	Area	Production	Yield	
Andhra Pradesh	- 3.52	16.45	20.67	578
Assam	—	—	—	—
Bihar	2.67	- 22.37	- 24.46	383
Gujarat	- 15.64	7.18	27.07	873
Haryana	1.35	- 25.77	- 26.68	448
Himachal Pradesh	—	—	—	—
J & K	- 3.77	25.30	30.27	680
Karnataka	13.27	35.56	19.80	490
Kerala	—	—	—	—
Madhya Pradesh	- 33.68	- 25.81	11.83	605
Maharashtra	- 16.03	- 13.03	3.39	366
Manipur	—	—	—	—
Meghalaya	—	—	—	—
Nagaland	—	—	—	—
Orissa	110.00	33.33	- 36.57	444
Punjab	- 39.97	- 45.84	- 9.75	1000
Rajasthan	- 13.05	- 17.78	- 5.63	268
Tamil Nadu	- 4.78	29.11	35.63	887
Tripura	—	—	—	—
Uttar Pradesh	- 7.88	- 8.54	00.73	684
West Bengal	200.00	300.00	33.40	667
A & N Island	—	—	—	—
Arunachal Pradesh	—	—	—	—
Chandigarh	—	—	—	—
D & N Haveli	—	—	—	—
Delhi	- 43.40	- 70.49	- 47.86	450
Goa, D & Diu	—	—	—	2000
Mizoram	—	—	—	—
Pondicherry	- 21.05	104.76	159.46	2867
INDIA	- 11.42	- 6.74	5.47	482

the rainfall) having lesser yield than the rabi crops except of rice. Other kharif crops are well adjusted with the amount and time of rainfall only the variability of rainfall and long dry spells district this adjustment and crops suffer both in terms of area and yield but largely in terms of yield per hectare. This unreliability in a large area (65% of the total gross cropped area) can only be removed and a new cropping pattern can be obtained with the expansion of irrigation facilities and rice can be expanded in a larger area with high yield level.

Jowar is one of the major kharif crops in India occupying about

13 per cent of the gross cultivated area and providing about 9 per cent of the total foodgrain production of India. Other kharif crops like bajra, maize, millets and kharif pulses are providing only about 4.3, 5.0, 1.5, 2.2, 1.5 per cent respectively. The yield of this crop is only 706 kg./hect. while the average yield of foodgrain is 1023 kg./hect. which is far below the national yield level.

The spatial expansion and its concentration variation is largely associated with the national pattern. In the country as a whole it occupies about 13 per cent area of the total cropped area and shares about 9 per cent of the total production of foodgrains of the country. But this percentage occupancy is not uniform in all the states of India. It occupies about 46 per cent of the gross cultivated area of Maharashtra and is a first ranking crop in the state. It shares about 40 per cent of the total production of the state while bajra and rice are the second and third ranking crop of the state and provides about 7 and 25 per cent of the total foodgrain production of the state. In terms of percentage area Karnataka, Andhra Pradesh and Gujarat occupied the respective ranks. In Gujarat it is a second major crop after maize, in Karnataka it is a first ranking crop occupying about 28 per cent of the gross cultivated area and providing about one-fourth of the total foodgrain production of the state. On the whole in two states of India (Karnataka, and Maharashtra) jowar occupies the first ranking crop, in Andhra Pradesh and Gujarat it is a second ranking crop occupying 24 and 22 per cent respectively. However, jowar is an important crop providing food at about 10 per cent for the country as a whole and at state-level this single crop is providing food at about 40 per cent to Maharashtra, 26 per cent to Karnataka, 13 and 14 per cent to Gujarat and Andhra Pradesh respectively.

Increase in Area (Growth)

In spite of the tremendous increase in yield level, the crop recorded negative growth rate, i.e., about 12 per cent during 1976–79. In absolute terms area decreased from 18 million to 16 million hectares. Among the major states of jowar producing Karnataka, Andhra Pradesh and Gujarat experienced negative growth in area by 35.0, 16.0 and 22 per cent respectively. The highest increase in area is recorded in J & K and Orissa but from area point of view these are the insignificant states as yield level decreased considerably, hence further increase in area is not possible in these states. In Maharashtra which occupies the highest percentage of jowar in India records only 8 per cent growth in area though the yield level is far below the national average. Therefore, it is evident from the Table 6.12 that major producing states of the country are experiencing reduction in area while increase is only in these states where it is an insignificant crop and worthless to count them as their contribution in terms of area and production. The decrease is worth mentioning in the states of Andhra Pradesh, Gujarat, Karnataka and Madhya Pradesh. In these states only two crops maize and rice recorded growth and possibly the area either encroached by maize or rice due to the higher yield of these crops than the jowar crop.

Increase in Production

In spite of the decrease in area at national level as well as decrease in area in major producing regions of jowar, the country experienced about 23 per cent increase in production. Except of Karnataka which is a major area for this crop experienced negative growth in production because of the high decrease in area though yield increased by 42 per cent in this state. Due to the overall increase in yield the absolute production of the country could not suffer. In Maharashtra which occupies the highest percentage of area and production and its major significance in the state as it has been stated earlier, requires major attention for analysis. In this state the increase in area is less significant (8%) than the increase in production as increased by about 24 per cent. It is because of the increase of yield by about 14 per cent. In the state of Karnataka decrease in area was so significant that even the 42 per cent increase in yield could not maintain the production record of 1968–71 and production fell down by about 8 per cent. Reverse is the case of Gujarat where area decreased by 22 per cent but production increased by 43 per cent because of the tremendous increase in yield (from 304 kg. to 533 kg./hec.) by 82 per cent. On the whole in spite of the decrease in area in most of the states production increased due to the high increase in yield level, i.e. from 506 kg. to 706 kg./hect. or by about 40 per cent in the country.

Increase in Yield

Among all the foodgrain crops of the country jowar recorded the highest growth in yield, i.e., by about 40 per cent, in spite of the decrease in area. While other crops which recorded negative growth in area but the increase in yield level was not so high. It is because of the use of HYV of jowar at large scale and traditional seeds area was reduced to a large extent and have been occupied by the HYV. The yield increase was more attractive in Gujarat, i.e., by 82 per cent though area decreased. Table 6.11 reveals that about 77 per cent area of the country is occupied by the medium level of yield lying in the states of Andhra Pradesh, Gujarat, J&K, Madhya Pradesh, Maharashtra, Orissa, Punjab, U.P., West Bengal. The highest yield level is recorded in the states of Karnataka & Tamil Nadu which occupies only 16.5 per cent of the jowar area. The lowest yield level is recorded in the states of Bihar, Haryana, Kerala, Rajasthan and Delhi. In spite of the low yield in Bihar and Kerala area increased. The contribution of each category in total production can also be seen from this Table 6.11. About 16 per cent area contributed about 24 per cent of the total production of the country while 6 per cent area of the lowest category contributed only 4 per cent of the production. The ratio of percentage area and production is more or less equal.

TABLE 6.10: Jowar — Growth Level (Fig. 11)

Yield Growth category	Area		Production	
	Million Hectares	% to India	Million Tonnes	% to India
A. >30	2.94	18.29	2.24	22.67
B. 20—30	3.65	22.71	2.47	25.00
C. 10—20	7.32	45.55	3.76	38.06
D. 0—10	1.94	12.07	1.35	13.66
E. 0—(-10)	0.02	0.13	0.01	0.10
F. (-10)—(-20)	neg.	neg.	neg.	neg.
G. >-20	0.20	1.25	0.06	0.51
Total	16.07	100.00	9.88	100.00

A. — Gujarat, Karnataka, Pondicherry.
B. — Andhra Pradesh, Tamil Nadu, Uttar Pradesh
C. — Maharashtra, Rajasthan.
D. — Kerala, Madhya Pradesh, W. Bengal.
E. — Bihar, Delhi.
F. — Punjab
G. — Haryana, Himachal Pradesh, J & K, Orissa.

TABLE 6.11: Jowar — Yield Level (Fig. 12)

Yield category	Area		Production	
	Million Hect.	% to India	Million Tonnes	% to India
A. >750	2.65	16.49	2.37	23.99
B. 500—750	12.44	77.41	7.15	72.37
C. <500	0.98	6.10	0.36	3.64
Total	16.07	100.00	9.88	100.00

A. — Karnataka, Tamil Nadu, Pondicherry.
B. — Andhra Pradesh, Gujarat, J & K, Madhya Pradesh, Maharashtra, Orissa, Punjab, Uttar Pradesh, W. Bengal, Dadra & Nagar Haveli.
C. — Bihar, Haryana, Kerala, Rajasthan, Delhi.

TABLE 6.12: Jowar — Growth in Area Production and Yield (1968—71 to 1976—79)

States	Percentage Growth			Yield kg./hect.
	Area	Production	Yield	
Andhra Pradesh	-16.02	3.43	23.16	569
Assam	—	—	—	—
Bihar	20.54	16.00	-3.59	430
Gujarat	-21.61	42.55	81.91	553
Haryana	-22.58	-39.53	-21.60	167
Himachal Pradesh	—	—	—	—
J & K	200.00	100.00	-33.33	667
Karnataka	-35.13	-8.19	41.52	876
Kerala	28.57	33.33	3.50	444
Madhya Pradesh	-21.84	-13.93	9.98	694
Maharashtra	7.91	23.39	14.35	526
Manipur	—	—	—	—
Meghalaya	—	—	—	—
Nagaland	—	—	—	—
Orissa	98.75	56.56	-21.23	601
Punjab	-31.58	-43.33	-17.11	654
Rajasthan	-28.13	-19.24	12.47	406
Tamil Nadu	4.05	32.36	27.13	943
Tripura	—	—	—	—
U. P.	-9.09	13.11	24.46	743
West Bengal	-62.50	-60.00	6.72	667
A & N Islands	—	—	—	—
Arunachal Pradesh	—	—	—	—
Chandigarh	—	—	—	—
D & N Haveli	—	—	—	571
Delhi	-12.50	-15.15	-2.93	364
Goa, D & Diu	—	—	—	—
Mizoram	—	—	—	—
Pondicherry	100.00	400.00	150.00	2500
INDIA	-11.96	22.77	39.53	706

The growth categories can be seen from the Table 6.10 where only 1.5 per cent area of the total jowar area experienced negative growth rate which is insignificant and there the crop was not a traditional (core area) one. Among all the states of India, Gujarat, Karnataka recorded highest growth in about 18 per cent of the jowar area of the country. Medium growth rate is recorded in only 23 per cent area consisting of Andhra Pradesh, Tamil Nadu, Uttar Pradesh. Low growth is recorded in the states of Maharashtra and Rajasthan which occupy about 45 per cent of the jowar area. Therefore, it is evident that higher rate of growth can further be achieved in the states where jowar is a traditional crop if proper step is taken for the spread of jowar HYV. It can also be seen from this table that higher growth rate is supported by the high percentage share in total production of the country.

Maize

Maize is one of the important crop of the country occupying sixth rank in terms of area and fourth rank in terms of total volume of foodgrains. One of the most important and striking characteristics of this crop is that it occupies either the first rank or second in all the hilly areas of the country. It is also an important crop of Punjab, Gujarat, Bihar, and Uttar Pradesh. On the whole maize occupies about 4.6 per cent of the gross cropped area and provides about 5 per cent of the total production of foodgrains of the country. Himachal Pradesh and Jammu & Kashmir states are the most important in terms of area and production. In both these states about 34 per cent of the GCA of each state is occupied by this crop and it shares about 46 per cent of the total production of Himachal Pradesh and 35 per cent of the J & K state. Arunachal Pradesh, Nagaland, Mizoram and Meghalaya cover at about 10.0, 12.0, 11.3 and 11.4 per cent respectively. In Punjab it is a second ranking crop which occupy about 10.5 per cent area of the GCA. The state of Manipur, Gujarat, Bihar, Rajasthan, U.P. and Pondicherry occupy less than 10 per cent of the GCA of each state. The higher concentration in these states are supported by the porous characteristic of the soil as well as the availability of needed amount of rainfall in the hilly areas. In hilly areas slopes are used for maize cultivation and valleys and flat lands for the rice cultivation.

The yield level varies from one region to another and from core region to peripheral region. Among the core areas the states of Mizoram, Nagaland and Meghalaya have much lower yield level than the state of J & K, Himachal Pradesh, Arunachal Pradesh and Punjab.

Increase in Area (Growth)

The country recorded 0.6 per cent growth during 1968–71 to 1976–79. Due to the area specialization, where geophysical conditions are more dominating as well as its concentration in peripheral regions where irrigation is needed, the growth in area is stagnant during this period though the yield level is considerably high, i.e., the crop ranks fourth in yield level after wheat, rice and barley in the country. The growth in area in the two major states (J & K and Himachal Pradesh) is less than 10 per cent while in other hilly states the situation is more or less like these two above mentioned states. In some peripheral maize regions the crop experienced a very high growth in area for instance in Karnataka, Manipur, Orissa and Tamil Nadu where an increase of more than 60 per cent was recorded due to the high yield of this crop. The states of Uttar Pradesh, Delhi and Punjab recorded negative growth rate due to the low yield of this crop in the respective states as compared to other crops like wheat and rice. The situation of Rajasthan where it is also a significant crop is balanced as area and yield under this crop is more or less same in both the periods. On the whole in all respects the crop is stagnant because of higher yield of the land occupied by this crop especially in the hill areas as there is no substitute of this crop on these particular lands.

Increase in Production

Due to the stagnant situation in area increase and slight decrease in yield by 1079 to 1053 kg./hectare, (or -2.4%) the country as a whole recorded 1.8 per cent decrease in production. This situation is not uniform in all the states of the country. The highest increase in production by 214 per cent was recorded in Karnataka which also recorded highest increase in area by 170.0 per cent. This increase in area is largely associated with the high yield (2853 kg./hect.) level. In this case the increase in area is responsible for such a high amount of production as yield recorded only 16.4 per cent during this period.

Similarly, the state of Maharashtra recorded 127 per cent growth in production with only 47 per cent growth in area and 54 per cent growth in yield. In this case increase in yield is responsible for such a high increase in production. The third highest growth in production is recorded (71%) in Orissa in spite of the decrease in yield but due to a very high increase in area (83%) a high increase in production was maintained. The states of Himachal Pradesh and Jammu & Kashmir, the traditional states for this crop, showed more or less a stagnant position. In J & K the increase in production is clearly associated with the increase in area as yield decrease is nominal and ineffective to the production. Similarly, the state of Himachal Pradesh experienced a nominal decrease in production by 0.7 per cent even after 9.2 per cent decrease in yield but the production level is maintained because of the 9.4 per cent increase in area.

Increase in Yield (Growth)

The country as a whole recorded 1053 kg./hect. yield in late 70's while it was 1079 kg./hect. in late 60's. This decrease is nominal, i.e. by -2.4 per cent. But in some of the states the yield decrease rate is very high such as in Uttar Pradesh (-22.3%), Manipur (-25.5%), Gujarat (-33.7%). A medium level of decrease in yield is recorded in the states of Haryana, Himachal Pradesh, Orissa, Punjab and Rajasthan at the rate of below 10 per cent. The state of Himachal Pradesh being one of the most important state for this crop recorded -11.2 per cent decrease in area. The general trend shows that in core areas the increase and decrease in yield is nominal, while in peripheral areas increase in some states is very high and very low.

Area and Production Share in different Growth Categories

It is evident from the Table 6.13 that about 37 per cent area under this crop is occupied by positive growth rate and about 63 per cent area falls under negative growth categories. The states of Maharashtra, Meghalaya, West Bengal, Delhi, Karnataka, Madhya Pradesh, Assam, Bihar and J & K, belong to the positive growth rate while the states of Andhra Pradesh, Tamil Nadu, Himachal Pradesh, Orissa, Punjab, Rajasthan, Gujarat, Haryana, Manipur and Uttar Pradesh belongs to the negative growth rate categories. These two categories shares about 43 per cent of production by positive growth

TABLE 6.13: **Maize — Growth Level** (Fig. 13)

Growth category (Yield)	Area		Production	
	Million Hectares	% to India	Million Tonnes	% to India
A. > 20	0.13	2.24	0.18	2.95
B. 10 — 20	0.84	14.48	1.07	17.51
C. 0 — 10	1.20	20.69	1.36	22.26
D. 0 — (-5)	0.32	5.52	0.39	6.38
E. (-5) — (-10)	1.66	28.62	1.87	30.61
F. > (-10)	1.65	28.45	1.24	20.29
Total	5.80	100.00	6.11	100.00

A. — Maharashtra, Meghalaya, W. Bengal, Delhi.
B. — Karnataka, Madhya Pradesh.
C. — Assam, Bihar, J & K.
D. — Andhra Pradesh, Tamil Nadu.
E. — Himachal Pradesh, Orissa, Punjab, Rajasthan.
F. — Gujarat, Haryana, Manipur, Uttar Pradesh.

TABLE 6.14: **Maize — Yield Level** (Fig. 14)

Yield category	Area		Production	
	Million Hectares	% to India	Million Tonnes	% to India
A > 1200	0.99	12.92	1.73	29.98
B. 1000-1200	3.39	44.26	1.44	24.96
C. 750-1000	1.70	22.19	1.45	25.13
D. < 650	1.58	20.63	1.15	19.93
Total	7.66	100.00	5.77	100.00

A. — Himachal Pradesh, Karnataka, Maharashtra, Manipur, Punjab.
B. — Andhra Pradesh, Bihar, Tamil Nadu, West Bengal, Arunachal Pradesh.
C. — Haryana, Madhya Pradesh, Nagaland, Orissa, Rajasthan, Delhi.
D. — Assam, Gujarat, Meghalaya, Uttar Pradesh, Mizoram.

rate and remaining 57 per cent production is shared by the negative growth rate categories. Among all these six categories, the area under low level of increase (8-10) occupied the highest area (21%) and provided maximum production (22.0%). In the highest level of growth only 2 per cent area is producing about 3 per cent of the total production of the country. On the other side the lowest level of decrease occupied by 5.5 per cent area with a production of about 6.4 per cent. A little less than one third area is occupied by the medium level of decrease with a production of about one third of the country. The concentration of area and production in negative growth rate indicate that even after a higher yield, except of rice, it is an stagnant crop and a aptitude of the farmer is to increase the area and yield of rice crop.

TABLE 6.15: Maize — Growth in Area Production & Yield (1968—71 to 1976—79)

States	Percentage Growth			Yield kg./hect.
	Area	Production	Yield	
Andhra Pradesh	23.87	22.92	- 0.81	1227
Assam	0.91	8.27	9.51	587
Bihar	- 5.83	- 2.02	4.01	1064
Gujarat	1.11	- 32.98	- 33.75	695
Haryana	- 4.59	- 15.18	- 11.14	933
Himachal Pradesh	9.41	- 0.67	- 9.21	1686
J & K	6.43	7.59	1.10	1384
Karnataka	169.91	214.16	16.40	2853
Kerala	—	—	—	—
Madhya Pradesh	11.41	31.64	18.02	904
Maharashtra	47.30	126.69	53.85	1740
Manipur	96.67	46.40	- 25.54	1551
Meghalaya	12.41	55.13	37.92	742
Nagaland	—	—	—	798
Orissa	82.83	70.91	- 6.50	777
Punjab	- 11.49	- 17.05	- 6.28	1417
Rajasthan	- 0.66	- 9.16	- 8.58	810
Tamil Nadu	63.36	60.56	- 1.75	1065
Tripura	—	—	—	—
Uttar Pradesh	- 16.76	- 35.27	22.30	742
West Bengal	- 5.72	26.86	34.51	1216
A & N Islands	—	—	—	—
Arunachal Pradesh	—	—	—	1138
Chandigarh	—	—	—	—
D & N Haveli	—	—	—	—
Delhi	- 61.54	- 50.00	- 30.08	800
Goa, D & Diu	—	—	—	—
Mizoram	—	—	—	707
Pondicherry	—	—	—	—
INDIA	0.57	- 1.81	- 2.41	1053

Area and Production Share in each Yield Levels

Among all these four categories of yield about 57 per cent area and 55 per cent production is concentrated in the two higher categories which is above the national yield level. The remaining 43 per cent area and 45 per cent share in production is concentrated in the yield below the national level. In this respect the performance of this crop is better than all the kharif crops of the country even the rice performance is not upto the level of maize. But on the basis of potentiality rice gives a better scope in larger areas than the maize as we have already achieved higher percentage of area with higher yield in maize crop than the rice where lower percentage of area is associated with high yield levels.

Ragi

Ragi is also one of the important crops of India both in terms of area and production. It occupies about 2.1 per cent of the gross cultivated area and provide 2.2 per cent of the total foodgrains production of the country. It is grown mostly in all the states of India except of Assam, Haryana, J&K and north-eastern hills. About 40 per cent area of this crop is concentrated in single state of Karnataka or in other words about 15 per cent of the gross cultivated area of Karnataka is devoted to this crop which is equal to the first ranking crop (rice) of the state. But in terms of production it shares only 18.2 per cent of the total production while rice shares about 31 per cent from the equal amount of land devoted to this crop. The yield of this crop is also higher than other crops except of rice and maize in this state. In Dadra & Nagar Haveli it occupies about 15 per cent area and ranks second after rice in terms of area and production share. But in this territory yield level is lower (966) than the national average of ragi yield, i.e. 1043 kg./hect. This crop is also important in Goa, Daman & Diu which occupies about 10.4 per cent of the gross cultivated area and ranks second after rice. But yield level is low (873 kg./hect.), therefore, it contributes only 5.6 per cent in the total foodgrain production. In Pondicherry it occupies only 5.1 per cent area in the state and contributes about 6.1 per cent in the total production due to the highest yield level in the country, i.e. about 2251 kg./hect. The states of Tamil Nadu is also important as it occupies about 6 per cent area of the GCA and ranks fifth in terms of area and third in terms of total production of the state after rice and jowar, while in terms of yield it ranks second after rice, hence ragi is an important crop for the state. Other states like Andhra Pradesh and Orissa is also important for this crop occupying about 3.5 and 4.2 per cent area respectively of the gross cultivated area of the state. In Orissa it is a second ranking crop but yield level is very low than the national average.

The yield rate varies from one state to another or for the country as a whole especially in all the states of northern India yield level is much lower than the states of south India. The lowest yield is recorded in Madhya Pradesh (240 kg./hec.) and 2251 kg./hect. in Pondicherry. The states of Karnataka, Tamil Nadu, Pondicherry where it is considered as a major crop have higher yield than the national average.

Increase in Area (Growth)

The country recorded only 3.4 per cent increase in area during this period, though increase in yield is 32 per cent which is the highest only after jowar but area could not increase in this proportion. A very high rate of increase in area is recorded from West Bengal and Orissa, i.e., about 63 and 84 per cent respectively, but yield rate decreased considerably, i.e., 30 and 36 per cent respectively. In this case area increase is not at all associated with the increase in yield. Thirdly, there are only few states like Andhra Pradesh, Bihar, Karnataka where both increase in area and yield is recorded. The situation requires detailed analysis of the factors affecting and creating such a complex pattern. In future it may happen that in those states where phenomenal increase in area and decrease in yield has been recorded may lower down the increase or occupancy of land under this crop. In reverse to this where yield has increased and area was either constant or decreased may catch more area under this crop in coming years. However, it is the only among all the inferior crops which recorded positive growth in area and high rate of increase in yield and production both. The future of this crop seems to be brighter than all the minor crops as yield is higher also.

Increase in Production and Growth

The country as a whole recorded about 37 per cent increase in production which is much higher than all the foodgrains crop of India except of wheat which recorded about 54 per cent increase in production while rice recorded only 22 per cent for production increase. It reveals that yield increase is only responsible factor for such a high increase in production when the increase in area is more or less constant.

In spite of the phenomenal decrease in area in many other states like Pondicherry, U.P. and Tamil Nadu an increase in production was recorded. There is only one state (Madhya Pradesh) where area increased but production decreased due to the decrease in yield level. While in majority of the states area and production both increased.

The increase in production is not uniform in all the states of India. The state of Karnataka, Tamil Nadu and Pondicherry showed a very high level of increase in production even after the decrease in area specially in Tamil Nadu and Pondicherry but the increase area in Karnataka was not so high as the increase in production. This is because of the high rate of increase in yield in all these three states. In the state of Kerala a very high rate of decrease in production (-70.0%) is recorded due to the high decrease in the area and yield both. On the whole such a high increase in production is due to the high increase in yield.

Increase in Yield (Growth)

As it has already been stated earlier that a high rate of increase in yield is recorded and is held responsible for the high level of increase in production but the contribution of each state in the increase of production is not equal. In this regard the contribution of Tamil Nadu, Karnataka and Pondicherry is most appreciable as they recorded 49 per cent, 37 per cent and 57 per cent increase in yield respectively even after the decrease in area. The contribution of Andhra Pradesh and Uttar Pradesh is also significant as each of them recorded about 29 per cent increase in yield as there was a phenomenal decrease in area in the state of Uttar Pradesh. There are some states like West Bengal, Orissa, Madhya Pradesh and Dadra & Nagar Haveli where area increased but the yield rate decreased but production could not decreased because of the high increase in area except of Madhya Pradesh where decrease in yield was more than the increase in area.

TABLE 6.16: **Ragi — Yield Level** (Fig. 15)

Yield	Area		Production	
	Million Hectares	% to India	Million Tonnes	% to India
A. > 1000	1.61	62.40	1.97	72.69
B. 800—1000	0.43	16.67	0.39	14.39
C. 600—800	0.50	19.38	0.33	12.18
D. 400—600	0.02	0.78	0.01	0.37
E. < 400	0.02	0.78	0.01	0.37
Total	2.58	100.00	2.71	100.00

A. — Andhra Pradesh, Karnataka, Tamil Nadu, Pondicherry.
B. — Himachal Pradesh, Kerala, Maharashtra, Uttar Pradesh, Dadra & Nagar Haveli, Goa, Daman & Diu.
C. — Bihar, Gujarat, Orissa.
D. — West Bengal.
E. — Madhya Pradesh.

TABLE 6.17: **Ragi — Growth Level** (Fig. 16)

Growth category (Yield)	Area		Production	
	Million Hectares	% to India	Million Tonnes	% to India
A. >40	0.30	11.63	0.45	16.73
B. 20—40	1.50	58.14	1.70	63.20
C. 0—20	0.42	16.28	0.30	11.15
D. 0—(-10)	0.05	1.94	0.04	1.49
E. (-10)—(-20)	0.02	0.78	0.01	0.37
F. >(-20)	0.29	11.23	0.19	7.06
Total	2.58	100.00	2.69	100.00

A. — (V. High) Tamil Nadu, Pondicherry.
B. — (High) Andhra Pradesh, Karnataka, Uttar Pradesh.
C. — (Medium) Bihar, Himachal Pradesh, Maharashtra.
D. — (Moderate) Gujarat, Dadra & Nagar Haveli.
E. — (Low) Madhya Pradesh.
F. — (V. Low) Kerala, Orissa, West Bengal.

Area and Production Share of the each Yield Levels

The situation and performance of this crop seems to be very satisfactory as about 62 per cent area of this crop is occupied by high yield category which is producing about 73 per cent of the total production of ragi. These states of high yield levels are Andhra

Pradesh, Karnataka, Tamil Nadu and Pondicherry where area under this crop is higher and occupying important position in terms of area also. The second high yield category is also occupying significant position especially in terms of production share. It is evident from this Table 6.16 that lower yield level categories are generally occupying lesser amount of area and low production. Among all the crops of India ragi is an unique crop and its performance and occupancy of land is related with the higher yield and low spread which is a major indication of developed cropping patterns.

TABLE 6.18: Ragi — Growth in Area Production and Yield (1968—71 to 1976—79)

States	Percentage Growth			Yield kg./hect.
	Area	Production	Yield	
Andhra Pradesh	1.64	31.33	29.16	1032
Assam	—	—	—	—
Bihar	3.84	23.31	18.70	603
Gujarat	- 8.73	- 14.92	- 6.99	745
Haryana	—	—	—	—
Himachal Pradesh	- 14.26	0.00	16.55	845
J & K	—	—	—	—
Karnataka	15.73	58.72	37.13	1204
Kerala	- 55.40	- 69.83	- 32.39	883
Madhya Pradesh	4.79	7.26	- 11.44	240
Maharashtra	0.00	6.39	6.47	823
Manipur	—	—	—	—
Meghalaya	—	—	—	—
Nagaland	—	—	—	—
Orissa	84.08	18.70	- 35.53	655
Punjab	—	—	—	—
Rajasthan	—	—	—	—
Tamil Nadu	- 3.64	43.84	49.30	14.90
Tripura	—	—	—	—
U.P.	- 18.47	5.50	29.40	964
West Bengal	63.16	14.40	- 29.94	563
A & N Island	—	—	—	—
Arunachal Pradesh	—	—	—	—
Chandigarh	—	—	—	—
D & N Haveli	17.20	10.12	— - 6.03	966
Delhi	—	—	—	—
Goa, D. & Diu	—	—	—	873
Mizoram	- 11.74	38.48	56.86	2251
INDIA	- 3.41	36.54	32.03	1043

Area and Production Share of Each Growth Levels

It is evident from the Table 6.17 that about 86 per cent area under this crop belongs to the positive growth rate of yield and about 14 per cent area falls into negative growth of yield. A high growth in yield is concentrated in 70 per cent of the ragi cultivated area which indicate that ragi is a well developed crop and in future inclusion of more area under this crop in place of other inferior quality of crops will be more useful in enhancing the total production of the country.

Gram

It is a fifth ranking crop in the country and occupies about 6.3 per cent of the gross cultivated area. In terms of total production it also occupies the same rank. Therefore, in terms of productivity it is not an inferior crop. It occupies about one-third of the total area of the pulses and produces more than fifty per cent of the total pulses production. Therefore, gram is one of the major and important crop of the country in all respects, i.e., its use as a pulses as well as cereals.

In terms of absolute area or per cent area under gram differ from one state to another. The state of Uttar Pradesh ranks first in late sixties and third in late seventies in terms of area share for the country as a whole. But within the state it occupies only 8.6 per cent area of the gross cultivated area or about 24 per cent area under this crop lies only in Uttar Pradesh. While in Haryana it is second ranking crop occupying about 26 per cent area of the gross cultivated area of the state. Therefore, in terms of concentration Haryana is the leading state where all the geographical conditions are favourable for this crop. In this term Rajasthan ranks second after Haryana where about 15 per cent of the GCA area of the state is devoted for this crop and shares about 21 per cent of the total production of the state. In the state of Madhya Pradesh it is a fourth ranking crop occupying about 10.8 per cent of the GCA. But in terms of absolute area it ranks first. The state of Punjab is also one of the important state of the country and occupies about 8 per cent of the gross cultivated area of the state.

These four states, (Haryana, Rajasthan, U.P. and Madhya Pradesh), occupies about 80 per cent of the total gram area as well as production of the country where all the geographical conditions are available for the better survival of the crop. The highest production is received from the state of Rajasthan though it ranks second in terms of area in the country due to the higher yield as compared to the Madhya Pradesh. The state of U.P. occupies second position in this respect and Madhya Pradesh ranks third while the area in this crop is highest than all these three states of India. Lastly Haryana occupies fourth position both in terms of area and production. Therefore, Madhya Pradesh attracts our attention for further analysis because of the first rank in area and third rank in production, it is because of the low yield of this crop in the state.

Other states of India occupy lesser than five per cent of the gross cropped area of the states. In Delhi and Himachal Pradesh it occupies about 4 per cent each of the GCA, while other states are occupying negligible area under this crop. Mostly all the hilly regions of the country are not favourable for this crop except of Himachal Pradesh and J & K state where it is grown in a negligible area only on the valley flours and uplands.

As it has already been stated earlier that gram is a low yield crop but its contribution in money term and use as pulses is very high, therefore, yield being very low in some of the states it is being grown and occupying a considerable size of area like in the state of Madhya Pradesh where the yield is about 538 kg./hect. which is far below than the national average and considerably very low than the states of high yield, i.e., states of Delhi (895 kg./hect.), Haryana (872 kg./hect.). Generally the states which have the highest area have the high yield unit of land.

The variation in yield level reveals the fact that in some of the states like Meghalaya where it is grown in an insignificant area yield is the highest in the country, therefore, it is not an attractive crop as expansion of this crop is not possible in the state. The low level of yield is received from the states of Andhra Pradesh, Karnataka and Maharashtra, therefore, increase in area due to this fact is not possible.

Increase in Area

The country as a whole experienced an increase in area by 7.4 per cent, but the increase is far less than the wheat which may be the substitute crop of Gram as it is a most important crop in terms of value. But still the gram is grown largely on unirrigated land where wheat cannot be grown so successfully.

The increase in area is not uniform in all the states of India. The states of Uttar Pradesh , West Bengal, Punjab, Karnataka, Bihar and Andhra Pradesh experienced decrease in area. The decrease is caused by the following factors –

(i) Due to the higher yield of wheat than gram, the crop could not attract the attention of the farmers as there is two to three times gap between the yield of these crops, especially in the states of Punjab and West Bengal.

(ii) Due to the spread of HYV seeds wheat gained more importance than gram especially in the states of U.P. and Bihar.

(iii) Due to the very low yield of gram than other crops especially in the state of Karnataka and Andhra Pradesh.

A special mention may be given to the states where gram is occupying high percentage of area like in Haryana, Rajasthan and Madhya Pradesh. In these states area increased due to the higher yield of the crop as well as increased irrigation facilities and being a major pulse crop for the state as in Haryana and Rajasthan other pulses are grown in a negligible area.

A very high increase in area is recorded in the states of Assam (76%), Gujarat (59%), Himachal Pradesh (128%), J & K (56%), Orissa (44%), and Tamil Nadu (13%). But these states occupy a negligible percentage of area of the country and does not exceed more than 2 per cent of the gram cultivated area of the country. Therefore, it is clear that high growth in area is associated with these states where area under gram is negligible. It indicates that gram area in future will increase both in major and minor states except those states where HYV, fertilizer and irrigation facilities are increasing rapidly as well as wheat being a substitute crop to gram.

Increase in Production

Increase in production is the result of two factors, i.e., increase in area and increase in yield. If the increase in area is low and even negative but the yield increase is very high, production will increase. But in most of the states the situation is very normal, i.e., where area decreased production also decreased due to the decrease in yield except of the states like Andhra Pradesh where area decreased but the yield increased in high percentage resulted an increase in production. Similarly the state of Orissa recorded about 20 per cent decrease in yield but due to the high increase in area production recorded an increase by 15 per cent. On the other side the state of Punjab experienced decrease in area but yield increased by 8 per cent resulted an increase in production. However, the country as a whole recorded about 10.0 per cent increase in production and the contribution of area increase is more important than the increase in yield as yield increase is much lower (2.5%) than the increase in area (7.4%) while in the case of wheat both the factors were more or less equally responsible for the high increase in production.

Increase in Yield

As we have already stated earlier that yield increase as compared to area increase is very low. But this increase is not equally distributed, in all the states of India. The highest yield is recorded in the states of J & K, i.e., about 195.0 per cent and production increased by 360 per cent when area increased only by 56 per cent. Therefore, in this state yield increase is more responsible for the increase in production. The states of West Bengal, Orissa, Karnataka, Bihar and Assam recorded decrease in yield but due to the decrease in area in most of the states production suffered.

A special mention should be made to the states which are more important for this crop, i.e., Haryana, Rajasthan, Uttar Pradesh, and Madhya Pradesh. In these states except of Rajasthan, yield increase is insignificant while in the states where area under this crop is insignificant yield increase is very high (Table 6.21). The situation of some of the states like Orissa, Maharashtra, Himachal Pradesh, Gujarat can be improved if irrigation facilities are provided with the increase in area. Other states like of J & K, Tamil Nadu have shown high increase in area and yield both but possibility of increasing more and more area under this crop is very less due to the geophysical conditions. The above analysis indicate that the important states for this crop can play a vital role if the increase in yield is considered as a major problem for this crop.

TABLE 6.19: Gram — Yield Level

Yield category	Area: Million Hectares	Area: % to India	Production: Million Tonnes	Production: % to India
A. > 800	3.23	40.89	2.73	49.28
B. 600—800	1.85	23.42	1.42	25.63
C. 400—600	2.14	27.09	1.16	20.94
D. < 400	0.68	8.60	0.23	4.15
Total	7.90	100.00	5.54	100.00

A. — Haryana, Meghalaya, Punjab, Rajasthan, Delhi.
B. — Gujarat, Himachal Pradesh, Uttar Pradesh, West Bengal.
C. — Assam, Bihar, J & K, Madhya Pradesh, Manipur, Orissa, Tamil Nadu.
D. — Andhra Pradesh, Karnataka, Maharashtra, Tripura.

TABLE 6.20: Gram — Growth Level (Fig. 18)

Growth category (Yield)	Area: Million Hectares	Area: % to India	Production: Million Tonnes	Production: % to India
A. > 30	0.04	0.51	0.03	0.54
B. 20—30	1.86	23.51	1.50	27.08
C. 10—20	0.53	6.70	0.20	3.61
D. 0—10	4.96	62.71	3.53	63.72
E. 0—	0.10	1.26	0.07	1.26
F. (-10)—(-20)	0.42	5.31	0.21	3.79
Total	7.91	100.00	5.54	100.00

A. — Himachal Pradesh, J & K.
B. — Andhra Pradesh, Rajasthan.
C. — Gujarat, Maharashtra, Delhi.
D. — Haryana, Madhya Pradesh, Meghalaya, Punjab, Tamil Nadu, Uttar Pradesh.
E. — West Bengal.
F. — Assam, Bihar, Karnataka, Orissa.

Area and Production Share in Each Yield Level

It is clear from the Table 6.19 that 41 per cent area lying in high yield level is contributing about 50 per cent of the total gram production of the country. The category at the national level of yield after occupying 23.4 per cent area of the country producing about 26 per cent of the national production. It indicates that about 75 per cent production of gram is received by the higher categories of yield and 25 per cent production of gram is received by the higher categories of yield and 25 per cent is received by the low yield categories, though the percentage share of area under high yield is about 64 per cent and 36 per cent in lower categories. The high yield states are Haryana, Meghalaya, Punjab, Rajasthan, Delhi, Gujarat, Uttar Pradesh and West Bengal (Table 6.19).

TABLE 6.21: Gram — Growth in Area Production and Yield (1968—71 to 1976—79)

States	Percentage Growth			Yield kg./hect.
	Area	Production	Yield	
Andhra Pradesh	- 13.67	8.96	25.95	330
Assam	76.47	55.56	- 11.72	467
Bihar	- 6.53	- 19.28	- 13.67	581
Gujarat	59.28	80.51	13.30	690
Haryana	11.88	12.60	0.69	872
Himachal Pradesh	127.89	205.56	34.04	693
J & K	56.00	360.00	195.00	590
Karnataka	- 15.71	- 29.12	- 15.97	363
Kerala	—	—	—	—
Madhya Pradesh	19.33	20.78	1.13	538
Maharashtra	20.32	33.33	10.62	323
Manipur	—	—	—	500
Meghalaya	—	—	—	1000
Nagaland	—	—	—	—
Orissa	43.78	15.22	- 19.76	475
Punjab	- 6.16	1.57	8.33	871
Rajasthan	38.69	72.98	24.81	825
Tamil Nadu	130.30	150.00	8.62	592
Tripura	—	—	—	333
Uttar Pradesh	25.71	- 22.54	3.63	771
West Bengal	- 41.98	- 44.43	- 4.22	772
A & N Islands	—	—	—	—
Arunachal Pradesh	—	—	—	—
Chandigarh	—	—	—	—
D & N Haveli	—	—	—	—
Delhi	- 35.30	- 49.50	13.58	895
Goa, D. & Diu	—	—	—	—
Mizoram	—	—	—	—
Pondicherry	—	—	—	—
INDIA	7.41	9.98	2.49	701

Share of Area and Production in Each Growth Categories

Table 6.20 indicates that about 93.5 per cent area recorded positive growth which contributed about 95 per cent of the total production of gram. The negative growth (or decrease in yield) is recorded only in the states of West Bengal, Assam, Bihar, Karnataka and Orissa. These states have a very low level of yield in late sixties which resulted in further decrease in yield per hectare in late seventies. The highest growth in yield was recorded in the states of J. & K and Himachal Pradesh but area under this crop is insignificant. A very low growth is recorded in those states where gram is a most important crop in the country which covers about 63 per cent of the gram cropped area and contributing about 64 per cent of the total production. Due to the high coverage of these states (Haryana, Madhya Pradesh, Punjab and Uttar Pradesh) and low growth in yield, production growth as a whole for the country is very low. These states are the most potential area for this crop and any strategy to be started for the pulses growth should be concentrated in these states.

Barley

Barley occupies one of the lowest rank in terms of area. But in terms of yield it ranks third after wheat and rice. However, it occupies about 1.6 per cent area of the GCA and shares 1.8 per cent of the total foodgrain crops.

Like other crops it is not an important or major crop of any state of the country. In the state of Uttar Pradesh, Rajasthan and Himachal Pradesh this crop occupies some significant position, i.e., sixth rank in U.P. and Rajasthan, fourth rank in Himachal Pradesh. During the post green revolution period the area under this crop is decreased at a phenomenal rate and during this period 1968–71 and 1976–79 it has recorded about 25.4 per cent decrease in area though yield has increased for about 12.7 per cent.

The yield rate is considerably higher in the states of Punjab and Haryana but area under this crop is very low as compared to the dominating states like U.P., Rajasthan, Himachal Pradesh where yield level is slightly higher than the national yield level except of Uttar Pradesh. About 70 per cent of the total barley area of the country is concentrated in Uttar Pradesh and Rajasthan and in these states yield increased but area decreased.

Increase in Area (Growth)

The crop, barley, recorded highest decrease in area than all other foodgrain crops of India, i.e., about 25.4 per cent though yield increased at a considerable higher rate than other crops but lesser than the wheat. It is evident that barley being a rabi crop and having higher yield rate than the rabi pulses, wheat has encroached the area of barley which is a higher yield giving crop than barley. Only in the states of Gujarat and Maharashtra the area under this crop has increased by 10.5 per cent and 141.0 per cent respectively but the area coverage is very low or negligible. Other states have shown a very high rate of decrease in area. The higher rate of decrease in area is recorded in Bihar, J & K, Delhi, West Bengal, Uttar Pradesh, Punjab and Haryana where irrigation facilities and HYV of wheat has encroached the barley area. But the area increase in gram and wheat both will reveal the actual fact. A state level analysis of this crop reveal that in gram 26 per cent area decreased indicate that wheat had captured the area of both the crops. Rajasthan is the second important state of barley where 39 per cent increase under gram and 34 per cent in wheat is recorded, therefore, it will not be a reliable fact that either gram or wheat has captured the barley area or the area of the other crops as there is only 2 per cent decrease in barley area in Rajasthan. Lastly, barley being a competitive crop to wheat a further decrease under this crop is possible if irrigation facility supplemented by HYV is developed. Therefore, an overall and high rate of decrease in area reveal that wheat and gram is attracting more attention of the farmers though per hectare yield of gram is relatively very low than barley but in terms of price, it is a high yield crop than barley.

Increase in Production (Growth)

It is evident from the Table 6.24 that after a high decrease in area production decreased only by about 16 per cent. The low proportion of the decrease in production is due to the yield increase by 12.7 per cent. In the major states of barley crop increase in production is very insignificant being a traditional states for this crop. In the state of Himachal Pradesh and U.P. a decrease by 16 and 23 per cent were recorded except of Rajasthan where it recorded only 21 per cent increase in production though yield increased but not in the proportion of area decrease.

In other states like Delhi, Punjab, J & K and Gujarat yield increase was phenomenal but due to the high decrease in area production could not increase except of Gujarat where area remained constant which resulted high increase in production. Therefore, high decrease in area is responsible for the overall decrease in production in spite of a considerable increase in yield.

Lastly, the states where absolute area in this crop is higher than other states like Bihar, Haryana, Madhya Pradesh, Rajasthan and Uttar Pradesh attracts our attention for analysis. It is evident from the Table 6.24 that except of Madhya Pradesh and Rajasthan where production increased due to the increase in yield. In other states production decreased even after increase in yield because of the high decrease in area.

Increase in Yield (Growth)

The analysis of area and production reveal that the production growth in negative is very less as compared to area because of the phenomenal increase in yield, i.e., about 13 per cent. But this yield increase is not uniform in all the states of India. Only in two states Bihar and Himachal Pradesh where yield decreased. The higher growth yield is recorded in the states of Delhi, Punjab, Gujarat and J & K., but absolute area is very low and ineffective in the contribution of total production. These states with higher yield level recorded high decrease in area and only minimized the level of decrease in production. Lastly the states where yield increase was low could not minimise the level of decrease in production. The state of Maharashtra where area and production both increased at a very high rate but due to the insignificant coverage of the crop should not attract our attention for analysis as the yield level and yield increase is also very low.

Area and Production Share of Each Yield Levels

It is clear from the Table 6.22 that about 32 per cent area under barley is producing about 39 per cent of the total production of the crop while about 68 per cent area producing about 61 per cent production which is below the yield level of national average. It indicates that the levels of development of this crop is not sound still there is a wide scope to include more and more area by increasing the yield of lower categories or the yield of the area below the national average.

TABLE 6.22: Barley – Yield Level (Fig. 19)

	Area		Production	
Yield category	Million Hectares	% to India	Million Tonnes	% to India
A. > 1100	0.68	32.23	0.88	39.11
B. 900–1100	1.22	57.82	1.22	54.22
C. 700–900	0.05	2.37	0.04	1.78
D. 500–700	0.16	7.58	0.11	4.89
Total	2.11	100.00	2.25	100.00

A. – Haryana, Himachal Pradesh, Punjab, Rajasthan, Delhi.
B. – Madhya Pradesh, Tamil Nadu, Uttar Pradesh.
C. – Maharashtra, West Bengal.
D. – Bihar, Gujarat, J & K.

TABLE 6.23: Barley – Growth Level (Fig. 20)

	Area		Production	
Growth category	Million Hectares	% to India	Million Tonnes	% to India
A. > 30	0.01	0.51	0.01	0.46
B. 20–30	0.01	0.51	0.01	0.46
C. 10–20	1.23	62.44	1.35	61.93
D. 0–10	0.54	27.41	0.67	30.73
E. 0–(-10)	0.14	7.11	0.09	4.13
F. (-10)–(-20)	0.04	2.02	0.05	2.29
Total	1.97	100.00	2.18	100.00

A. – Gujarat, Delhi.
B. – J & K
C. – Haryana, Madhya Pradesh, Uttar Pradesh.
D. – Maharashtra, Rajasthan, West Bengal
E. – Bihar
F. – Himachal Pradesh, Karnataka.

The high yield states are Haryana, Himachal Pradesh, Punjab, Rajasthan and Delhi where yield level is high or above the national average. The lowest yield states are Bihar, Gujarat and Jammu and Kashmir, where only 4.9 per cent production is received after devoting 7.6 per cent area of the country for this crop.

Area and Production Share in Each Growth Levels

In the country as a whole positive growth is recorded in about 91 per cent area under barley while only 9 per cent area is under negative growth rate or the positive growth states are producing about 93 per cent of the total production of Barley. The list of the states under positive and negative growth are mentioned in the Table 6.23.

TABLE 6.24: Barley — Growth in Area, Production and Yield (1968—71 to 1976—79)

States	Percentage Growth			Yield kg./hect.
	Area	Production	Yield	
Andhra Pradesh	—	—	—	—
Assam	—	—	—	—
Bihar	- 46.29	- 47.40	- 2.06	665
Gujarat	10.46	56.00	41.29	527
Haryana	- 29.71	- 20.48	13.13	1361
Himachal Pradesh	- 5.56	- 15.82	- 10.87	1238
J & K	- 41.54	- 25.00	28.27	658
Karnataka	—	—	—	—
Kerala	—	—	—	—
Madhya Pradesh	1.71	14.52	12.63	990
Maharashtra	140.54	144.44	1.64	742
Manipur	—	—	—	—
Meghalaya	—	—	—	—
Nagaland	—	—	—	—
Orissa	—	—	—	—
Punjab	- 30.54	- 2.87	38.95	1327
Rajasthan	- 2.00	2.09	4.20	1298
Tamil Nadu	—	—	—	1000
Tripura	—	—	—	—
U.P.	- 32.70	- 23.06	14.32	1094
West Bengal	- 36.78	- 31.33	8.73	847
A & N Islands	—	—	—	—
Arunachal Pradesh	—	—	—	—
Chandigarh	—	—	—	—
D & N Haveli	—	—	—	—
Delhi	- 41.67	- 18.18	40.24	1286
Goa, D. & Diu	—	—	—	—
Mizoram	—	—	—	—
Pondicherry	—	—	—	—
INDIA	- 25.43	- 15.96	12.68	1111

The characteristic of the growth indicate that higher yield states are also reducing the area under this crop due to the availability of a substitute crop with a more high yield giving (wheat) of the same ecological conditions though the yield of this crop as compared to other crops are significantly higher.

Small Millets

Mostly in all the states and Union Territories of India small millets are produced in an area of about 3.5 per cent of the gross cultivated area of India. In terms of area occupied it is one of the important crops in the states of Andhra Pradesh (ranks III after rice and jowar), Karnataka (ranks V), Madhya Pradesh (V), Nagaland (III), Orissa (III), Tamil Nadu (III) and Arunachal Pradesh (III). But in terms of production share it occupies the lowest rank in the country or on the whole it shares only 1.5 per cent of the total production after occupying about 3.5 per cent area of the country. It is a lowest yield giving crop of the country, i.e., 419 kg./hectare.

The maximum concentration of this crop is in the states of Andhra Pradesh (8%), Madhya Pradesh (9%), Tamil Nadu (9%), Arunachal Pradesh (14%), and Nagaland (7%) of the gross cropped area. Other states occupy less than 5 per cent of the gross cropped area. It occupies most of the inferior and unirrigated land of the cultivated area. Hence the use of marginal cultivated areas is based on this crop. The highest yield is found in Meghalaya (1048 kg./hectare) and Gujarat (809 kg./hect). The states of Andhra Pradesh, Assam, Gujarat, Himachal Pradesh, Jammu & Kashmir, Karnataka, Kerala, Maharashtra, Meghalaya, Nagaland, Tamil Nadu, U.P., West Bengal, Arunachal Pradesh and Pondicherry are about the average yield level of the country. The lowest yield is received from Madhya Pradesh (214 kg./hect) which occupy about 9.3 per cent of the gross cultivated area of the state and occupies highest amount of area in the country.

Increase in Area (Growth)

At national level the crop recorded 5.8 per cent decrease in area. The higher decrease in area is noticed in the states of U.P., Rajasthan, Kerala, Bihar and Gujarat. During the period 1968–71 in the states of Punjab and Haryana the crop is being grown in a very small area but in 1976–79 there is no existence of this crop. But in the states of Assam and Orissa this crop recorded 37.3 and 33.6 per cent growth respectively though in both the states yield level is very low and even at a decreasing rate during this period. The major states (Tamil Nadu, Madhya Pradesh and Andhra Pradesh) of millets growing also recorded negative growth in area. With the development of irrigation facilities the crop may further be reduced in area as other high yielding crops will encroach the millets area especially in northern plain states.

Increase in Production (Growth)

In the country as a whole the decrease in area could not lower down the total volume of production during this period 1968–71 to 1976–79 due to the increase in yield by 11 per cent though production could not increase at the rate of yield increase. About 4.3 per cent growth in production is recorded during this period. Among the major state of millets producing only Andhra Pradesh recorded 88.4 per cent increase in production even after 9 per cent decrease in area because of the 106 per cent increase in yield during this period as yield increased from 219 kg./hect. to 451 kg./hect. The second highest growth in production is recorded from Karnataka, i.e., about 68.4 per cent with an increase in area by 2 per cent. This high growth in production received is due to the 65 per cent increase in yield from the level of 260 kg./hect to 429 kg./hect. Other major states like Tamil Nadu and Madhya Pradesh recorded negative growth in production due to the decrease in area and yield both. The state of Assam recorded 35 per cent growth in production even after a decrease in yield because of the high rate of increase in area, i.e., 37 per cent.

Increase in Yield (Growth)

As it has already been discussed earlier that due to the high increase in yield production increased even after the decrease in area. It is evident from the Table 6.27 that about 11.0 per cent growth in yield is recorded in the country. This average growth rate is not uniform for all the states of India. The highest growth (106%) is recorded from Andhra Pradesh which is one of the major states for this crop while Madhya Pradesh and Tamil Nadu recorded negative growth in yield being one of the major states for this crop. The lowest decrease in yield is recorded from Bihar and Orissa though area increased by 34 per cent in Orissa in this crop. Only four states (West Bengal,

Karnataka, Andhra Pradesh, Kerala and Gujarat) recorded growth in yield above the national average of 11.0 per cent. Other states recorded a very low growth in yield such as Himachal Pradesh, Rajasthan and Uttar Pradesh. The states of Assam, Bihar, J & K, Madhya Pradesh, Orissa and Tamil Nadu recorded negative growth rate at a very low rate.

TABLE 6.25: Small Millets — Growth Level (Fig. 21)

Yield Growth category	Area		Production	
	Million Hectares	% to India	Million Tonnes	% to India
A. > 40	1.10	24.66	0.49	26.49
B. 20—40	neg.	neg.	neg.	neg.
C. 5—20	0.34	7.62	0.21	10.81
D. 0—5	0.54	12.11	0.33	17.84
E. 0—(-5)	0.47	10.54	0.34	18.38
F. (-5)—(-15)	1.61	36.10	0.34	18.38
G. (-15)	0.40	8.97	0.15	8.10
Total	4.46	100.00	1.85	100.00

A. — Andhra Pradesh, Karnataka
B. — Kerala
C. — Gujarat, Maharashtra, West Bengal
D. — Himachal Pradesh, Rajasthan, Uttar Pradesh
E. — Assam, J & K, Tamil Nadu
F. — Madhya Pradesh
G. — Bihar, Haryana, Orissa, Punjab.

TABLE 6.26: Small Millets - Yield Level (Fig. 22)

Yield category	Area		Production	
	Million Hectares	% to India	Million Tonnes	% to India
A. > 700	0.57	12.69	0.43	22.87
B. 600—700	0.52	11.58	0.34	18.09
C. 500—600	0.02	0.45	0.01	0.53
D. 400—500	1.31	29.18	0.58	30.85
E. < 400	2.07	46.10	0.52	27.66
Total	4.49	100.00	1.88	100.00

A. — Gujarat, Meghalaya, Tamil Nadu
B. — Himachal Pradesh, Kerala, Nagaland, Uttar Pradesh, West Bengal, Arunachal Pradesh, Pondicherry.
C. — J & K
D. — Andhra Pradesh, Assam, Karnataka, Maharashtra, Dadra & Nagar Haveli.
E. — Bihar, Madhya Pradesh, Orissa, Rajasthan.

Percentage Share in Area and Production in Each Growth Categories

The highest growth (above 40%) in yield is found in 25 per cent areas of the country and producing about 26.5 per cent of the total millets production of the country. On the other hand about 36 per cent area contributed only 18 per cent of the total production is found in a very high negative growth rate. On the whole about 44 per cent area contributing about 55 per cent of the total production fall in positive growth of yield while 56 per cent area contributing about 45 per cent production belongs to the negative yield growth rate.

TABLE 6.27: Small Millets — Growth in Area, Production and Yield (1968—71 to 1976—79)

States	Percentage Growth			Yield kg./hect.
	Area	Production	Yield	
Andhra Pradesh	8.54	88.44	105.94	451
Assam	37.29	34.48	- 2.24	481
Bihar	- 22.80	- 32.60	- 19.07	382
Gujarat	- 19.12	- 7.93	13.78	809
Haryana	—	—	—	—
Himachal Pradesh	- 7.72	- 6.81	1.04	677
J & K	1.55	- 19.43	- 2.05	569
Karnataka	2.09	68.43	65.00	429
Kerala	- 48.39	- 36.36	23.31	656
Madhya Pradesh	- 2.91	- 8.14	- 5.31	214
Maharashtra	- 4.91	1.48	6.83	438
Manipur	—	—	—	—
Meghalaya	—	—	—	1048
Nagaland	—	—	—	697
Orissa	33.58	10.73	- 16.25	397
Punjab	—	—	—	—
Rajasthan	- 17.06	- 15.70	1.49	341
Tamil Nadu	- 8.80	- 11.56	- 3.03	737
Tripura	—	—	—	—
Uttar Pradesh	- 17.96	- 14.04	4.79	656
West Bengal	3.79	17.28	12.87	693
A & N Islands	—	—	—	—
Arunachal Pradesh	—	—	—	654
Chandigarh	—	—	—	—
D & N Haveli	—	—	—	429
Delhi	—	—	—	—
Goa, D. & Diu	—	—	—	—
Mizoram	—	—	—	—
Pondicherry	—	—	—	667
INDIA	- 5.81	4.27	10.85	419

The positive growth rate states are Andhra Pradesh, Karnataka, Gujarat, Maharashtra, West Bengal, Himachal Pradesh, Rajasthan and Uttar Pradesh where yield increase is responsible for the higher contribution in total production (Table 6.25).

Percentage Share in Area and Production in Each Yield Level

It is clear from the Table 6.27 that about 75 per cent area is concentrated in a low yield categories which provide about 58 per cent of the total production of this crop. While the higher yield level occupies only 25 per cent area and contributing about 42 per cent of the millets production of the country. The high yield level states (Gujarat, Meghalaya, Tamil Nadu, Himachal Pradesh, Kerala, Nagaland, U.P. West Bengal, Arunachal Pradesh and Pondicherry) have more rainfall than the states of low yield level (Andhra Pradesh, Karnataka, Maharashtra, Madhya Pradesh, Orissa and Rajasthan). As millets are the kharif season crops depends largely on rainfall amount and variability. The crop is devasted easily than any other kharif crops after a short duration of dry spells.

Tur

It is one of the important pulses of the country which occupies about 2.1 per cent of the gross cultivated area of the country. The states of Andhra Pradesh, Bihar, Karnataka and Uttar Pradesh are the major growing states of the country. These states occupy about 90 per cent of the total area under this crop. In all the hill states of India this crop is absent. It is grown on a very inferior quality of land and generally it is grown mixed with other crops also.

In terms of area Maharashtra occupies the highest area of the country or about 4.4 per cent of the GCA of the state. It ranks fourth in terms of area in the state. The state of Uttar Pradesh ranks second in terms of area in the country supported by a very high yield. The state alone occupies about 20 per cent of the cultivated area of the country and produce about 40 per cent of the total production of this crop. The state of Madhya Pradesh and Maharashtra combindly occupy more or less double area but produces lesser than U.P. because of the very low yield of this crop in these states.

The yield level varies from one state to another. The highest yield is recorded in U.P., i.e., 1357 kg./hect. which is about two times higher than the national average, i.e., 702 kg./hect. The lowest yield is recorded in Andhra Pradesh which is about one fifth of the national average. Only four states namely Haryana, Meghalaya, Uttar Pradesh, and West Bengal have more than the national average yield. But the area under this crop is very low except of Uttar Pradesh. One of the chief characteristic of this crop is that the major tur producer states have a very low level of yield and far below the national average.

Increase in Area

The country experienced negative growth in area by only 0.3 per cent during the period 1968–71 and 1976–79. It indicates that more or less the area under this crop remained stagnant. But a state level situation reveals that there are some states where area increased for more than 45 per cent in the states of Tamil Nadu, Dadra & Nagar Haveli, Rajasthan, Punjab, Orissa and Assam but the area under this crop is very low. An analysis of the major tur producing states reveal the fact that those states show a very critical situation as they recorded negative growth rate in area except of Madhya Pradesh where area increased only by 1.6 per cent which is negligible. It is because of the low and declining yield in most of the states. A special mention may be made regarding Maharashtra and Uttar Pradesh where area declined in both the states but production increased due to the increase in yield. Though Punjab recorded an abnormal growth in area by 4.90 per cent but the area under this crop is negligible.

Increase in Production

The increase and decrease in production is the result of decrease and increase of yield and area. But at national level due to the decrease in area and yield both production decreased by - 1.0 per cent during this period. But at state level a number of states like Assam, Gujarat, Haryana, Karnataka, Orissa, Punjab, Rajasthan, Tamil Nadu & Dadra and N. Haveli recorded a very high increase in area. But the area under this crop is very low in these states which could not affect the volume of total production. In the states of Andhra Pradesh, Bihar, Kerala and West Bengal production decreased at high rate but in these states also the area under this crop is very low which could not affect largely the total volume of production except of Andhra Pradesh and Bihar states. The situation of major states of tur crop is more or less stagnant where the decrease and increase in production is not phenomenal except of Karnataka where production increased by 25.5 per cent due to the increase in yield at the same rate.

Increase in Yield

Out of six major Tur producing states of India namely Andhra Pradesh, Bihar, Karnataka, Madhya Pradesh, Maharashtra and Uttar Pradesh only three states (Karnataka, Maharashtra and Uttar Pradesh) recorded positive growth in yield. The highest growth is recorded in Tripura and Meghalaya but the area under this crop is too small to mention. Similar in the case of Haryana where yield increased just double but the area decreased. Therefore, it is evident that even with high increase in yield area could not increase, the future of this crop is not very prospective due to the problem of expansion of area. The nation as a whole recorded negative growth in yield by 0.7 per cent over this period. Generally the high decrease in yield is recorded in the states of lesser significance for this crop with the exception of few states like Tripura, Dadra & N. Haveli and Haryana.

Share of Production and Area in Each Yield Level

It is clear from the Table 6.28 that about 85 per cent area under this crop is occupied by higher yield level which produces about 94 per cent of the total production of tur crop. Only 15 per cent area lying in low yield level is producing about 6 per cent of the total production of the country. It indicates that tur is a well developed crop and its future may be bright if we increase either area or yield in high yield level states.

Share of Area and Production in Each Growth Level

It is clear from the Table 6.28 that about 65 per cent area with 75 per cent production is occupied by positive growth rate, only 35 per cent area with 25 per cent production falls under negative growth level. The growth rate between 15–30 occupies more than half of the area of the country and producing about 69 per cent of the total production of this crop.

TABLE 6.28: Tur (Arhar) — Yield Level (Fig. 23)

Yield category	Area		Production	
	Million Hectares	% to India	Million Tonnes	% to India
A. > 750	0.55	21.40	0.75	41.21
B. 500—750	1.63	63.42	0.96	52.75
C. 250—500	0.19	7.39	0.08	4.40
D. < 250	0.20	7.79	0.03	1.64
Total	2.57	100.00	1.82	100.00

A. — Haryana, Meghalaya, Uttar Pradesh, West Bengal.
B. — Assam, Bihar, Gujarat, Himachal Pradesh, Karnataka, Madhya Pradesh, Maharashtra, Punjab, Tripura, Dadra & Nagar Haveli.
C. — Orissa, Rajasthan, Tamil Nadu.
D. — Andhra Pradesh, Kerala.

TABLE 6.29: Tur (Arhar) — Growth Level (Fig. 24)

Growth category (Yield)	Area		Production	
	Million Hectares	% to India	Million Tonnes	% to India
A. > 30	0.01	0.39	0.01	0.55
B. 15—30	1.45	56.42	1.26	68.85
C. 0—25	0.21	8.17	0.10	5.46
D. 0—(-10)	0.50	19.46	0.32	17.49
E. (-10)—(-20)	0.10	3.89	0.04	2.19
F. > (-20)	0.30	11.67	0.10	5.46
Total	2.57	100.00	1.83	100.00

A. — Haryana, Meghalaya, Tripura, Dadra & N. Haveli.
B. — Karnataka, Maharashtra, Uttar Pradesh, W. Bengal.
C. — Gujarat, Himachal Pradesh, Tamil Nadu.
D. — Assam, Madhya Pradesh.
E. — Orissa, Rajasthan.
F. — Andhra Pradesh. Bihar, J & K, Kerala, Punjab.

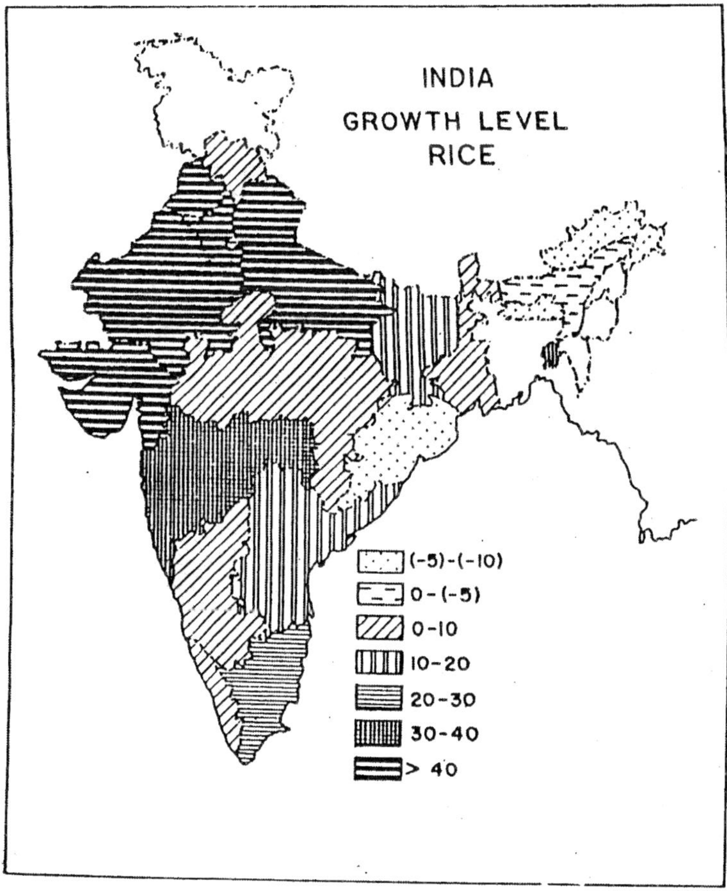
INDIA
GROWTH LEVEL
RICE
(-5)-(-10)
0-(-5)
0-10
10-20
20-30
30-40
> 40

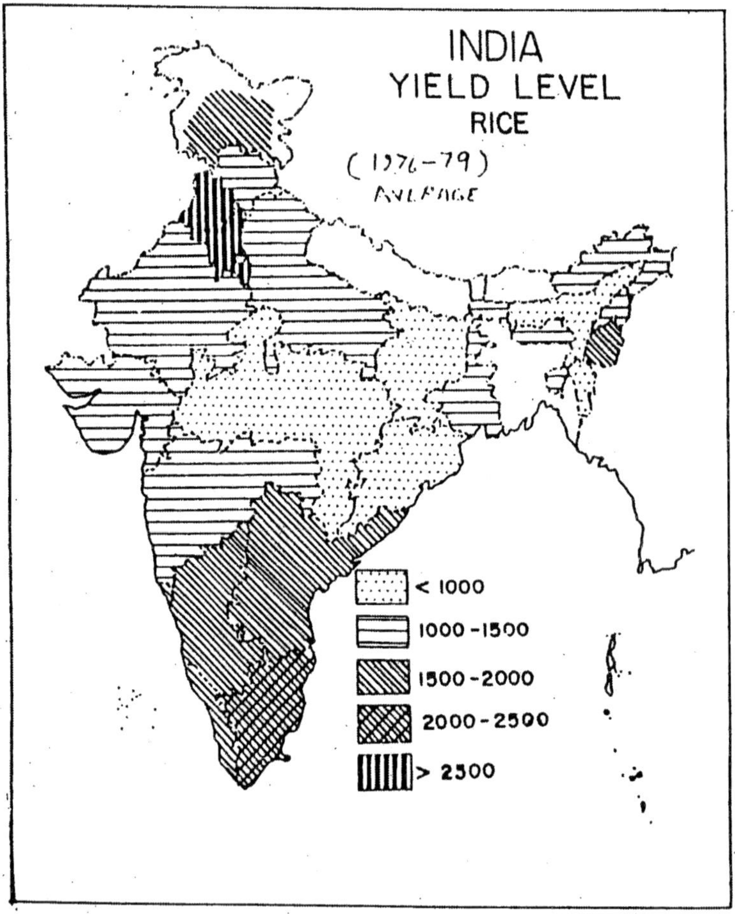
INDIA
YIELD LEVEL
RICE
< 1000
1000-1500
1500-2000
2000-2500
> 2500

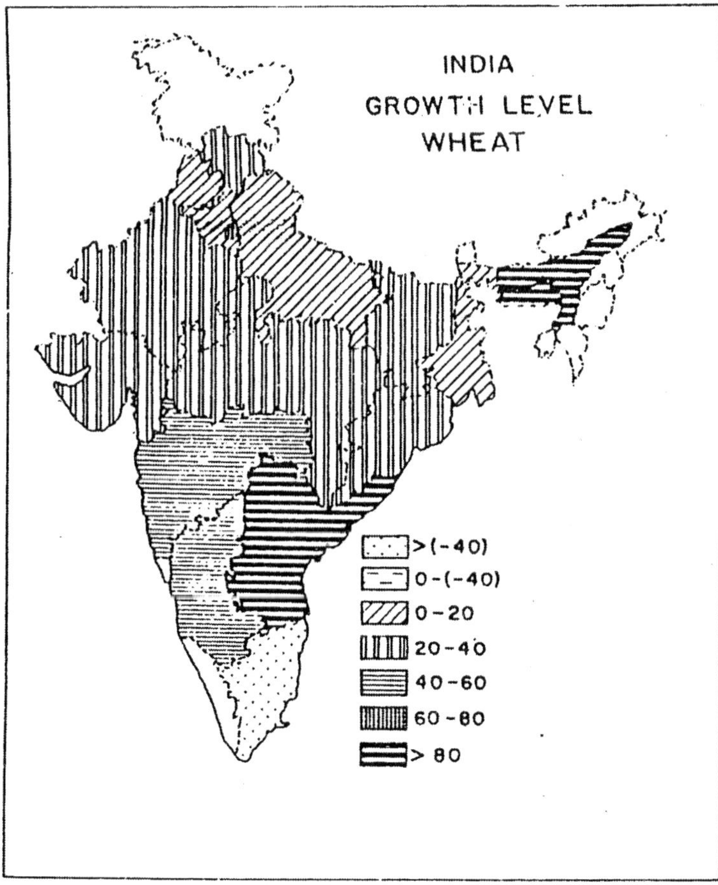
INDIA
GROWTH LEVEL
WHEAT
>(-40)
0-(-40)
0-20
20-40
40-60
60-80
> 80

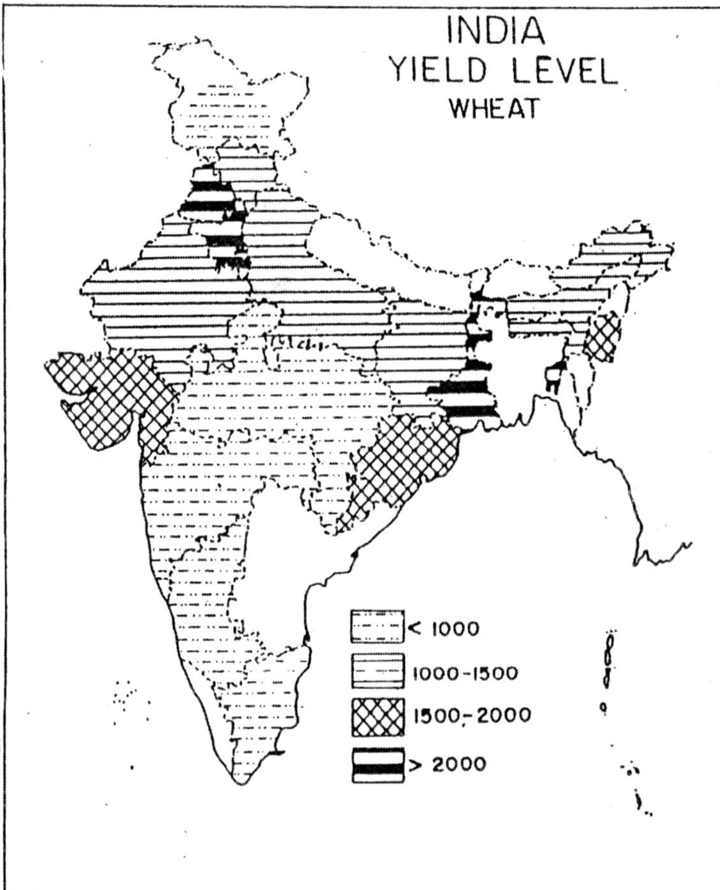
INDIA
YIELD LEVEL
WHEAT
< 1000
1000-1500
1500-2000
> 2000

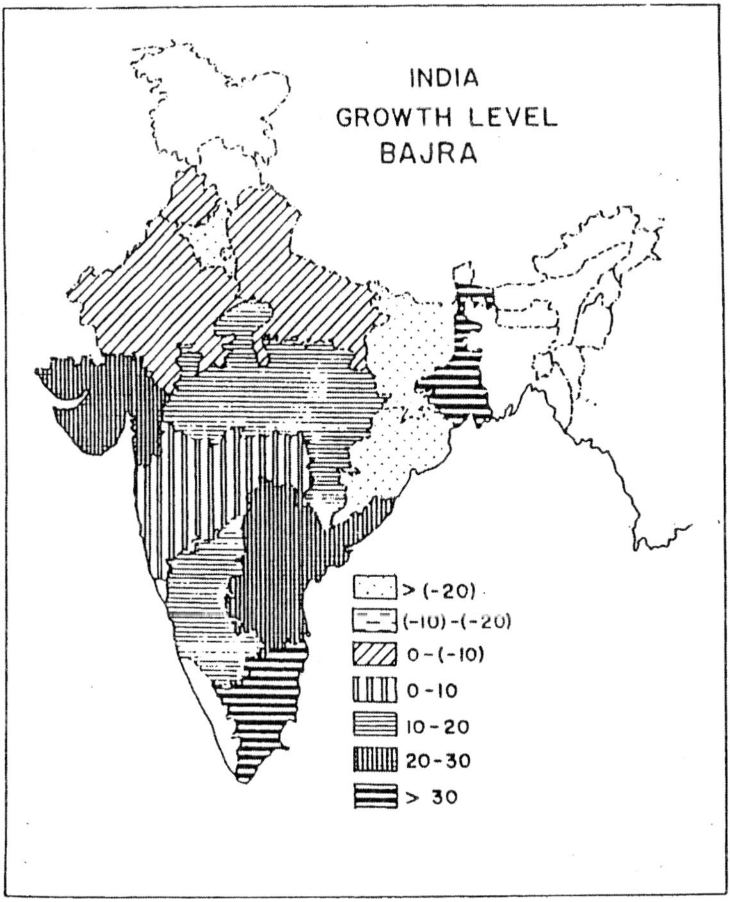
INDIA
GROWTH LEVEL
BAJRA
> (-20)
(-10) - (-20)
0 - (-10)
0 - 10
10 - 20
20 - 30
> 30

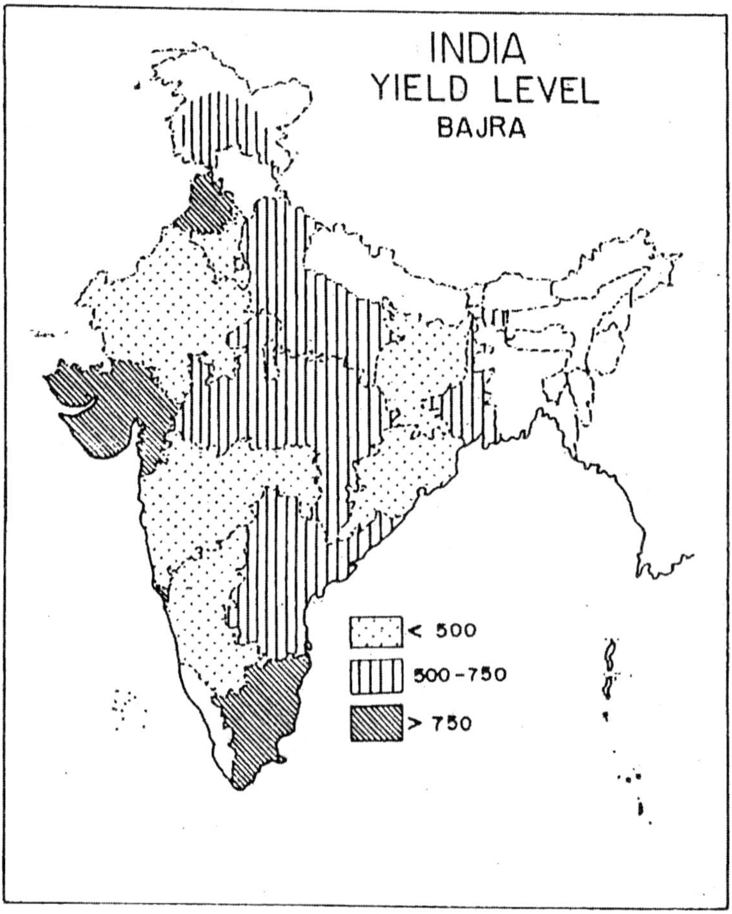
INDIA
YIELD LEVEL
BAJRA
< 500
500-750
> 750

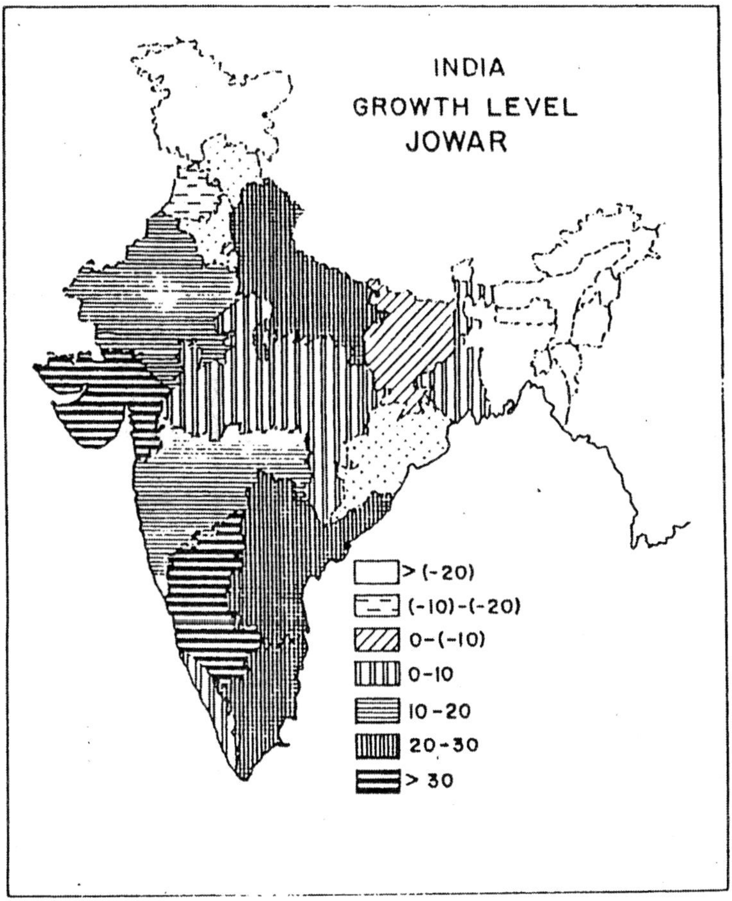
INDIA
GROWTH LEVEL
JOWAR
> (-20)
(-10)-(-20)
0-(-10)
0-10
10-20
20-30
> 30

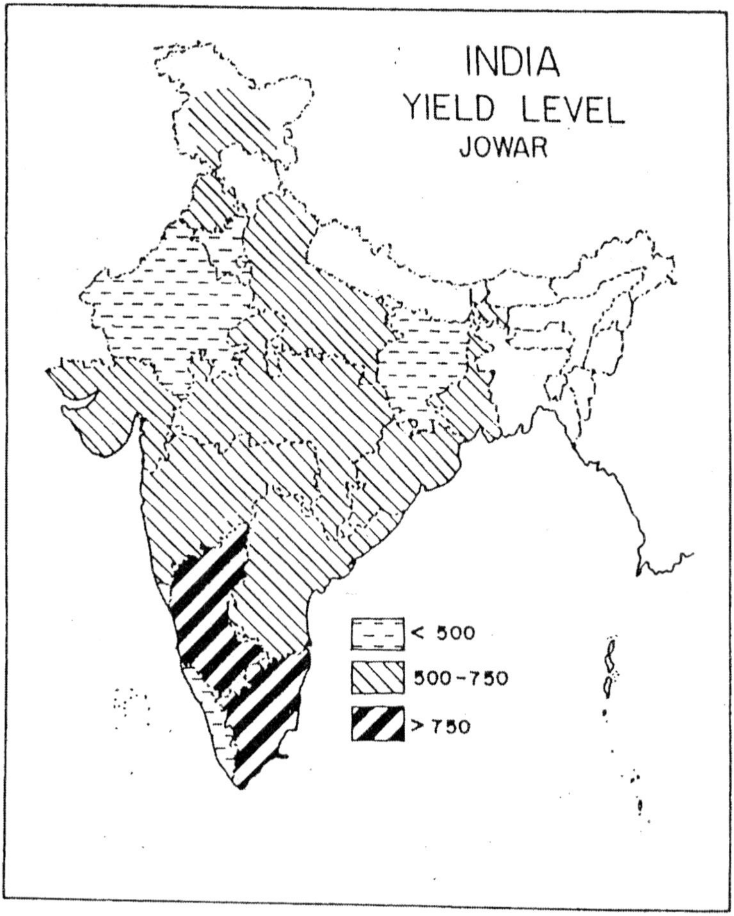
INDIA
YIELD LEVEL
JOWAR
< 500
500-750
> 750

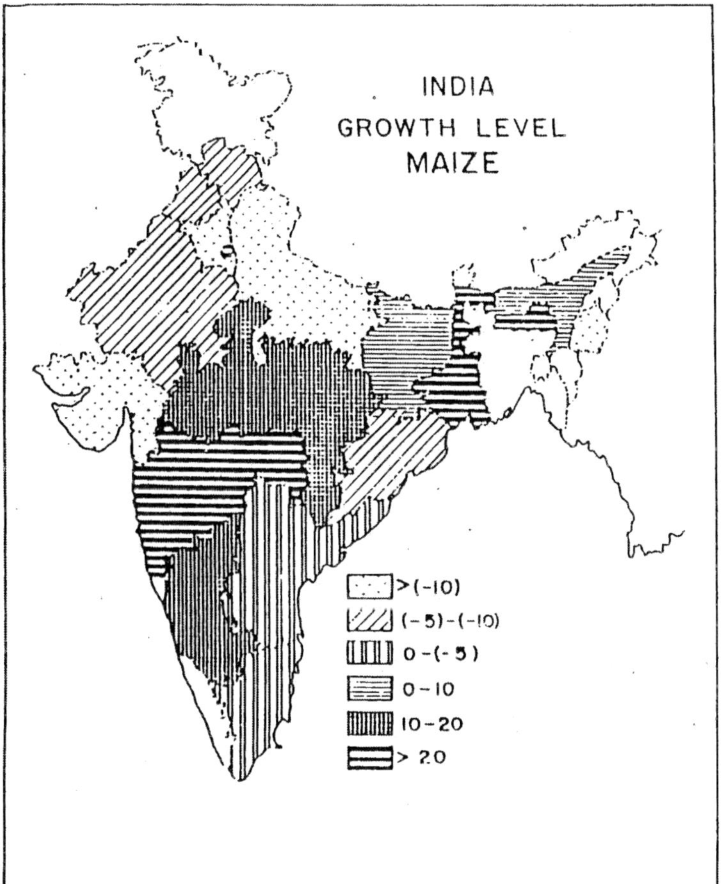
INDIA
GROWTH LEVEL
MAIZE
>(-10)
(-5)-(-10)
0-(-5)
0-10
10-20
> 20

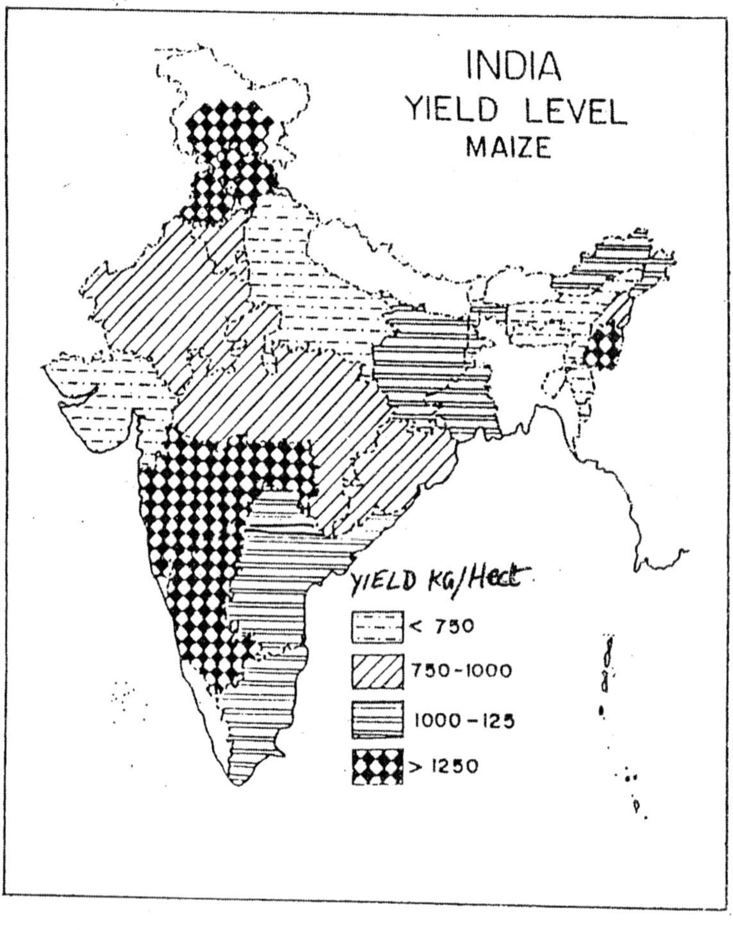
INDIA
YIELD LEVEL
MAIZE
YIELD KG/Hect
< 750
750-1000
1000-125
> 1250

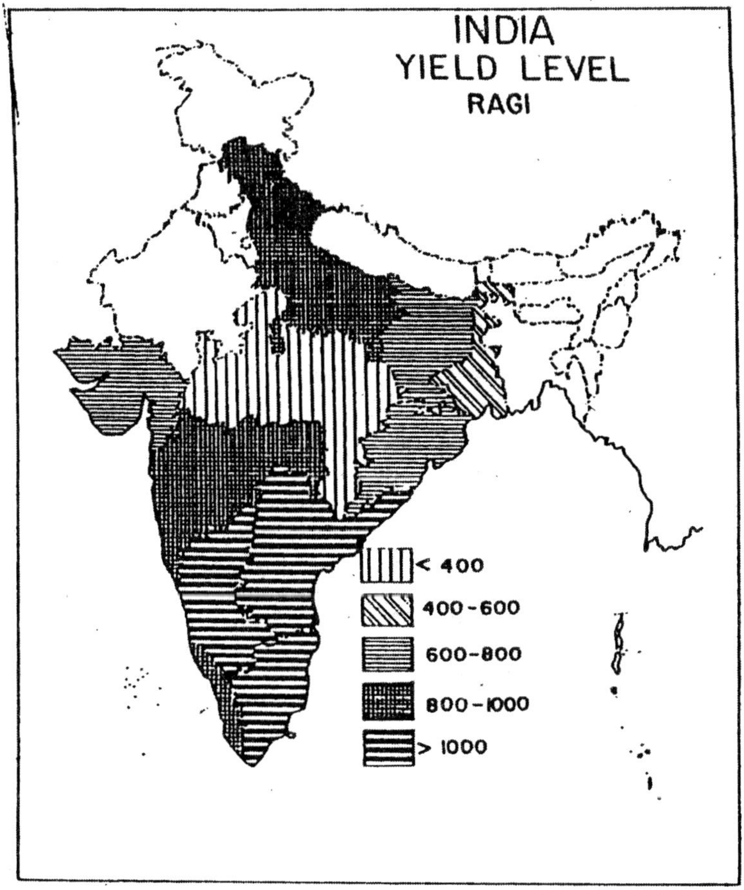
INDIA
YIELD LEVEL
RAGI
< 400
400-600
600-800
800-1000
> 1000

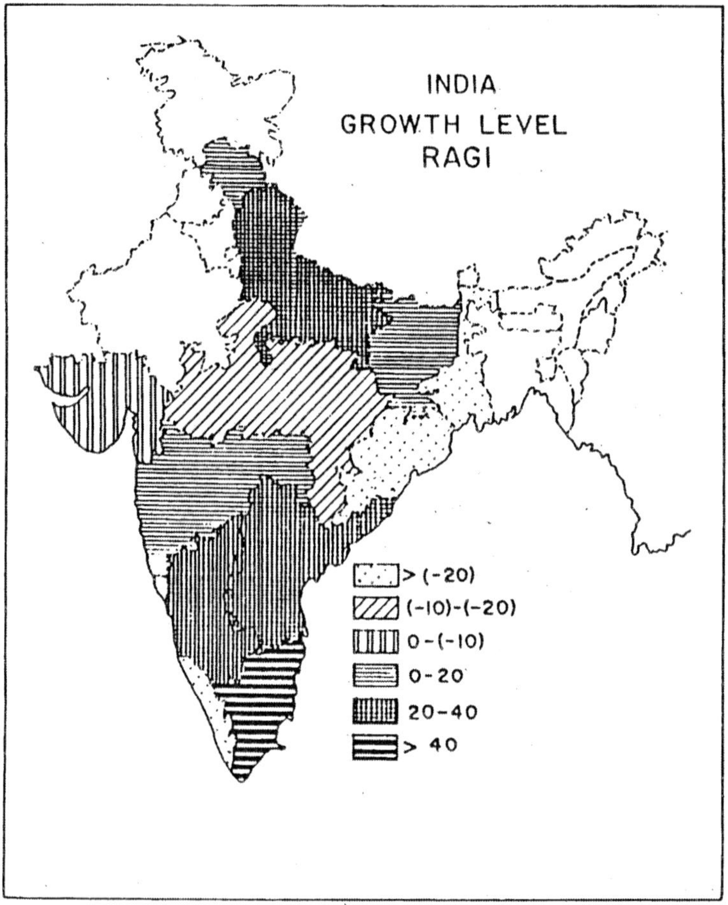
INDIA
GROWTH LEVEL
RAGI
> (-20)
(-10)-(-20)
0-(-10)
0-20
20-40
> 40

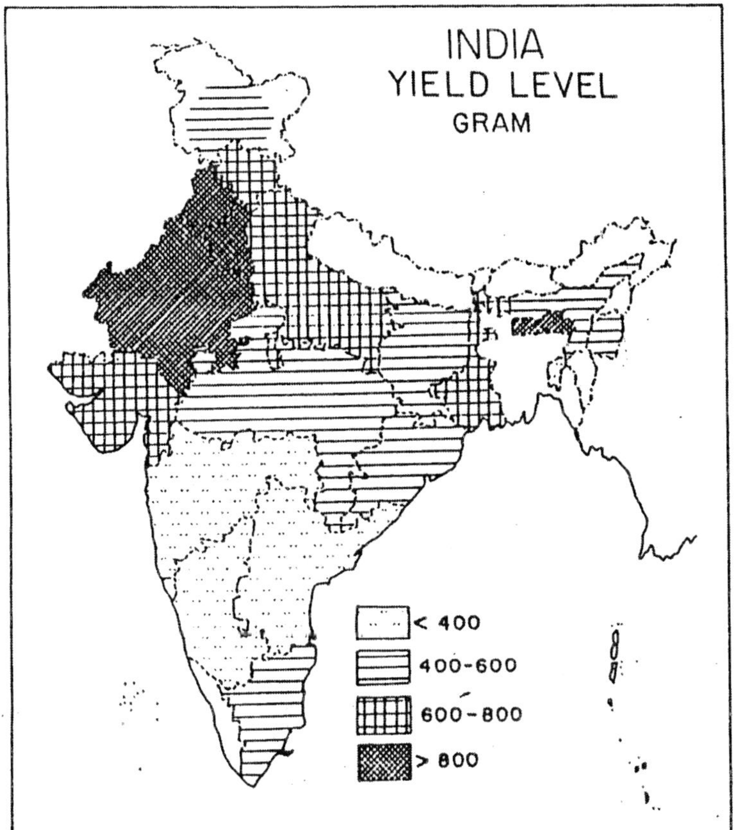
INDIA
YIELD LEVEL
GRAM
< 400
400-600
600-800
> 800

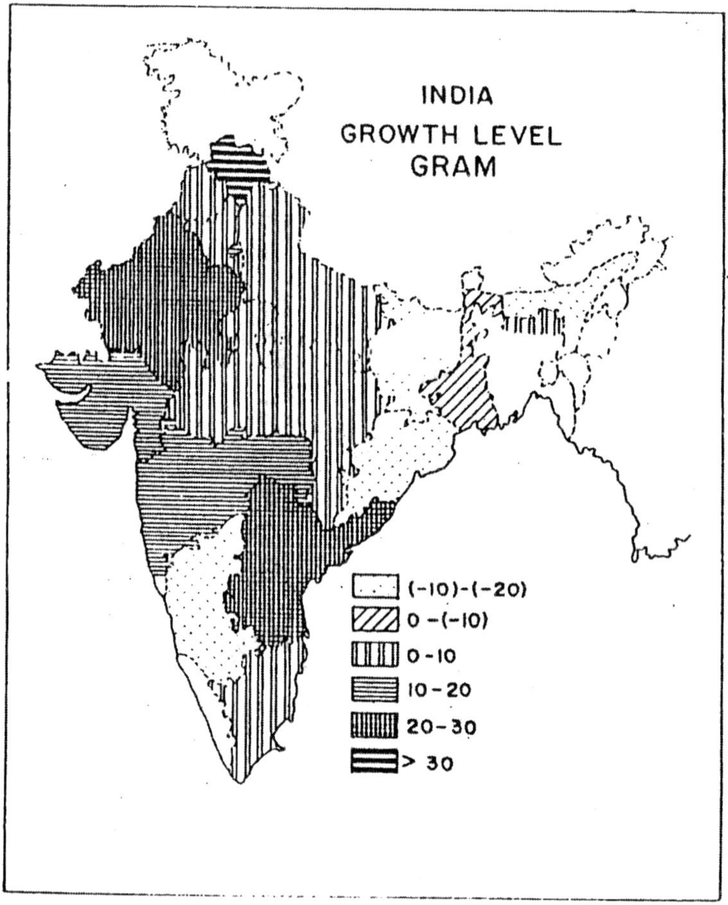
INDIA
GROWTH LEVEL
GRAM
(-10)-(-20)
0 -(-10)
0-10
10-20
20-30
> 30

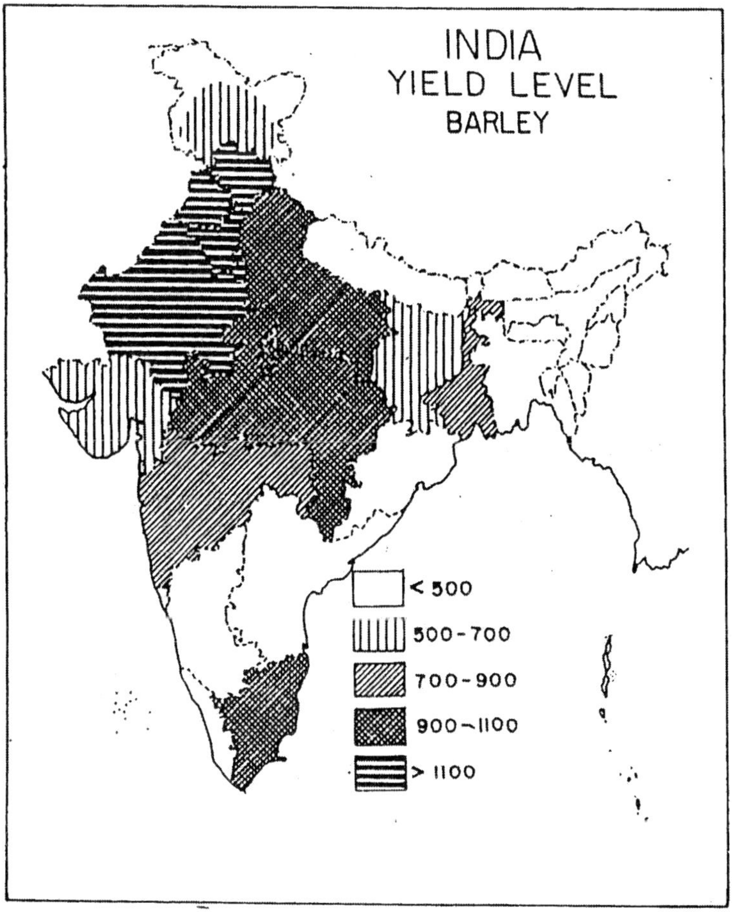
INDIA
YIELD LEVEL
BARLEY
< 500
500-700
700-900
900-1100
> 1100

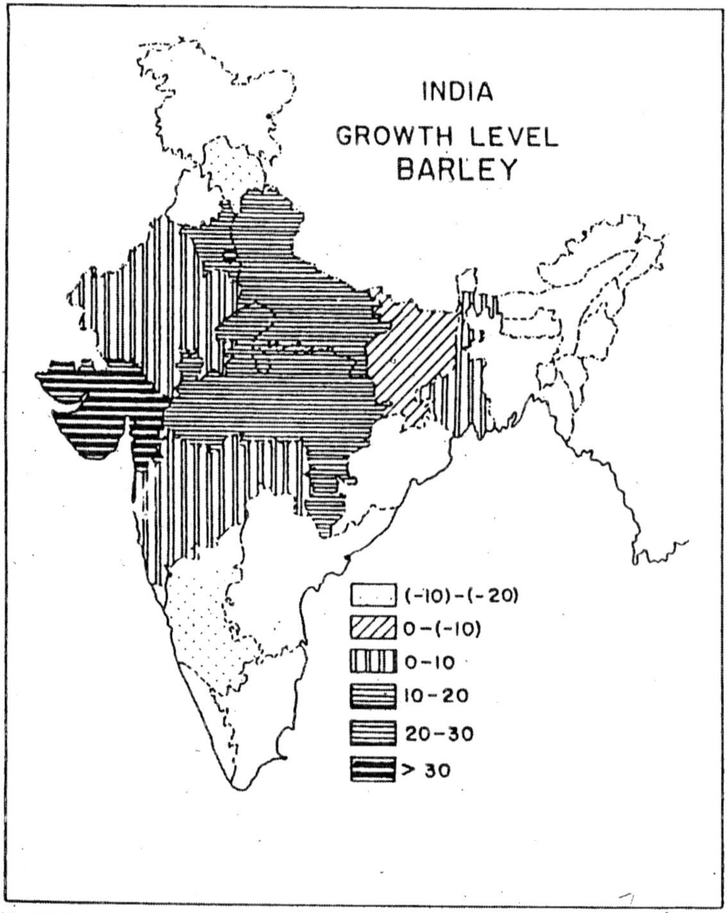
INDIA
GROWTH LEVEL
BARLEY
(-10)-(-20)
0-(-10)
0-10
10-20
20-30
> 30

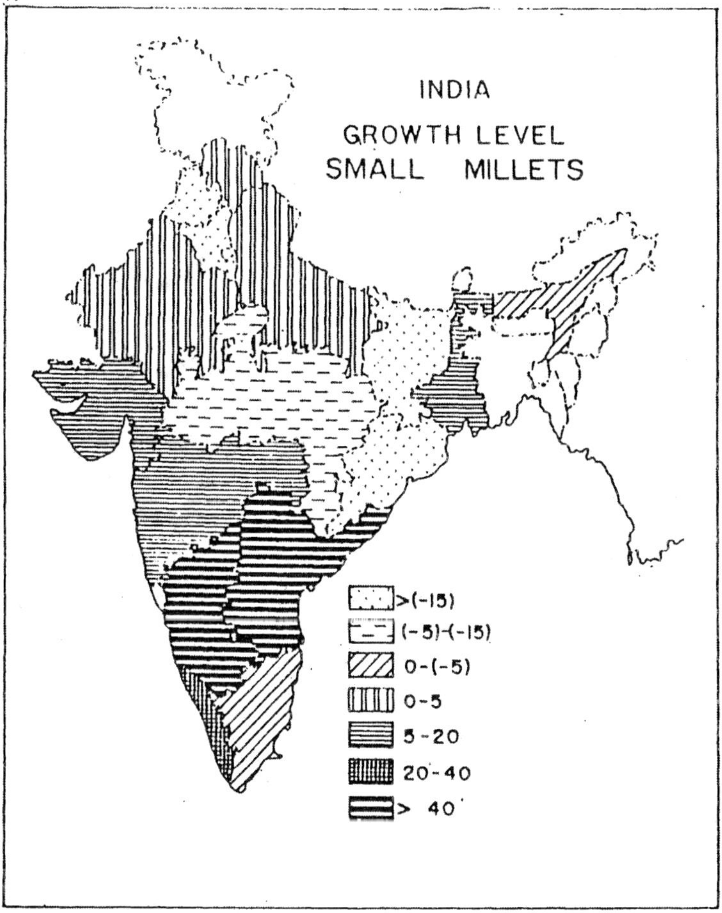
INDIA
GROWTH LEVEL
SMALL MILLETS
>(-15)
(-5)-(-15)
0-(-5)
0-5
5-20
20-40
> 40

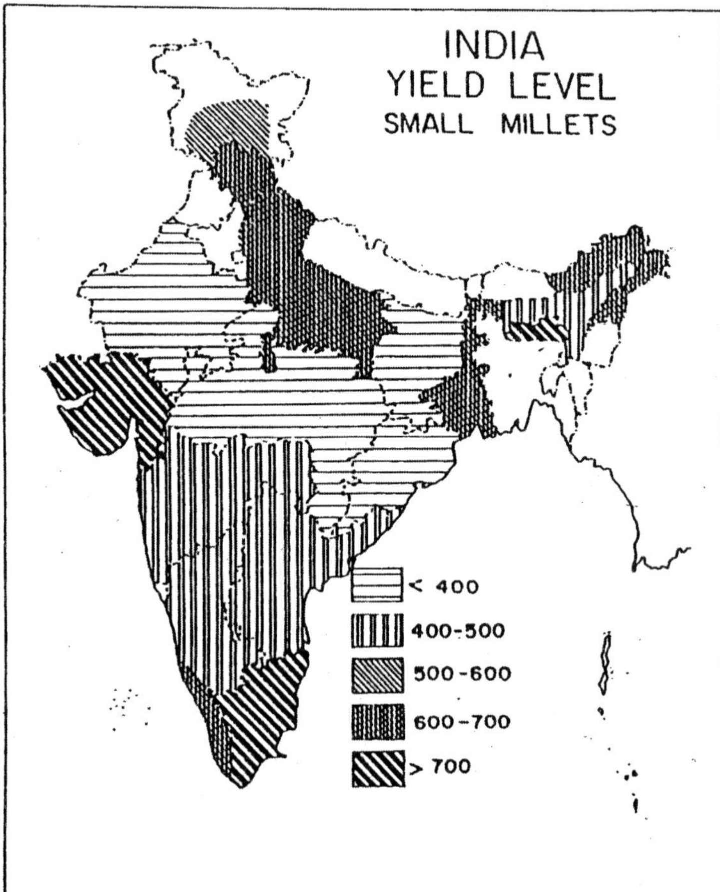
INDIA
YIELD LEVEL
SMALL MILLETS
< 400
400-500
500-600
600-700
> 700

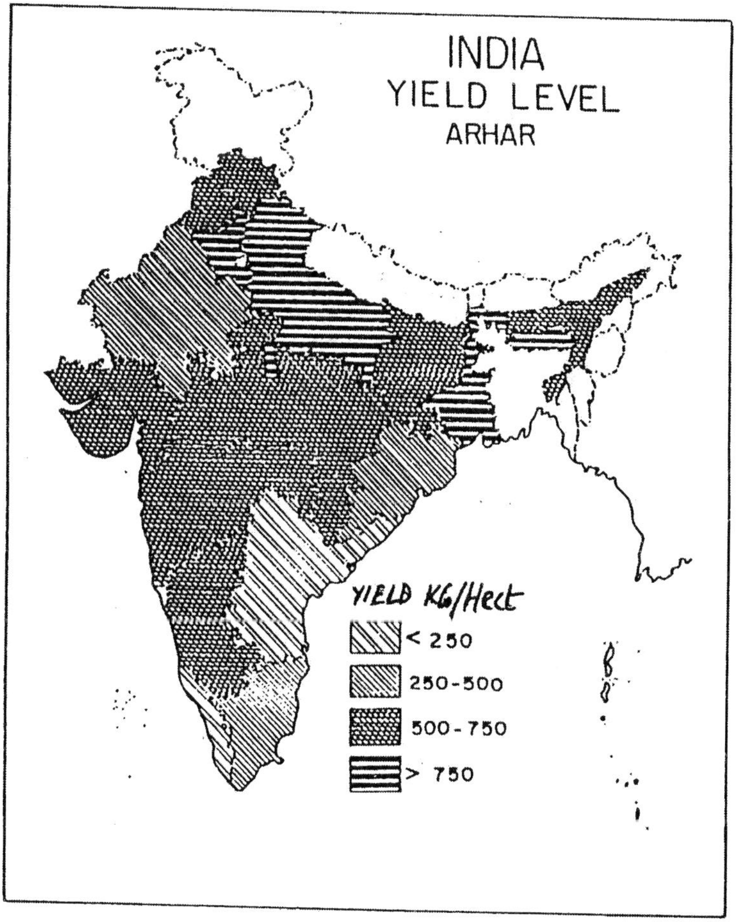
INDIA
YIELD LEVEL
ARHAR
YIELD KG/Hect
< 250
250-500
500-750
> 750

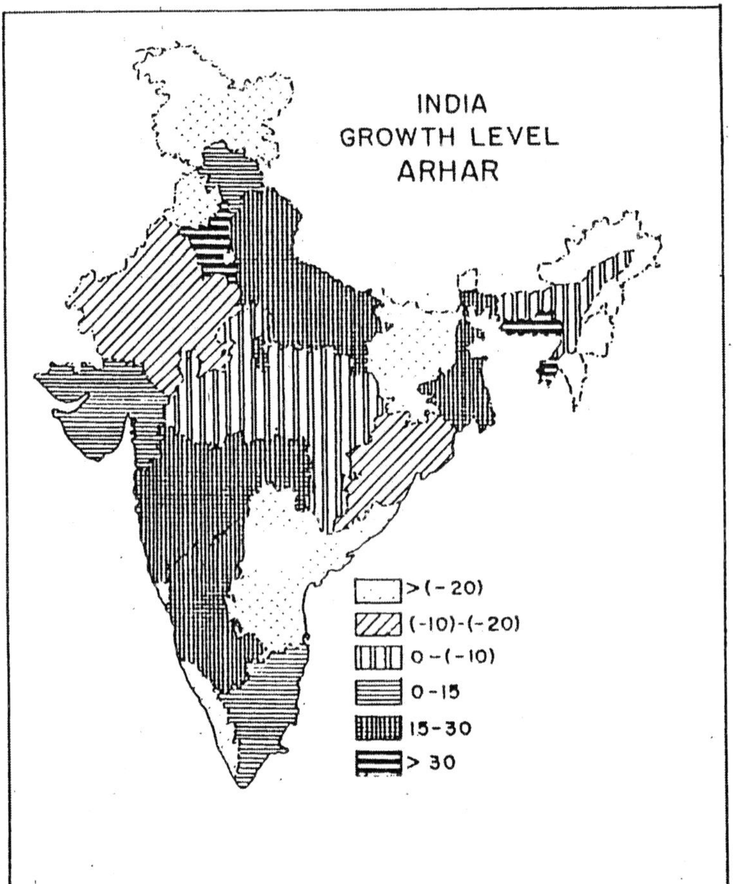
INDIA
GROWTH LEVEL
ARHAR
>(-20)
(-10)-(-20)
0-(-10)
0-15
15-30
> 30

7

Supply and Demand for Foodgrains

The problem of food in India is a very complicated and serious one. It is not a recent phenomenon, nor created by the widely-accepted malady of population growth. A historical study of famines goes to prove this. The evidence is available in the economic history of India which records numerous instances of crop failures, and lack of proper food supply. The country has experienced about 30 major famines during the last 300 years, and of the 34 great famines of the world 18 have occurred in India.

The frequency and the cyclic order show the peculiar susceptibility of this country to crop failures and recurrent shortage of food supply. Even after the development of the means of irrigation and a network of communication only the character of famine changed. There is permanent food shortage in some pockets of India especially in the regions both high and low productivity. In the high productivity states it is because of the high density of population and low man-land ratio while in the region of low productivity it is because of the erratic monsoon and lack of irrigation facilities. Secondly, in some of the regions whether it is of high yield level or a low level one, there exist disadvantaged groups in the agricultural sector, known as agricultural labourers, marginal farmers and uneconomic land holders, etc. They always suffer from food shortage. Therefore, food scarcity for the nation as a whole as well as among the disadvantaged groups has become a normal feature of national life. It is also arising out of a normal overall deficit or a gap between total output and requirements of the population resulting into a chronic state of underfeeding and malnutrition. Apart from this the fluctuating character of the total output accentuates food shortages in the form of short cycles almost everywhere and in some localities quite frequently. Again taking a regional view of the food scarcity one finds more than a dozen pockets of chronic scarcity. These lie in the drought-prone and the frequently flooded areas.

The above mentioned aspect of food problem is a quantitative consideration showing inadequacy of common average diets with reference to physiological adequacy or living near the starvation line. But in qualitative terms the common diets being cereal, they are unbalanced lacking in the essential requirements of protective foods, vitamins and minerals. This results in a chronic state of diseases resulting from malnutrition (nutritional deficiency). Therefore, the combined effects of the quantitative and qualitative deficiency are poor growth of body, low working capacity and a number of nutritional deficiency diseases which cause enormous sufferings. Lastly it erodes the human resources needed for economic development. Thus the vicious circle continues.

In historical perspective which can be considered as a base for todays development, the magnitude of the problem was first realised after the Bengal Famine (1943) and the extent of the shortage was estimated at about one-third of its population. Specific attention to the problem was paid by Sir John Megaw and Radhakamal Mukherjee. The former estimated that in the beginning of the 1930's of the total population 39 per cent was adequately nourished, 41 per cent poorly nourished, and 20 per cent was very badly nourished; and during abnormal periods the situation still worsened. The latter thought that there was a shortage for about one-third of its population, the remaining two-third was fed adequately. The Advisory Planning Board of Indian Council of Agricultural Research assessed in 1947, with reference to a balanced diet, the extent of shortage in the country in various items of food in terms of daily individual diets. The results obtained show that there was a deficiency of each items of foods in this country on an average per head per day. It was estimated that cereals deficiency was 7.1 per cent, pulses 36.7 per cent, leafy vegetables 84 per cent, ghee and vegetable oil 82 per cent, milk and its products 52 per cent, meat, eggs and fish 90 per cent, fruits and nuts 36.7 per cent, and sugar and gur was deficient by 30 per cent.

During the First Five Year Plan only the temporary aspects of the problem and not the fundamental ones have been recognised. But after a number of Five Year Plans the problem of food has been recognised at national level which is known as 'self-sufficiency in food', but we never recognised this problem at the regional level or state level, the village level and the household level as a household is a basic unit of food production and consumption as there is a large disparity in operational and size of holding from one household to another household.

Now the magnitude of the problem at regional level struck by the famines and large quantity of food import has been modified to a considerable extent, but the actual problem still exists at local level due to the vast disparity in the size of land holdings. This is such a problem which is not going to be solved only through increasing the transport network and irrigation facilities. Keeping in view the idea of social justice, as about 72 per cent of the total operational holdings are the small holdings, the problem should be tackled not at the state or regional level but at household level to remove the actual problem existing among the group of small land holdings.

TABLE 7.1: Rate of Population and Food Growth

States	Population Growth	Food Growth
Assam	3.3	1.7
Haryana	3.3	6.5
West Bengal	2.6	2.7
Gujarat	2.5	5.0
Rajasthan	2.4	3.4
Madhya Pradesh	2.4	2.1
Kerala	2.3	1.9
Maharashtra	2.3	2.0
Karnataka	2.1	1.9
Punjab	2.1	1.2
Orissa	2.1	1.8
Bihar	1.9	2.6
Himachal Pradesh	1.9	2.5
J & K	2.8	5.0
Andhra Pradesh	1.7	1.1
U.P.	1.7	1.9
Tamil Nadu	1.6	3.8
INDIA	2.1	2.9

In recent years we have been made more aware of the problems arising from our expanding population and relatively slow rate of growth of food production in many parts of India. This situation has led an increasing number of people to recognise that one of the pressing problems facing India today is that of maintaining a balance between the population and its food supply. In most of the regions the situation has become so critical and complex that there are no sufficient productivity surpluses for investment, if there is any that surplus is generally used for increasing the land holding by making others landless instead of investing to increase per unit productivity.

There is a large variation between growth of population and food production. There are some states where population growth is more than the foodgrains growth. For example in Assam and Kerala, the growth of population is much higher than the foodgrains growth. Except for a few states, i.e., Haryana, Punjab, Tamil Nadu and Jammu & Kashmir where agricultural growth is more than the population growth while other states are following the trend of equal growth of population and agriculture.

On the basis of the Table 7.1 production of foodgrains and per head share in foodgrains production it can be easily identified that which year produced lesser amount of foodgrains in terms of requirement per annum per head, i.e. 176 kg. per head.

The Table 7.2 indicates that out of thirty years about twelve years produced lesser amount of foodgrains than the requirement. To obtain this value production was divided by the total population of that year. The trend of self-sufficiency seems to be more satisfactory after the year 1968. After this period only two years 1973 and 1975 were noticed a fall in total production because of the environmental abnormalities. The position seems to be more satisfactory after 1959 because production fall short of the requirement marginally except of two years, i.e., 1966 and 1967. In these years production fell tremendously from 89 million tonnes to 70 million tonnes because of the widespread drought throughout the nation. The overall situation seems to be very satisfactory regarding the per head per annum share but the imports of foodgrains as well as the fertilizer import indicate that the nation is not self-sufficient regarding the overall foodgrains production.

On the basis of the Table 7.3 'per cent share of production and population to the total of India' it can be identified easily that which state is disbalanced regarding the share of foodgrains production and population. On the whole three types of pattern emerges: (i) the states which have higher percentage share in production than the population, (ii) the states having lesser percentage of production than the population (iii) the states having balancing performance between production and population shares on the basis of these above categories the states of Haryana and Punjab are having more production than the population share which constitute only 4.3 per cent population of the country, or in other words only 4.3 per cent

TABLE 7.2: Production of Foodgrains and per head Share in Foodgrain Production

Year	Production of Foodgrains (in metric tonnes)	Foodgrains per capita (Kg.)
1950	60.8	(-) 170.19
1951	55.0	(-) 151.50
1952	55.6	(-) 150.60
1953	61.8	(-) 164.50
1954	72.3	189.10
1955	70.7	181.50
1956	69.3	(-) 174.50
1957	72.4	178.70
1958	66.6	(-) 160.90
1959	78.8	186.30
1960	77.1	178.30
1961	82.3	186.10
1962	82.4	182.[illegible]
1963	80.3	(-) 173.90
1964	80.7	(-) 170.90
1965	89.4	185.20
1966	72.3	(-) 146.70
1967	74.2	(-) 147.20
1968	95.0	184.40
1969	94.0	178.40
1970	99.5	184.60
1971	108.4	196.80
1972	105.2	186.90
1973	97.0	(-) 168.90
1974	104.8	177.70
1975	100.9	(-) 166.96
1976	121.0	195.40
1977	111.6	175.88
1978	126.1	193.94
1979	131.4	197.22
1980	108.9	185.10
1981	132.0	197.11

Note: The sign (-) indicates the deficit year of production according to the standard requirement of 176 kg./per head per annum.

population have more production than the consumption. It is only because of the two factors, i.e., high yield per hectare and high man-land ratio. The states of Assam, Bihar, Gujarat, Kerala, Maharashtra and West Bengal have higher population than the per cent share of production. It is largely because of the single factor, i.e., high density of agricultural population though the yield level is considerably high.

TABLE 7.3: Per cent Share of Production and Population at State Level to the Total of India

States	Years											% share in population (1979)
	1969	1970	1971	1972	1973	1974	1975	1976	1977	1978	1979	
	(in % share in Production)											
1	2	3	4	5	6	7	8	9	10	11	12	13
Andhra Pradesh	7.3	7.4	6.5	6.9	6.9	8.3	9.0	7.8	6.7	7.1	7.8	7.8
Assam	2.4	2.1	1.9	1.9	2.5	2.1	2.0	2.0	2.0	1.9	1.8	2.9
Bihar	9.4	7.6	7.5	9.4	9.6	7.4	8.2	7.6	8,2	7.9	7.6	10.1
Gujarat	2.5	3.3	4.0	4.0	2.3	3.8	2.1	3.8	3.6	3.1	3.4	4.9
Haryana	3.2	4.6	4.3	4.3	4.2	3.7	3.3	4.2	4.7	4.3	4.8	1.9
Himachal Pradesh	1.0	1.0	0.9	0.9	1.0	0.9	1.1	0.9	1.0	0.8	0.8	0.6
J & K	1.2	1.2	1.0	0.9	1.0	1.0	1.0	0.8	0.8	0.9	0.9	0.9
Karnataka	5.4	5.9	5.5	5.7	4.7	6.2	6.7	5.9	4.2	5.8	5.8	5.4
Kerala	1.5	1.3	1.2	1.3	1.5	1.2	1.4	1.2	1.1	1.1	1.0	3.7
M.P.	10.0	9.7	10.0	10.0	11.0	10.2	9.9	9.8	9.7	9.7	7.6	7.6
Maharashtra	7.6	7.0	6.7	4.7	3.2	6.8	7.5	7.5	8.7	8.3	7.6	9.2
Manipur	0.4	0.3	0.2	0.2	0.2	0.3	0.3	0.3	0.3	0.3	0.3	0.2
Meghalaya	—	—	0.1	0.1	0.1	0.1	0.1	0.1	0.1	0.1	0.1	0.2
Nagaland	0.1	0.1	0.1	0.1	0.1	0.1	0.1	0.1	0.1	0.1	0.1	0.1
Orissa	5.8	5.1	4.7	4.1	5.0	5.0	3.9	4.6	3.6	4.4	4.4	3.8

(Contd.)

1	2	3	4	5	6	7	8	9	10	11	12	13
Punjab	6.6	7.0	6.4	7.5	7.9	7.4	7.9	7.3	8.3	8.2	8.8	2.4
Rajasthan	4.6	5.0	8.1	6.2	5.6	6.6	5.0	6.4	6.7	5.7	6.0	5.0
Tamil Nadu	5.8	6.3	6.4	6.5	7.4	7.0	4.7	5.9	6.3	6.2	6.3	7.1
Tripura	0.2	0.3	0.2	0.3	0.2	0.4	0.3	0.3	0.3	0.3	0.3	0.3
U.P.	17.3	17.7	17.8	16.7	18.7	14.9	17.4	16.1	17.5	16.6	17.4	16.2
West Bengal	7.6	7.4	6.7	7.4	7.0	6.6	7.8	7.1	6.8	7.2	5.8	7.9
A & N Islands	—	—	—	—	—	0.01	0.02	0.02	0.01	0.01	0.01	—
Arunachal Pradesh	0.1	0.1	0.1	0.1	0.1	0.1	0.1	0.1	0.1	0.1	0.1	—
Chandigarh	—	—	—	—	—	—	—	—	—	—	—	—
Dadra N. Haveli	—	—	0.01	0.01	0.01	0.02	0.02	0.02	0.02	0.02	0.02	—
Delhi	0.1	0.1	0.1	0.1	0.1	0.1	0.1	0.1	0.1	0.1	0.1	—
Goa, D. & Diu	0.1	0.1	0.1	0.1	0.1	0.1	0.1	0.1	0.1	0.1	0.1	—
Mizoram	0.1	0.1	0.1	0.1	0.1	0.1	0.1	0.1	0.1	0.1	0.1	—
Pondicherry	0.1	0.1	0.1	0.1	0.1	0.1	0.1	0.1	0.1	0.1	0.1	—

While the other states like U.P., Tripura, Tamil Nadu, Rajasthan, Orissa, M.P., Karnataka, J.&K., Himachal Pradesh and Andhra Pradesh are on a balancing position with a negligible variation. However, it is obvious that about 40 per cent of the total population of India requires more production than the consumption. Similarly about 56 per cent population is at the balancing state they can face the food scarcity at anytime of environmental abnormalities.

Demand and Suppiy

During the period 1950 and 1979 there have been, for various reasons, a wide range of variations between the estimated and the actual levels of demand for foodgrains. The demand for foodgrains during the end of First Five Year Plan period (1955-56) was estimated at 62 million metric tonnes on the basis of the assumed availability of 447 grams per adult per day. But the actual availability was much higher as the production of foodgrains exceeded the target and reached 69 million tonnes. The demand for foodgrains during the period of Second Five Year Plan (1960-61) was estimated at 75 million tonnes on the basis of the assumed availability of 518 grams per head per day and the calories consumption of 2200 in 1955-56 was expected to rise to 2450 by 1960-61. But our availability exceeded the target and reached to 82 million tonnes. The demand for foodgrains during the Third Five Year Plan period (1965-66) was estimated at 102 million tonnes on the basis of the 510 grams per head per day. But the availability was about 90.7 million tonnes including supplies from imports. During this period weather played an adverse role and the country passed through an acute shortage of food situation in 1966 and in this third plan period the country imported 25 million tonnes of foodgrains and in the year 1966 about 10 million tonnes of foodgrains was imported. According to B.M. Bhatia the total imports for the third plan period (1961–65) was 25.4 million tonnes, 10.34 million tonnes for 1966, the worst drought year, 8.66 million tonnes for 1967, the next worst drought year, 5.69 million tonnes for 1968. The original Draft Fourth Year Plan (1966–71) put the target of production for the terminal year 1970–71 at 129 million tonnes. This was on consideration of prospective growth in population and in per capita income. The total availability of 108 million tonnes in 1970-71 including imports fell short of the estimated demand by a considerable margin. The actual availability for 1968-69 was 94 million tonnes and for 1969-70 it was 99.5 million tonnes. This resulted in almost doubling of wholesale prices during the period 1966–71. The target of production for 1971-72 was set at 112.0 million tonnes (the Fourth Plan Mid-term Appraisal, 1971) but the production fell short to a considerable extent as the availability was only 105 million metric tonnes.

The Fourth Five Year Plan estimated the target of production at about 129 million tonnes. It was assumed that per capita expenditure would go up by 16 per cent and population would increase by 15.7 per cent during the period 1969–75. But during this period however, the increase in per capita income fall considerably short of the target and the lower level of availability led by unprecedented rise in the price of foodgrains. On the other hand, the population count in 1971 registered a level lower than that of projected in 1960's by the expert committee on projection. The actual availability for consumption in 1974 has been obtained 104.8 million metric tonnes.

The Fifth Five Year Plan 1974–79 assumed the base level of demand for the year 1973-74 at 114 million tonnes and considered the building up of an adequate buffer stock essential. The target of production for the year 1978-79 was fixed at 140 million tonnes. But the total production achieved about 131.5 million tonnes. The Draft Five Year Plan 1978–83 estimated a demand for 1982-83 of 140 to 144 million tonnes and excepted a similar availability through production in that year in which the success is achieved. The estimates of output for 1987-88 has been put at 164 to 169 million tonnes. On the basis of as high as 2 per cent growth in population between 1978 and 1988, together with an income elasticity for demand of 0.6, the demand in 1987-88, on a base level of 126 million tonnes in 1978, would, however, be less than this figure.

On the basis of the present policies of the government of India, i.e., adding to its buffer stock in recent years suggests that the demand for foodgrains has not been increasing as anticipated and that the incentive for greater production has been provided more by the higher guaranteed procurement prices than demand proper. Nonetheless, there must be more to the demand pattern apparently meets the eye because prices in the open grain market are often higher than the procurement prices. One obvious reason, of course, is that the better quality grain is offered in the open market for which the demand is higher while the inferior quality is offered to government procurement. Nonetheless, the tardiness with which demand for foodgrains has behaved in recent years, especially since 1975, calls for a hard look at the prospects of foodgrains production in the coming years. While the technological impediments to higher agricultural productivity have been identified and are being more and more efficiently attended to, the consumption and distribution pattern of foodgrains will demand more attention in the context of prospective incomes and their distribution.

8

Surplus and Deficit in Food Availability

Measurement of Surplus and Deficit

There are various limitations of this problem as what should be the criteria to measure the surplus and deficit level of food availability. The various methods have been evolved like the total availability of cereals of the level of standard requirement, either in terms of calories or various recommended allowances of nutrients, namely, protein, calcium, carbohydrates, fats, iron, minerals and vitamins. Secondly, these allowances vary with each age groups, sex, body weight, occupation and temperature. The distary habits of normal healthy people in different parts of the country and among different ethnic groups, their total food intakes and the proportions of ingredients in the total intake, reveal significant differences. To what extent the uniform norms of desirable cereals and pulses requirements for the country as a whole, irrespective of regions of varied climate conditions, communities and cultures are untenable. This exercise does not take into account foods that are locally available and enter into the common diet, often unpaid for or unaccounted in diet or consumption surveys, like fish and home grown tapioca, coconut or fruits or vegetables, or even those local foods, most often rightly chosen, which have an economising effect on the food budget. The exercise does not go into the question of availability or requirements of vegetables, fates and oils, milk and other animal foods. Nor does the study attempt to determine how much of the surplus protein in the diets of common man in different parts of the country is broken into for meeting calorie deficiency. On account of difficulties in choosing the right year of reference and in allocating food values between the intake of cereals and pulses on the one hand and oils and fats, sugar, etc., on the other, we have not found, for this statewise exercise, the NSS consumption surveys series readily tractable, particularly for the purpose of allocating the districts or states to NSS Zones, although the level of disaggregation of data in the NSS surveys is much more attractive.

Standard Requirement level

The present attempt begins by assuming that the requirements of cereals for the entire population throughout the country will be uniform. It makes a virtue of necessity – data for other ingredients being not so readily available for purposes of disaggregated study – by sticking to cereals and pulses requirements alone, as though cereals were the only important thing for diet and nutrition. Therefore, this study relies rather heavily on the argument that what is more important in the Indian situation of a legume culture is the adequacy of calories rather than of proteins. It, therefore, attempts to find answers only in terms of cereals and pulses intakes and requirements. An even more serious and questionable assumption is that all cereals and pulses have been taken as equal, first, because no data was made available at state level to the relative shares of wheat, rice, millets, maize etc. in the total production as each cereals have different amount of nutrients per unit and, secondly, because no satisfactory standardised conversion factor in terms of rice could be worked out for other cereals. For this problem a micro-level study is needed to correlate the results from micro-level to meso-level. In this way a village survey should be introduced to find out the crop-wise share in terms of various nutrients in various sections (economic classes) of the Village Community. However, the present exercise, at state level have some limited and in some ways misleading exercise, but it would still have significant messages for understanding the situation of hunger, nutrition and malnutrition in the country on the basis of availability and requirements of cereals and pulses alone. And this exercise will be useful at least for state planners. Keeping in view the limited scope of this exercise any conclusion would be subject to, an estimation was undertaken of the daily per capita food consumption required for balanced diet for five broad age and biological groups on all India basis. These five population sub-groups are: (i) below the age group of 15 years (ii) adult males 15 years above (iii) females pregnant above 15 years (iv) lactating adult females 15 years and above, (v) other adult females. The basic data for this estimation has been taken from *Diet Atlas of India* published by the Indian Council of Medical Research.[1] The limitation of this study is that only the foodgrains, like cereals and pulses which form the bulk of the average Indian diet have been considered. The consumption of fats and oils and sugar have not been taken into account because a very little information is available on their conversion factor. In recent years, again the availability of these crops has heavily dependent upon import and export fluctuations. The table, Estimates of Daily average Indian Balanced Diet Required presents the details of estimation of foodgrains required for sustenance by five different population subgroups. According to the current diet habits of the Indian population and according to the availability of foodgrains supply in the country, it has been broadly estimated that each child of age below 15 years requires on an average 288 grams of foodgrains intake daily. According to the Diet Atlas the age group 15–18 is supplied to consume 451 grams. But we have here considered two main age groups 0–14/15 and above, on the assumption that since an overwhelming proportion of boys and girls of the ages 15–18 work for their livelihood, their consumption ought to be closer to the adult mark than the adolescent mark. In addition a considerable proportion of boys and girls aged 10–14 also work almost full time for a living. It would therefore, be only fair to weight this additional consumption on the age group 15–18 and club it with adult populations.

Age Structure and Food Requirement

The figures are the minimum amount of foodgrains required daily per capita for the barest sustenance, below which level malnutrition may set in. These indicate the foodgrains needs of average persons. No refinement has been made for hard manual workers, or ailing persons or growing persons in the early years of adulthood. It is curious to note that, even according to the norms of the Indian Council of Medical Research the food requirements of the pregnant and lactating women (whose nutrition requirement one would imagine should be more) is supposed to be definitely less than that of an adult male. Covered into estimates of annual requirements of foodgrains, the figure come to:

TABLE 8.1: Age Structure and Food Requirement

1.	A child	— 105.12	kg.	per	year
2.	Adult male	— 209.05	kg.	per	year
3.	Pregnant women	— 175.06	k.g.	per	year
4.	Lactating women	— 197.05	kg.	per	year
5.	Adult women	— 157.03	kg.	per	year

If the per cent share of each population group is made available the total requirement of foodgrains can be estimated. The average requirement per head per day can be calculated on this basis. The difference between average foodgrains production and the total foodgrains required in a district or state can be calculated. This will provide the surplus or deficit in foodgrains. If the amount of foodgrains availability happened to be greater than the foodgrains demand, the state or district can be rated surplus. If the amount of foodgrains demand happened to be greater than the foodgrains available from production the region will be rated deficit. These estimates of food surplus and deficit provide a measure of nourishment and malnutrition in India.

Share of Pulses and Cereals in Food Production

The Table 8.2 entitled pulses and cereals – per head per day distribution in terms of grammes and kg. reveals that the states of Andhra Pradesh, Assam, Bihar, Kerala, Madhya Pradesh, Maharashtra, Meghalaya, Nagaland, West Bengal and other Union Territories have lesser production than the requirement per head per day. While on the other side the states of Haryana, Himachal Pradesh, J & K, Karnataka, Madhya Pradesh, Manipur, Orissa, Punjab, Rajasthan, Tamil Nadu, Tripura, U.P., Arunachal Pradesh and Dadra & Nagar Haveli have more production than the requirement per head per day. The average picture for the country as a whole is sufficient and slightly more than the requirement, i.e., in spite of the standard requirement by 482 the country is receiving 519 grams per head per day.

The magnitude of the deficiency is recorded at high level from the states of Assam, Gujarat, Kerala, Meghalaya, Nagaland A & N Islands, Delhi, Goa, D. & Diu, Mizoram and Pondicherry. While other states are marginally deficient like Andhra Pradesh, West Bengal, Bihar and Maharashtra. In these states top priority for the improvement of agriculture should be given to fulfil at least the standard requirement of not to generate any surplus. In the states of Kerala, Delhi, Goa Daman & Diu and Mizoram other source of income should be created so that the increased purchasing power will help to solve the problems.

The situation of pulses is very critical in all the states except of Haryana, Madhya Pradesh and Rajasthan. The country as a whole is receiving only 50 grammes pulses per head per day while the standard requirement is 84 grammes. A high level of deficiency is recorded where the average intake is lesser than the national average, these states are Andhra Pradesh, Assam, Bihar, Gujarat, Himachal Pradesh, J & K, Kerala, Manipur, Meghalaya, Nagaland, Tamil Nadu, Orissa are marginally below than the standard requirement.

TABLE 8.2: Cereals and Pulses (Per Head Per Day Share in Production) (Grammes)

States	Total Grammes	Kg. Cereals	Kg. Pulses	Grammes	
				Cereals	Pulses
	1	2	3	4	5
1. Andhra Pradesh	(-) 472	165.58	6.82	454	18 (-)
2. Assam	(-) 346	124.13	2.11	340	6 (-)
3. Bihar	(-) 398	134.83	10.30	369	19 (-)
4. Gujarat	(-) 354	123.42	5.92	338	16 (-)
5. Haryana	1268	382.59	80.40	1048	220
6. Himachal Pradesh	698	245.35	9.27	672	26 (-)
7. J & K	526	186.95	5.13	512	14 (-)
8. Karnataka	509	171.22	14.44	469	40 (-)
9. Kerala	(-) 146	52.51	0.68	144	2 (-)
10. Madhya Pradesh	615	183.39	41.26	502	113
11. Maharashtra	(-) 398	128.16	17.03	351	47 (-)
12. Manipur	641	232.36	1.74	637	4 (-)
13. Meghalaya	(-) 327	118.70	0.80	325	2 (-)
14. Nagaland	(-) 348	121.30	5.64	332	16 (-)
15. Orissa	559	179.14	24.91	491	68 (-)
16. Punjab	1787	631.72	20.65	1731	56 (-)
17. Rajasthan	611	161.82	61.36	443	168
18. Tamil Nadu	503	179.32	4.29	401	12 (-)
19. Tripura	529	192.05	1.15	526	3 (-)
20. U.P.	532	171.08	22.95	469	63 (-)
21. West Bengal	(-) 429	150.34	6.14	412	17 (-)
22. A & N Island	(-) 304	–	–	–	–
23. Arunachal Pradesh	514	–	–	–	–
24. Chandigarh	–	–	–	–	–
25. D & N Haveli	647	–	–	–	–
26. Delhi	(-) 62	–	–	–	–
27. Goa, D. & Diu	(-) 278	–	–	–	–
28. Mizoram	(-) 228	–	–	–	–
29. Pondicherry	(-) 319	–	–	–	–
INDIA	519	171.09	18.21	469	50 (-)

1. Standard Requirement of Cereals = 398 grams
2. Standard Requirement of Pulses = 84 grams
3. Total requirement of foodgrains = 482 grams

(-) Deficit (availability of foodgrains).

On the basis of the above statement we can say that in India there is a pulse crisis as compared to the cereals because there is a cereals shortage not a crisis. Pulses are the only major source of protein in Indian dietary system and still the pressure on pulses demand is as high as it was before and will continue in future also because there is no hope in the change of dietary system as well as lack of the production of any substitute to it. There are certain pulses, (khesari) and on that basis the state like Madhya Pradesh is self-sufficient, the production of it can be banned because some of the desastrous diseases. Now the situation will again worsened in India in terms of total intake and availability of pulses because of this khesari pulses.

The immediate priority should be given to tackle the crisis and a scientific method should be adopted to include the high yield giving pulses in the present cropping pattern.

Foodgrains Production Per Head Per Annum in terms of Surplus and Deficit

The Table 8.2 'Statewise Foodgrains per head production' will reveal the positive and negative states of foodgrains production. The state below 176 kg. per head production per annum is the limit according to the standard requirement per head per annum. The states like Assam, Bihar, Gujarat, Kerala, Maharashtra, Meghalaya, Nagaland, Mizoram, Pondicherry, Delhi, Goa, D. & Diu and West Bengal are below the standard requirement. The per cent departure from the standard requirement among these states are not equal but it varies in different magnitude, i.e., among the major states Assam, Gujarat, and Kerala, the departure is much than the Bihar and Maharashtra, Mizoram and Delhi the situation is very critical. The situation for the country as a whole is very satisfactory and per head per annum production is 14 kg. more than the standard requirement. Among the deficit states no doubt that the yield is very high but due to the high density of population especially in the states of Bihar, West Bengal, Kerala and in many other hilly states, the situation has become very critical. The states of Haryana, Punjab, Himachal Pradesh, J & K, Rajasthan, Uttar Pradesh, Madhya Pradesh, Karnataka, Manipur, Orissa, Tripura, Arunachal Pradesh and Dadra & Nagar Haveli are under the surplus producing states and magnitude of the surplus differs from one state to another states. Among these states the highest surplus is shown by the Haryana and Punjab where the surplus is more than the three times higher than the standard requirement.

Surplus and Deficit States

The amount of surplus and deficits have been calculated at state level. The Table 8.2 'State level surplus and deficit' with per cent contribution of each state to the Net surplus of India reveals the amount of surplus and deficit. The calculation is based at district level which will give more authentic picture. At district level every state have some districts deficient in food production per head except of Haryana & Punjab. At state-level in some of the states it seems that there is an overall deficit but in each states there are some district where deficit and surplus districts are also located.

TABLE 8.3: No. of Deficit Districts in Per Head Food Production

States	Deficit District	Total No. of Districts
Andhra Pradesh	16	21
Assam	5	7
Bihar	13	17
Gujarat	15	18
Haryana	0	7
J & K	0	2 (units)
Kerala	10	10
Madhya Pradesh	3	43
Maharashtra	23	26
Karnataka	4	19
Punjab	0	11
Tamil Nadu	6	12
West Bengal	4	14
U.P.	11	48
Rajasthan	5	26
Orissa	3	13

The amount of deficit and surpluses have also been indicated against each state both in absolute picture in lakh metric tonnes and percentage surplus available. The states of Punjab and Haryana alone have 41 per cent share in total surplus of the country. The states of Uttar Pradesh and Madhya Pradesh contribute about 32 per cent surplus in total surplus sharing about 16 per cent each, while Rajasthan have about 12 per cent of total surplus. Other states have a very insignificant amount of surplus.

TABLE 8.4: Statewise Foodgrains Production and per Head Production per Annum (1976-77—78-79)

(Production in metric tonnes)

States	Cereals	Pulses	Foodgrains		Per Head Production Per Annum (KG)
Andhra Pradesh	8613600	354900	3968500	(-)	172.40
Assam	2297200	39100	2336300	(-)	126.23
Bihar	9016500	688600	9705100	(-)	145.12
Gujarat	3939900	188900	4128800	(-)	129.34
Haryana	4676000	982700	5658700		462.99
Himachal Pradesh	992200	37500	1029700		254.62
J & K	1045600	28700	1074300		192.07
Karnataka	6024700	508200	6532900		185.66
Kerala	1263900	16300	1280200	(-)	53.18
Madhya Pradesh	9013200	2027700	11040900		224.64
Maharashtra	7584100	1007900	8592000	(-)	145.18
Manipur	307600	2300	309900		234.06
Meghalaya	147900	1000	148900	(-)	119.50
Nagaland	86000	4000	90000	(-)	126.93
Orissa	4469600	621400	5091000		204.04
Punjab	10067100	329100	10396200		652.37
Rajasthan	5209100	1975100	7184200		223.18
Tamil Nadu	8279900	198300	8478200		183.61
Tripura	367000	2200	369200		193.19
U. P.	18586300	2493800	21080100		194.03
West Bengal	7749600	316400	8066000	(-)	156.47
A. & N. Islands	13100	600	13700	(-)	110.96
Arunachal Pradesh	112700	—	112700		187.61
Chandigarh	—	—	—		—
D & N Haveli	17800	2600	20400		236.16
Delhi	136800	4000	140800	(-)	22.63
G D & Diu	98100	—	98100	(-)	101.47
Mizoram	41300	—	41300	(-)	83.22
Pondicherry	71600	2800	75400	(-)	116.44
INDIA	111191100	11834400	123025500		189.38

Note: (-) Indicate Deficit States.

It is evident from the Table 8.5 'state level surplus and deficit and percentage share in surplus production' that almost all yield level states have some surplus and deficit production. Though the main reason of surplus can be due to the high yield level states have more surplus production in spite of the small size of the state like Punjab and Haryana. But even the low and medium yield level states have some surplus production because of the low density of population like Madhya Pradesh, Rajasthan, Uttar Pradesh and West Bengal. The state of Kerala having high yield level falls under the deficit production per head because of the high concentration of population. Therefore, the policies of agricultural development should be based not on high and low yield level and improve the yield level of low yield giving states or high yield giving states but it should largely based on the surplus and deficit production per head in spite of the high or low yield. For example in Kerala there is a need for the improvement in yield level while in Rajasthan and Madhya Pradesh priority should be given after the Kerala in terms of social justice and inequality of per head food production.

TABLE 8.5: State Level Surplus and Deficit Production

(Lakh metric tonnes)

States	Surplus	Deficit	% Surplus to the total Surplus
Andhra Pradesh	—	3.64	—
Assam	—	1.08	—
Bihar	—	10.37	—
Gujarat	—	7.54	—
Haryana	29.17	—	14.28
Jammu & Kashmir	1.97	—	0.96
Kerala	—	19.20	—
Karnataka	7.57	—	3.71
Madhya Pradesh	33.84	—	16.57
Maharashtra	—	35.18	—
Punjab	55.06	—	26.96
Tamil nadu	9.47	—	4.64
Orissa	8.00	—	3.92
Rajasthan	24.19	—	11.86
West Bengal	2.38	—	1.16
Uttar Pradesh	32.58	—	15.95
INDIA	204.23	77.01	100.00
Net Surplus	127.22	—	—

TABLE 8.6: State Level Surplus and Deficit Production

(% contribution of each state)

States	Surplus	% Surplus	Deficit	% Deficit	Total	
					Surplus	Deficit
Andhra Pradesh	6.00	2.43	9.63	7.89	—	3.64
Assam	0.44	0.18	1.52	1.25	—	1.08
Bihar	5.31	2.16	15.68	12.85	—	10.37
Gujarat	2.11	0.86	12.85	10.53	—	7.54
Haryana	29.17	11.86	0.00	0.00	29.17	—
J & K	1.97	0.80	0.00	0.00	1.97	—
Kerala	0.00	0.00	19.20	15.74	—	19.20
Karnataka	11.04	4.49	3.47	2.84	7.57	—
Madhya Pradesh	34.12	13.87	0.28	0.23	33.84	—
Maharashtra	0.91	0.37	36.09	29.58	—	35.18
Punjab	55.06	22.38	0.00	0.00	55.06	—
Tamil Nadu	13.67	5.56	4.20	3.44	9.47	—
Orissa	8.16	3.30	0.16	0.13	8.00	—
Rajasthan	25.92	10.54	1.73	1.42	24.19	—
West Bengal	13.85	5.63	11.47	9.40	2.38	—
U. P.	38.31	15.57	5.73	4.70	32.58	—
INDIA	246.03	100.00	122.01	100.00	127.22	—

Surplus and Deficiency at District Level

In the period of district and block level planning it is more important to find out the magnitude of deficiency at micro unit. Though the data is available at district level, therefore, deficiency and surplus level have been calculated and total amount of deficiency and surplus is given in the Table 8.3 and 8.6 as well as the number of the district at state level.

Reference

1. C. Gopalan, et al; *Diet Atlas of India*, National Institute of Nutrition, ICMR, Hyderabad, 1971.

9

Potentials for Development and Perspectives for 1980–2000 A.D.

It is estimated on the level of 1971 population census that the population will double during the end of the century and the situation of food will become more critical and worse than today as well as the Green Revolution will not fulfil the need of the day. We are also witnessing the widespread poverty at the increasing trend and a substantial section of the population being unable to have enough food to eat. We are very far from the self-sufficiency regarding the availability of balanced nutrients and there is a widespread occurrences of nutritional deficiency diseases and at least about more than thirty (3) nutritional deficiency diseases have been noticed. The Green Revolution embodied in the new seeds and widespread use of fertilizers changed the context. Can we project with confidence the gains of green revolution into the future? Or shall we once again face the menacing situation of widening foods gaps when population expands in the coming two decades?

This exercise involves two problems, i.e., population increase and food production increase. In the past thirty years population increased at the rate of 2.15 per cent per annum between 1951 and 1961 and 2.48 per cent per year between 1961 and 1971 and 2.22 per cent between 1971 and 1981. Though the increase in trend is not very steep but if we analyse this increase after 1981 it will be considered steep rather it is described as population explosion. The increase is held responsible due to the steep decline in the death rate from 29 per thousand to 16 per thousand between 25 years after independence, and secondly, there was only a gentle reduction in the birth rate from 42 to 39 per thousand between this period. Even if we adopt the modest estimate of population growth the country is likely to add about 25 crores of population by the year A.D. 2000. The medium estimate will be about 6 crores more during this period. In other words more than 55 crores more people will be in the country by the turn of the century. The population will be nearly double to A.D. 2000.[1]

No doubt with the increase of population there will be an increase of food production with an encouraging rate as we have noticed after 1951 that population increased by 2.03 per cent and food production increased by 2.65 per cent. In other words we have noticed that farm production as a whole outpaced population growth. But the consumption outpaced production which required imports of foodgrains. With the low level of consumption of foodgrains (395 grams per head per day) in 1951, the country developed strain on supply with rising incomes as the per capita income increased by 30 per cent and the availability of foodgrains increased by 18 per cent during 1951–71 even this performance was made possible with imports. However, at the lowest the requirement of foodgrains by the year A.D. 2000 is likely to be close to 200 million tonnes with the upper limit of requirement is likely to be in the neighbourhood of 238 million tonnes or 261 million tonnes (depending on the assumptions). The challenge is to attain about double the present level of foodgrains production to the end of the century.

The Possibilities to increase the Foodgrains Production

The challenge of population explosion can only be solved by increasing the production of food. The rate of growth of foodgrains production during 1951–61 was 2.7 per cent per annum. It is now discouraging to note that over half of the total increase was received from the increased area under cultivation because during 1961–71 the contribution of area increase was very low because of the exhaustion of potentiality of expansion of area under cultivation and largely the increase was received from the increased yield in some major crops of green revolution. Hence the future growth of production will have to come almost entirely through increased productivity. We can adopt various approaches to face this challenge, and the major among them will be the technology and the consumption behaviour of the people. For this we need change both in technology as well as in consumption behaviour. A suitable agricultural technology for each region and its large scale availability as well as the taste and the preference of the consumers should be considered which is because of the increase in per head income likely to be changed. To do full justice to the dynamics of the situation on the demand and the supply side, we require a project of the entire system, or in terms of model a system of equations that would bring out the relationships of prices, production inputs, tastes, preferences and technology.

It requires a number of lengthy exercises like to measure the trends regarding land use, areas under irrigation, cropping intensity, area under individual crops and crop yield. No doubt, if all the cultivable wastelands are brought under cultivation and its yield level is obtained to the level of high yield regions the contribution in total production will be very high, if all the cultivated land is brought under irrigation upto A.D. 2000 as it has been indicated by the Irrigation Commission that all the water resources will be tapped by A.D. 2000 to irrigate the present cultivated area definitely the production increase will be more than the requirement because the proportion of irrigation to the total cropped area is very low. The increased irrigation facilities will increase the intensity of cropping. The major problem of today is the lack of irrigation. However, water is a crucial factor in Indian agriculture. It will also allow the introduction of HYV and fertilizer and other technology. The role of individual crop is very significant in increased production as it is evident from the cropwise yield level. If the cropping pattern is changed and high yield giving crops are introduced over larger area the total production achieved through this will be enough to feed the growing population. If the land is coaxed well the country can feed more than five times of the present population. Lastly other inputs like fertilizers, labours, market etc. will be largely available if we are able to tackle the above mentioned situation. But on the whole the present trend of the availability of various infrastructure facilities and the present system does not seem very encouraging. Therefore, the analysis of the present trend is necessary to project for future.

The trend of foodgrains production indicate that it experienced a growth rate of 2.64 per cent per annum after the planning till now. The growth rate varied according to the period considered. During the first decade of planning, higher growth rate was experienced primarily as the area under crops rapidly expanded. Subsequently, the growth of production slowed down as it depended largely on yield expansion. A slow rate of production growth, a little above the population growth rate, worked as a constraint on the expansion of the overall economy. In an inter-sectoral balanced growth, the growth rate of agriculture should be around 6.6 per cent per year to support an annual growth rate of 10.5 to 10 per cent in the industrial sector. In the plan period of 1978–83 the compound growth of agriculture is envisaged to be 3.98 per cent per annum and we have been able to achieve this goal, the corresponding growth rate for the overall economy is envisaged to be 7.4 per cent per annum.[2] Therefore, the projections for farm production for the year A.D. 2000 are to be considered in the above background.

With the assumption of continuation of past trends in regard to the expansion of area under crops, the irrigated area, crop yields and allocation of land to different crops, the crop production would increase annually at a compound rate of 1.76 per cent. The growth rate is likely to slow down in the future as compared to that observed in the past mainly because the limit to the expansion of land under crops will be reached much before the end of the present century. The expansion of irrigation in the past has not been at a rate adequate enough to support a high rate of growth of yield per hectare. With the assumption that the irrigation potential will be full exploited before the end of this century, the growth rate jumps to 2.5 per cent which is mainly the result of increased yields per hectare. The technology has undergone a change in the past one decade. The HYVs represent a major breakthrough in regard to wheat. A slow but perceptible progress has been achieved in regard to paddy. Though some problems have been faced regarding bajra, jowar and maize, new strains on the basis of hybridisation have been successfully developed for these crops.

According to the infomed sources, the technological breakthrough witnessed during the late sixties may be repeated on a similar or a little lower scale for different crops, on an average, at an interval of 5-7 years. The 3-5 new breakthroughs may, therefore, be expected in the next two decades.[3] It may therefore be possible to cover almost the entire land under foodgrains with HYVs. Though the newly introduced varieties may have higher yield levels, while the other varieties may be on the way out, the average yield per hectare which may be assumed with some confidence may average around the yield levels now obtaining for HYVs in the farmers fields. With these assumption the growth rate of production jumps upto a little less than twice, while the growth rate of gross cropped area remains unchanged, the major expansion is witnessed in the case of yields per hectare.[4]

Expecting per capita income to double in the A.D. 2000 may not be considered as an ambitious goal. This goal implies that the per capita income should expand at a compound rate of 2.7 per cent per annum. To make an allowance for linkages, the rate of growth of per capita income may have to be close to 3.0. If the population on an average is expected to double till A.D. 2000, the compound rate of growth of population would be around 2.34. It may even be slightly higher, as some of the estimates suggest that population may increase by 7.7 per cent. To attain the goal of doubling the per capita income and also to keep pace with the growth of population, the overall growth rate of the economy would be above 5 per cent. A safe margin would suggest that the rate should be closer to 5.5 per cent. A growth rate of 4 per cent for agriculture, therefore, may be considered the minimum necessary, and a little higher than 4 per cent may be considered desirable. We should, however, remind ourselves that the rate of growth of crop production envisaged by us presumes much faster increase in the area under irrigation, a much higher rate of increase in the research activity to improve the technology and a much faster expansion in the use of fertilizers.

Foodgrains — Demand and Supply

We have not worked out demand projection because several independent estimates of demand for foodgrains and other crops are available on the basis of exercises done by other scholars and agencies. The National Commission on Agriculture in its report gives projections of gross and net demand for different crops. In the case of foodgrains, the difference between the gross and the net is about 18 per cent and is accounted by the requirement for seed, feed and wastage.

TABLE 9.1: Crop Production in A.D. 2000 (Million Tonnes)

Crops	Average (1969—71)	A.D. 2000
Rice	41.8	201.0
Wheat	23.5	62.9
Jowar	8.5	78.9
Bajra	6.2	9.7
Cereals	92.7	433.5
Pulses	11.5	16.1
Foodgrains	104.2	450.5

V.M. Rao Projected the consumption levels on the basis of National Sample Surveys (NSS) data. His projection is based on the assumption that the lowest 30 per cent of the total population eventually will move upward and that their level of per capita consumption of foodgrains will improve at least upto the level now enjoyed by families in the middle income groups. The National Commission on Agriculture has assumed different expenditure elasticities of demand for different items of foodgrains for rural and urban areas these are based on NSS data for 1971. Its demand projections are based on the assumption that the proportion of urban and rural population would change. As envisaged by the National Commission, the quantity of foodgrains consumed would increase between 1971 and the year A.D. 2000 at a compound rate of 2.16 per cent at the lowest and 2.47 per cent per annum at the highest, which would, however, give a lower increase of 0.32 and 0.75 per cent respectively in calorie intake. Kirit Parikh's estimates suggest a higher level of demand for foodgrains at 474 million tonnes and as low as 288 million tonnes (under different assumption) compared to the 1971 level, implying an annual compound rate of growth of demand for foodgrains of 5 per cent at the highest and 3.31 per cent at the lowest respectively. While the demand projections of Kirit Parikh seem to be on the higher side, those of the National Commission on Agriculture seem to be rather low. Rao's projections give an annual compound rate of growth of 2.99 per cent. If population grows at the rate of 2.11 per cent then the per capita rate of growth for foodgrains intake implied in the demand projections of Rao would be 0.88 per cent. Parikh's demand projection estimates indicate a per capita increase in foodgrains consumption of 1.80 per cent at the lowest which is about double that of V.M. Rao; but a little more than double that projected by the National Commission on Agriculture. The highest growth rate of demand per capita of 2.66 per cent projected by Parikh is three time the rate estimated by Rao.

Pulses

While the overall foodgrain position may suggest comfortable supply in the year A.D. 2000. Almost all supply projection suggest a low level of production of pulses, leaving a wide margin between the projected demand and the projected supply of pulses. In almost all the projection indicated supply seems to be fairly comfortable regarding the level of protein intake per day per capita. This is partly due to the fact that there might be a shift in the consumption from inferior to superior cereals. Grains like wheat have a high protein content. Wheat for instance, gives around 11.8 per cent protein; maize, bajra and jowar have protein content varying between 22 and 25 per cent, the gap that may be left by lower supply of pulses may perhaps be adequately filled up by increased consumption of superior cereals.

We have assumed the relative prices of commodities to remain unchanged. However, a serious gap between the demand for and the supply of pulses may create pressures on prices of pulses. This pressure of rising prices may be inadequate to initiate the transfer of land from cereals to pulses, if the former enjoy a big technological advantage. But if prices rise drastically at some stage, the area under pulses may tend to increase. Though the reallocation may result in a slightly lower calorie intake, it may not affect the protein level to a substantial extent.

TABLE 9.2: Demand Projections for foodgrains for A.D. 2000 (Million Tonnes)

Crops	Projection by operational Research Group		Projection by Kirit Parikh		Projection by National Commision on Agriculture		projection by V.M. Rao
	High	Low	High	Low	High	Low	
Rice	93.9	80.0	197	121	91.0	84.6	103.0
Jowar	14.9	13.6	49	28	—	—	—
Bajra	14.1	11.8	19	11	—	—	—
Maize	—	—	28	16	—	—	—
Millets	22.2	19.5	28	17	—	—	—
Wheat	59.8	45.5	77	51	56.5	50.4	71.0
Total cereals	204.8	170.4	398	244	193.6	181.6	—
Total Pulses	—	—	76	44	30.4	25.5	39.0
Total Foodgrains.	237.8	196.0	474	288	225.3	205.3	261.0

References

1. Jaipal, P.A., Second India Studies: Population, Macmillan Co. of India Ltd., Bombay, 1975, p. 122.
2. Govt. of India, Draft Five Year Plan, 1978–83, Vol. II (Planning Commission), New Delhi, 1978, p. 7.
3. National Commission on Agriculture, Rice Development in India: Problems and prospects (Report of the Study team) constituted by the National Commission on Agriculture, New Delhi (mimco) p. 45.
4. Agricultural Development of India, Policy and Problems, Orient Longman, 1979, p. 607.

10

Summary, Conclusion and Recommendations

This monograph has attempted a state level analysis of trends in area, production and yield of foodgrain crops, supply and demand for foodgrains, food availability, surplus and deficit situation in the country as well as potentials for development and perspectives for A.D. 2000 and lastly the various agricultural development strategies. It has also discussed a number of policy questions arising out of the result. The following main observations can be deduced from this investigations:

(1) In India about 81 per cent area is devoted to cereal crops to the total foodgrain crops of the country and this distribution is not uniform in all the states of India but it is observed that in all the states cereals are the dominating crops. It is because of the higher yield level of cereals than the pulses crops as cereals are contributing about 90 per cent by devoting only 81 per cent of the gross cultivated area and pulses only 10 per cent to the total foodgrain production of the country by devoting about 20 per cent land. A state level analysis has been done for this problem.

(2) The yield level of cereals and pulses per hectare of cultivated area very largely, i.e., for the country as a whole it is 1078 kg. for cereals and 504 kg. for pulses, which is the main reason for the domination of cereal crops in all the states of the country. All the possible lands have been devoted to cereals and it has realised that there was a big encroachment of land from pluses crops to the cereals. The highest yield of cereal is received from Punjab, i.e., 2431 kg./hect. while 855 kg./hect. for pulses from Haryana.

(3) Growth level of cereal during this period is about 22 per cent while pulses recorded a negative growth by 2.14 per cent in spite of high demand of cereals in the country.

(4) Various factors have been associated with the increase and decrease of yield and production of foodgrains such as environmental, institutional and technological. It was realised that it is impossible to overlook the role of environmental factors because 93 per cent area is still under the control of environmental factors and only 7 per cent area is without the control of environmental phenomenon. It is because of the environmental factors the yield level varies from one geophysical regions to another which is shown in the Table 10.1. The higher yield is received from those physical complex where there is no environmental control or the negative role is less rigorous. These regions can be used for planning purposes to give priority for mechanization to control the physical factors.

TABLE 10.1: Yield kg. per hectare in each Regions

(A)	Northern Mountains	980	kg./hect.
(B)	North Eastern Mountains and Valleys	1252	kg./hect.
(C)	East coast	993	kg./hect.
(D)	West coast	1636	kg./hect.
(E)	Gujarat Plain	1253	kg./hect.
(F)	N.W. Arid Zone	561	kg./hect.
(G)	N.W. Semi Arid Zone	910	kg./hect.
(H)	Peninsula Plateau South	1519	kg./hect.
(I)	Peninsula Plateau Central	682	kg./hect.
(J)	Peninsula Plateau North East	792	kg./hect.
(K)	Peninsula Plateau North West	628	kg./hect.
(L)	Lower Ganges Plain	1235	kg./hect.
(M)	Upper Ganges Plain	1353	kg./hect.
(N)	Punjab Plain	1410	kg./hect.

(5) Various technological factors have been analysed like tractors per thousand of cultivated area, fertilizers use per hectare, irrigation machinery and per cent area irrigated in each yield and growth categories. It was observed that high yield level region is occupying high concentration of various inputs and similar situation was also observed regarding the high and low growth rates. It was noticed that the role of various inputs are more vital because there is large variations in yield level between the mechanized and non-mechanized area and the gap can be noticed at least more than three times in yield.

(6) In this monograph various institutional factors have been studied like land ownership (high and low land holding) and its relationship with the yield level, agricultural labourers (demand and labour), land tenure system and agricultural productivity and agricultural income per head and its relationship with agricultural productivity as well as to plan the area for its future regarding the investment policy and aptitude for investment. It was noticed that large size of land holdings have lower yield than the small size of the land holdings which direct us to plan and distribute the landholdings to get more production for the existing cultivated land. The problem of tenancy is one of the major problem and was held for low production in the country. Agricultural labourers are available in abundance in those areas where medium level yield is found and medium level of concentrations of agricultural labourers are found in the regions of high yield level. This observation creates a doubt either agricultural labourers are considered as an input or not. No doubt its role is not equivalent to the mechanization but its role is held positive in the high concentration of agricultural labourers regions with agricultural productivity.

(7) India's population has been rapidly increasing. In the year A.D. 2001 it will be close to 950 million. This spurt in growth will bear directly on all aspects of agricultural growth, productivity, food deficit and food surplus.

(8) In the year (1979) food surplus occurred in a number of States and food deficit in some states also. This situation was observed at district level and it was realised that in all the states of India except of Haryana and Punjab food deficit occurred in a number of districts.

(9) In this year (average '1979' for three years) food surplus was recorded about 20.42 million metric tonnes and food deficit was about 7.7 million tonnes, thus creating a net surplus of roughly 12.72 million tonnes. Though for a single year of 1979 the net surplus was calculated at about 21.5 million tonnes because of the very good weather while in other two years weather was not so good, therefore, the average picture for surplus came down on average basis of three years including 1979 also.

(10) It is observed that food surplus occurred mainly due to the high yield and higher growth rate and food deficit which is mainly associated with the low yield and stagnant growth. The population is held one of the major factor to measure the deficit and surplus situation as it was realised that low yield with low density of population create a situation of surplus in food while high yield and high density of population may create a situation of food deficit and this situation was observed in West Bengal, Kerala, Bihar and Eastern Uttar Pradesh etc. For example in Kerala with much higher yield than Rajasthan, the caloric intake per head per day was calculated at about 3000 for Rajasthan and 1500 for Kerala.

(11) It is observed that food production largely depends more on irrigation than on fertilizer. Therefore, in order to enhance food surplus and reduce food deficit, we should emphasize more on irrigation than on other inputs. On Irrigated land higher productivity can be achieved through fertilizer use only. Without irrigation facilities fertilizer use is not possible. Therefore, in all respect irrigation is the base to transform the agriculture and the expansion of irrigation facilities is possible at large scale.

(12) The availability of investments and inputs for growth purposes are concentrated only in about 20 per cent area.

(13) The concentration of land ownership gives some confusing results, i.e., a high productivity is occurring in some areas in spite of high land inequality. On the other hand low level productivity has been occurring in 45 per cent area in spite of relatively less land inequality. It is because of the lesser investments by way of inputs, leading to greater fragmentation of holdings and effect of various factors like social and cultural.

(14) The amount of food deficit progressively decreases with the rise in irrigated area. Conversely, the amount of food surplus increases with the increase in irrigated area.

(15) Due to the lack of data of castes in India it is very difficult to find out the effect of caste system on agricultural productivity at macro- and meso level as different castes have different cropping pattern and aptitude for agricultural operations. Therefore, a sample micro-level (village) study should be undertaken to get a representative picture for the country as a whole.

(16) A great deal of penetrating research is urgently needed to throw light on the crucial questions of interrelationship between the measure of land inequality and indices of agricultural growth and development in India. In this respect some homogeneous natural regions and sub-regions should be considered to collect data for this problem. No doubt that land distribution on equality basis is necessary but it should be provided with required inputs and checking the fragmentation of a land holding. The first temporary effect of such redistribution will very possibly be a fall in productivity unless it is simultaneously buttressed by legislation preventing alienation and fragmentation, and by positive steps for consolidation, irrigation, and institutional availability of inputs along with enforcement of productivity and output delivery norms.

The above mentioned hurdles should be crossed through technological, institutional, managerial and agrarian policy side. The 'National Commission on Agriculture' (1976) estimated that "the total cereal requirement on the basis of data on improved diets for 1976 that is, on the assumption that everybody, irrespective of Social or economic status or geographical location, would eat his due requirement of cereals, was about 88.8 million tonnes. To this may be added about 12 million tonnes of requirements by way of pulses. The total comes to about 100-101 million tonnes. Allowing for seeds, feed, waste, industrial use and for annual increase in population at the rate of 2 per cent and a figure of 0.6 for increase in the annual income elasticity of demand, we find, particularly since 1975, that the demand for cereals is not keeping up with their production.

In India the agricultural land is used for the maximization of personal profits and not of production. The production of foodgrains has grown from a mere 50 million tonnes in 1950 to 131 million tonnes in 1979 with about 20 million tonnes of buffer stocks, but a large proportion of the population still goes hungry. No more than 150 mandays per acre are worked in India compared to 450 in Japan and about 650 in Tachai. Yet with strictly equitable distribution a mere 110 million tonnes would give adequate nutrition to everybody. The buffer stocks of about 20 million tonnes are therefore, in a way fictitious and in another way catastrophic, on the basis of the rates of cereal consumption recommended by the National Institute of Nutrition, 20 million tonnes of foodgrains can keep roughly 40 million of the urban and rural poor-infants, children, women and men-adequately fed for calories for three years together. This can make a major difference between the current picture of starvation and malnutrition in India on one side and adequate nutrition for the bulk of her deprived population on the other. The food-for-work programme for building up national and community assets can easily be lifted from its below market, semistarvation-wages-in-kind to a full-wage-in-kind programme, and put enough of self-respecting purchasing power in the hands of those who are at present unemployed.

The way to 2000 will be undoubtedly uphill and strenuous. The Indian peasant has demonstrated that he can make it, even if the circumstances are not all that propitious, let alone ideal. It all the more stands to reason, therefore, that given the will and the requisite social and political organization the target should be reasonably within reach (A. Mitra 1978).

Other charges against India's Agricultural Policy should be removed such as neglect of agriculture, deliberate underinvestment in this sector as a whole and in some particular regions and under pricing of agricultural commodities. The increasing rate of cost of production and due to the diminishing return in some agriculturally advanced pocket the farmers are under frustration. Therefore, the inputs cost should be controlled. The supply of various inputs to small and marginal farmers should be made easily available to increase the agricultural productivity especially among the 'small and the marginal farmers' which is the most disadvantageous group of the Indian Society.

Selected Bibliography

Acharya, K.C.S. (1983), *Food Security System of India*, Concept Pub. Co. New Delhi.

Agarwal, N.C. (1961), *The Food Problem of India*, Bombay.

Agarwal, P.C., (1965), Measurement of Agricultural Efficiency in Bastar Distt. A Factional Approach, *Proceedings of Summer School in Geography* (mimeo), Aligarh Muslim University, Aligarh, pp. 50-59.

Agarwal, S.K., (1966), Intensive Cultivation Programme in Uttar Pradesh: A Retrospect, *Indian Journal of Agricultural Economics*, 21(4), pp. 134-160.

Ahmad, Z. (1966), The Measurement of Productivity and Farming Efficiency in Village Manupura, *The Geographical Observer*, 2, pp. 68-82.

Ahmad, Z. M. (1972), The Social and Economic Implications of the Green Revolution in Asia, *International Labour Review*, January, Geneva.

Ali Mohammad (1977), *Food and Nutrition in India*, Rajesh Publications, New Delhi

Ali Mohammad (1978), *Dynamics of Agricultural Development in India*, Concept Publishing Co., New Delhi.

Ali Mohammad (1978), *Situation of Agriculture Food and Nutrition in Rural India*, Concept Publishing Co., New Delhi.

Ali Mohammad (1978), *Studies in Agricultural Geography*, Rajesh Publications, New Delhi.

Ali Mohammad (1980), Regional Imbalances in Levels and Growth of Agricultural Productivity – A Study of Assam, *The Geographer*, Aligarh Geographical Society, Aligarh.

Ali Mohammad (1984), Growth Structure in Indian Agriculture – Assam, Bihar, Uttar Pradesh, Rajasthan and Jammu & Kashmir, (mimeo), *Department of Geography & Regional Development*, Kashmir University, Srinagar (J & K).

Ali Mohammad, (1981), Regional Imbalances in levels of Agricultural Productivity, *Perspective in Agricultural Geography* (ed.), Concept Pub. Co. New Delhi.

Ali Mohammad, (1981), Sources of Variations in Agricultural Productivity, *Perspective in Agricultural Geography* (ed.), Concept Pub. Co., New Delhi.

Amani, K.Z. (1977), *Agricultural land use in Aligarh Districts*, Aligarh.

Angrish, A.C. (1966), Some Aspects of Food Problem in India *Congress Committee Economic Review*, Vol. 18.

Aykroyd, W.R. (1951), The Nutritive Value of Indian Foods and the Planning of Satisfactory Diets, *Health Bulletin*, No. 23.

Bardhan, P., (1970), Green Revolution and Agricultural Labourers, *Economic and Political Weekly*, 5, (29-31) July, pp. 1239-46.

Bhalla, G.S. (1979), *Performance of Indian Agriculture*, Sterling Publishing Co., New Delhi.

Bhalla, G.S. and Chadha, G.K. (1983), *Green Revolution and the Small Peasant*, Concept Pub. Co. New Delhi.

Bhalla, Shiela (1977), Agricultural Growth - Role of Institutional and Infrastructural Factors, *Economic and Political Weekly*, Vol. III, No. 45, Nov. 5-12.

Bhatia, B.M. (1970), *India's Food Problem and Policy Since Independence*, Bombay, 1970.

Bhatia, S.S., (1967), Spatial Variations Changes and Trends in Agricultural Efficiency in Uttar Pradesh, 1953--1963, *Indian Journal of Agricultural Economies*, 22, (I), pp. 66-88.

Borck, K. (1955), Input-output Analysis as Basis for Productivity Measurement, *Productivity Measurement Review*, OECD, No. 1.

Bose, P.K., (1968), Human Factor is the Main Cause for Stagnation in Agricultural Productivity. *Science & Culture*, 34 (4), pp. 155-58.

Brown, L.R. (1960), The Agricultural Revolution in India, *Foreign Affairs,* July.

Brown, L.R., (1975), The World Food Prospect, *Science*, 190 (4219), 12 Dec., pp. 1053-59.

Carding, T., (1967), No Food, No Water, No Clothes: These are the Facts of Life of Bihar, *Guardian*, June 1.

Chaterji, A. and Maitreya, P., (1964), Some Aspects of Regional Variations in Agricultural Productivity and Development in West Bengal, *Indian Journal of Agricultural Economics*, 19 (1) pp. 207-12.

Chatterjee, P., (1966), Productivity in Indian Agriculture, *All India Congress Working Committee Economic Review*, (Special No.). 17 (14 & 15), pp. 157-62.

Clark, C. and Haswell, M.R. (1957), *The Economics of Subsistence Agriculture*, 3rd ed., MacMillan, London.

Clark, C., (1967), *Population Growth and Landuse*, MacMillan, London.

Crosson, T.R., Institutional obstacles to Expansion of World Food Production, *Science*, 188, (4188), pp. 519-24.

Crowe, P.R., (1933), The Analysis of Rainfall Probability: A Geographical Method and its Application to European Data, *Scottish Geographical Magazine*, 49, pp. 73-91.

Dandekar, V.M. (1964), Regional Variations in Agricultural Development and Productivity, Summary of Group Discussion, *Indian Journal of Agricultural Economics*, 19 (1), pp. 263-66.

Dantwala, M.L. (1951), *India's Food Production*, Bombay.

Davies, C., (1950), *Mechanized Agriculture*, London.

Dayal, Edison, (1978), A Measure of Crop Intensity, *The Professional Geographer*, 30 (3), August, pp. 289-96.

Deb, P.C. and Agrawal, B.K. (1974), Rural Leadership in Green Revolution, *Research Publication*, Delhi.

Department of Agriculture, (U.P.) (1972), Small Farmers and Landless Labours Problems and their Solution, Lucknow.

Desai, Mubarik, V.R., (1969), *Strategy of Food and Agriculture in India*, Lalvani, Madras.

Dewan, M.L. (1982), *Agriculture and Rural Development in India: A Case Study on the Dignity of Labour*, Concept Pub. Co., New Delhi.

Dharm, N. (1972), Growth and Imbalances in Indian Agriculture, *Economic and Political Weekly*, 7 (13).

Dhondyal, S.P. (1964), Regional Variation in Agricultural Development and Productivity, *Ind. J. of Agr. Eco.* 19 (1); pp. 190-202.

Directorate of Economics and Statistics, *Indian Agriculture in Brief* (fifteenth edition), Ministry of Agriculture and Irrigation, New Delhi, 1976.

Directorate of Economics and Statistics, Estimates of Area and Production of Principal Crops of India, 1975-76, 1977-78 1978-79, Govt. of India, New Delhi.

Dixit, R.S. (1973), High Yielding Varieties Programme in Aligarh, *Kurukshetra*, 21 (16), pp. 14-15.

Dixon, J.A. and Gavan, J.D., India: A Perspective on the Food Situation, *Science*, 188 (4188), pp. 541-49.

Dominador, Z.K. (1969), Geography of Food and Population, *The Philippine Geographical Journal*, July - August - September, Vol. 13, No. 3.

Dovring, F. (1967), Productivity of Labour in Agricultural Production, *Agricultural Experiment Station Bulletin* No. 726, University of Illinois College of Agriculture Urbana, Illinois.

Dumont, R. (1957), *Types of Rural Economy*, London.

Dwivedi, R.C. (1972), *New Strategy for Agricultural Development in India*, Loyal Book Depot, Meerut.

Edde, A.D.M., Phillips and Tarton, B.J. (1975), *Environment, Man and Economic Change*, Longman, London.

Eicher, C. and Witt, L. (ed.) (1964), *Agriculture in Economic Development*, McGrow Hill Series.

Emergency Agricultural Production Programme, *Lok Rajya*, May 1973, pp. 16-46.

Enyedi, G.Y. (1964), Geographical Types of Agriculture, *Applied Geography in Hungary* (ed. M. Pecsi), Budapest.

Evenson, R.E. and Kislen, Y. (1975), Agricultural Research and Productivity, *New Haven*, Yale University Press.

Everybody is Hungry, *Time*, Dec. 25, 1972.

F.A.O. (Annually), *State of Food and Agriculture*, Rome

Face of Hunger, *Indian Express*, April, 9, 1967.

Failure of Two Crops Leads to Distress, *Financial Express*, June 16, 1969.

Famine Conditions in Villages, *Link*, Vol. 8 (10) October 17, 1965, pp. 13-15.

Farmer, B.H., The Pioneer Peasant in India, *Ceylon Geographer*, 17, 49.

Farmer, B.N., (1974), *Agricultural Colonization Since Independence*, Oxford University Press, New York, Published for the Royal Institute of International Affairs.

Feeding the Hungry, *Times of India*, Sept. 23, 1972.

Fighting Scarcity on War-Footing, *Financial Express*, No. 3, 1972.

Food and Agriculture Organisation of the United Nations, *Inter-Relationship Between Agrarian Reforms and Agricultural Development*, Rome, 1953.

Food and Agriculture Organisation of the United Nations, *Agricultural Credit for Small Farmers*, Rome, 1952.

Food and Agriculture Organisation of the United Nations, *Essential Considerations in Mechanization of Farming*, Washington, 1950.

Food and Agriculture Organisation of the United Nations, *Community Organisation for Irrigation in the United States*, Rome 1952.

Food and Agriculture Organisation of the United Nations, *Farm Management Investigations for Agricultural Improvement*, Rome, 1952.

Food and Agriculture Organisation of the United Nations, *Progress of Economic Problems in Farm Mechanisation*, Rome, 1952.

Food and Agriculture Organisation of the United Nations, *Crop-Production Levels and Fertilizer Use*, Rome, 1962.

Food and Agriculture Organisation of the United Nations, Basic Factors Affecting the Growth of Productivity in Agriculture, *The State of Food and Agriculture*, Rome, 1963.

Food and Agriculture Organisation of the United Nations, *Smaller Farmlands Can Yield More, Raising Agricultural Productivity by Technical Change*, Rome, 1969.

Food and Agriculture Organisation of The United Nations, *Planning for Agricultural Development, The State of Food and Agriculture,* Rome, 1970.

Food and Drought, *Indian Express*, February, 2, 1970.

Ganguli, B. (1938), *Trends of Agriculture and Population in the Ganges Valley*, London.

Ghosh, D. (1946), *Pressure of Population and Economic Efficiency in India*, Calcutta.

Gopalan, C. (1966), Major Nutritional Problem of India and South-East Asia, *Proceedings of Seventh International Geographical Congress*, Vol. 3.

Govinda Rajan, S.V., and Gopala Rao, H.G., (1971), *Soil and Crop Productivity*, New Delhi.

Gowverneur, J. (1971), *Productivity and Factor Proportion in Less Developing Countries*, Oxford.

Greenland, D.J. (1975), Bringing the Green Revolution in the Shifting Cultivator, *Science*, 190 (4217), 28, Nov., pp. 841-44.

Griliches, Z. (1968), *Productivity and Technology, International Encyclopaedia of Social Sciences,* 1, pp. 241-45.

Gupta, B.D. (1976), Agrarian Change and New Technology in India, *U.N. Research Institute for Social Development*, Geneva.

Hatch, J. (1967), Hunger and Thirst in Bihar, *New Stateman*, Sept. 1.

Hauser, P.M. (1963), *The Population Dilemma* (ed.) Englewood Cliffs, Prentice Hall, New Jersey.

Hayami, Y. and Kinuya, I. (1969), International Comparison of Agricultural Productivities, *Farm Economists*, 11 (10), pp. 407-19.

Hayamı, Y. and Ruttan, V.W. (1970), Agricultural Productivity Differences Among Countries, *The American Economic Review*, 60 (5), Dec. pp. 895-911.

Haystead, L. and Fite, G.C. (1955), *The Agricultural Regions of United States*, Norman, Oklahama.

Heady, Earl O. (1964), *Economics of Agricultural Production and Resource Use*, New Delhı.

Hirsch, H.G. (1943), Crop Yielding Index, *Journal of Farm Economics*, 25 (3) p. 583.

Holst, W. (1967), Planning for Self-sufficiency in Foodgrains, *Eco. and Pol. Weekly*, 2 (27), 8 July, pp. 1211-27.

Horring, J. (1964), *Concept of Productivity Measurement in Agriculture on a National Scale*, OECD, Documentation in Food and Agriculture, Paris.

Horring, J. and Von Den Noort, P.C. (1963), The Trends of Productivity Income in Dutch Agriculture 1949–61, *Productivity Measurement Review*, 33, pp. 34-63.

Hsieh, S.C. and Ruttan, V.W. (1967), Environmental, Technological and Institutional Factors in the Rice Production: Philippine, Thailand and Taiwan, *Food Research Institute Studies*, 7 (3), pp. 304-41.

Hutchinson, J. B., (1965), *Essays on Crop Plant Evaluation*, Cambridge University Press.

Hutchinson, J.B. (1956), Land and Human Populations, *The Advancement of Science*, January 23.

India, Directorate of Economics and Statistics, *Food Situation in India*, 939-53, Manager of Publications, 1954.

India, Directorate of Economics and Statistics, *Indian Food Statistics*, New Delhi 1949.

India, Ministry of Food and Agriculture, *Review of the Food Situation and Food Statistics*, February, 1964.

Indian Council of Agricultural Research, *Handbook of Agriculture*, New Delhi, 1961.

Indian Council of Agricultural Research, *Handbook of Manures and Fertilizers*, New Delhi, 1964.

Indian Council of Medical Research, *The Nuritive Value of Indian Foods and Planning of Satisfactory Diets*, New Delhi, 1964.

Indian Council of Medical Research, *Results of Diets Survey in India*, New Delhi, 1957.

Indian Food Facts (tasle), *Economic Studies* Vol. 7, 1967.

International Labour Organisation, *Hunger and Social Policy*, Geneva, 1963.

Jain, S.C. (1966), *Agricultural Policy in India*, Allied, New Delhi.

Jain, S.C. (1967), *Changing Indian Agriculture*, Vora, Bombay.

James, O.B. (1963), Farm Tenancy and Productivity in Agriculture: A Case Study of U.S., *Food Research Institute Studies*, 4(1), pp. 25-38.

John, P.V., Impact of Cropping Pattern on Agricultural Output, *Indian Journal of Agricultural Economics*, 22(3), pp. 72-75.

Johnson, P. (1970), Where there are No Fat Villagers, Ceres, FAO, *Review*, (Italy), Vol. 3(4), July-August, pp. 35-39.

Just, R.E., et.al. (1979), Technological Change in Agriculture, *Science*, 206 (4424), 14 Dec. pp. 1277-80.

Kamath, M.G. (1954), Rice Cultivation in India, *Indian Council of Agricultural Research*, New Delhi.

Kanitkar, S. and Gokhle (1968), *Dry Farming in India*, Indian Council of Agricultural Research, New Delhi.

Kanwar, J.S. (1969), Fertilizer – The Kingpin in Agriculture, *Indian Farming*, 18 (12).

Kanwar, J.S. (1970), The Role of Machinery in Modernization of Agriculture, *Indian Farming*, 19 (11).

Kaul, J.L. and Johl, S.S. (1967), Differentials in Productivity Growth in Punjab, *Agricultural Situation in India*, 22(1), pp. 3-7.

Kendall, M.G. (1939), The Geographical Distribution of Crop-productivity in England, *Journal of the Royal Statistical Society*, 162, pp. 21-48.

Kendrick, J.W. (1961), Productivity Trends in the United States, General Series 71, *Princeton National Bureau of Economic Research*.

Khan, W. (1971), Papers and Proceedings of the Workshop Cum - Seminar or Rural Institutions and Agricultural Development, *National Institute of Agricultural Development*, Hyderabad.

Kherdikar, D.N. (1967), Supplying Agricultural Machinery and Improved Implements for Agriculture, *Indian Journal of Public Administration*, 13 (3).

Khusro, A.M. (1965), Measurement of Productivity at Macro and Micro Level, *Journal of Indian Society of Agricultural Statistics*, 17 (2), pp. 278-83.

Kostrowicki, J., *A Geographical Typology of Agriculture: Principles and Methods* (Abstract), 20th I.G.U.

Kostrowicki, J., Agricultural Typology, *Bulletin of International Geographical Union*, 20.

Kostrowicki, J., *Principles, Basic Notions and Criteria of Agricultural Typology*, Conclusion Drawn from the Answers to the Commission's Questionnaire, I.G.U.

Krishan, R. (1973), *Intensive Agricultural Programme,* Aligarh – The Beacon Light (Special issue), Directorate of Agriculture, U.P. Lucknow.

Krishna, D. (1971), *The New Agricultural strategy,* Delhi.

Krishna, R. (1980), The Economic Development in India, *Scientific American* (New York), 243 (3) Sept., pp. 166-78.

Krishnaswamy, S.Y. (1958), *Food Production in India: Principles and Problems,* Bharti Books, Madras.

Lalvani, K. (1954), Food and Famines in India, *Arthvijnana*, Gabesana Mandir.

Leake, H.M. (1932), *The Foundation of Indian Agriculture*, Cambridge.

Lewis, A.B. (1969), Economic Land Classification in the Far East with reference to Basic Studies elsewhere, *World Agricultural Economics and Rural Sociology*, Abstracts, Review Articles, Nos. 9, 11.

Loomis, R.A. and Barton, G.T. (1961), Productivity of Agriculture United States 1870--1958, *Technical Bulletin No. 1238*, Agriculture Research Service, United States Department of Agriculture, Washington, D.C.

Macdonald, A.L. (1976), *Agricultural Technology in Developing Countries*, Rotterdam

Mackenzie, W. (1962), The Impact of Technological Change on the Efficiency of Production in Canadian Agriculture, *Canadian Journal of Agricultural Economics*, 10 (1), pp. 41-53.

Majid Hussain (1981), *Agricultural Geography*, Concept Publishing Co. New Delhi.

Majid Hussain (1983), *Crop-combination in India*, Concept Publishing Co., New Delhi.

Majumdar, D. (1965), Size of Farm and Productivity: A Problem of Indian Peasant Agriculture, *Economica*, 32.

Mathur, B.S. (1968), Increasing Agricultural Productivity: Role of Institutional Credit, *Productivity*, 9 (2), pp. 97-100.

Mathur, S.C. (ed. 1970), *Agricultural Policy and Food Self-sufficiency in India*, New Delhi.

Mauldin, W.P. (1980), Population Trends and Prospects, *Science*, 109 (4452), 4 July, pp. 148-57.

Meiburg, C.O. and Bandt, K. (1962), Agricultural Productivity in the United State: 1870-1960, *Food Research Institute Studies*, 3 (2).

Millar, C.E. (1963), *Soil Fertility*, New York.

Mills, P.C. (1952), Productivity and Economic Progress, *National Bureau of Economic Research*, Occasional Paper No. 38, New York.

Ministry of Food and Agriculture, Report on Location and Utilization of Wasteland in India, Part X, U.P., Govt. of India, 1962.

Ministry of Food and Agriculture, Intensive Agricultural Distt. Programme, Report (1961–63), *Expert Committee on Assessment and Evaluation*, Govt. of India, 1963.

Ministry of Irrigation and Power, *Report of the Irrigation Commission* 1972, 3, Part I, New Delhi.

Misra, Pratibha (1984), *Soil Productivity and Crop-potentials*, Concept Pub. Co., New Delhi.

Morgan, W.B., Munton, R.J.C. (1971), *Agricultural Geography*, Methuen, London.

Mubarik, D.V.R. (1969), *The Strategy of Food and Agriculture in India*, Lalvani Pub. House.

Mukerjee, S.K. (1968), Fertilizer Requirements for Increasing Food Production, *Science and Culture*, 34 (5), pp. 191-97.

National Council of Applied Economic Research, India, (1966). *A Strategy for Agricultural Planning*, New Delhi.

Neale, W.C. (1962), *Economic Change in Rural India, Land Tenure and Reform in U.P.*, 1800–1955, Yale University.

Nichollas, L., Sinclair, M.M. and Jalliffe, D.A., *Tropical Nutrition and Dietics*, Balliere Tindall and Co. London.

Noor Mohammed, (1980), *Agricultural Land Use in India*, Concept Publishing Co., New Delhi.

Noor Mohammmed, (Ed.) (1981), *Perspectives in Agricultural Geography*, 5 Vols. Concept Publishing Co. New Delhi.

Ohlin, G. (1967), Population Control and Economic Development, *Development Centre of the Organisation for Economic cooperation and Development*, Paris.

Oommen, M.A. (1962), Agricultural Productivity Trends in Kerala, *Agricultural Situation in India*, 17 (4), July, pp. 333-36.

Page, H.J. (1959), Trends in Fertilizer Consumption in Relation to World Food Supply, *Outlook on Agriculture*, 2.

Pandit, S.N. (1983), *Critical Study of Agricultural Productivity in Uttar Pradesh 1951-75*, Concept Pub. Co. New Delhi.

Patel, G.D. (1954), *The Indian Land Problem and Legislation*, Bombay.

Pearson, F. and Harper, F.A. (1945), *The World's Hunger*, New York.

Plimmer, R.H.A. (1955), *Food, Health and Vitamins*, London.

Poleman, T.T., World Food: A Perspective, *Science*, 188 (4188), pp. 510-18.

Pradhan, S.N. (1971), Role of Improved Agricultural Implements and Machinery in Rice Production, *Science and India's Food Problem*, New Delhi.

Prasad, V.L. Srinivasan, Measurement of Agricultural Efficiency in Andhra Pradesh with Respect to Food Crops, *Southern Economist*, Vol. 9, No. 16, pp. 13-15.

Proceedings of the Symposium on Cropping Patterns in India, *Indian Council of Agricultural Research* (ICAR), 1972.

Quigley, D.T., (1959), The National Malnutrition, Milwauki.

Rajamani, A.N. (1966), Approaches to Solving the Food Problem, All India Congress Committee, *Economic Review*, Vol. 17. April 15.

Rajgopalan, C., Singh, J. (1971), *Adoption of Agricultural Innovations*, National Pub. House, Delhi.

Randhava, M.S. (1959), *Farmers of India*, 4 Vols., Indian Council of Agri. Res.

Randhava, M.S. (1974), *The Green Revolution*, New Yrok, John Wiley and Sons.

Rangaswamy, P. et al., (1972), *India's Changing Farmers*, Allahabad.

Rao, C.H.H. (1975), *Technological Changes and Distributional Gains in Indian Agriculture*, Macmillan Co. India.

Rao, V.K.R.V. (1966), *India's Long Term Food Problem: An essay in Food and Nutrition*, Kerala University, Trivendrum.

Raychaudhari, S.P. (1975), *Problems of Fertilizer Use and Crop Production*, New Delhi.

Report on Indias Food Crisis and Steps to Meet it, Ministry of FACD & C (1959).

Revelle, R. (1974), Food & Population, *Scientific American*, 231 (3), pp. 160-70.

Richard, L.M. and Ernest. H.W. (1971), *The Geography of Poverty in the United States*, McGraw-Hill.

Rogers, E.M. (1962), *Diffusion of Innovations*, Glencoe.

Roy, S.E. (1971), Increasing Agricultural Production Through the Adoption of Improved Machinnery, *Science and India's Food Problem*, New Delhi, 1971, pp. 280-283.

Roy, T.C., New Horizon of Food Production, *Fertilizer News*, Vol. 2 No. 8, pp. 9-11.

Sajid, H. Zaidi (1982), *Rural India and Malnutrition: Implications Problems and Prospects,* Concept Pub. Co., New Delhi.

Sancheti, D.C. (1964), Productivity of Principal Cereals in Dry Area of Rajasthan, *Ind. J. of Agr. Eco.* 19 (1), pp. 202-7.

Sanderson, F.H., The Great Food Fumble, *Science*, 188 (4188), pp. 503-9.

Sapre, S.G. and Deshpande, V.D. (1964), Inter-district Variations in Agricultural Efficiency in Maharashtra State, *Indian Journal of Agri Economics*, 19(1), pp. 242-52.

Saran, R. (1965), Production Function Approach to the Measurement of Productivity in Agriculture, *Journal of the Indian Society of Agricultural Statistics*, 17 (2), pp. 265-78.

Sarin, L.L. (1968), Mechanization of Farming, *Yojana* 12(14), pp. 15-16.

Sarma, J.S. (1965), Measurement of Agricultural Productivity – Concepts, Definitions etc. *Journal of the Indian Society of Agricultural Statistics* 17(2), pp. 253-57.

Schultz, T.W. (1964), *Transforming Traditional Agriculture,* New Haven.

Sen, S.N. (1966), Trends in Agricultural Production and Growth Rate, *Changing Indian Agriculture* (ed. S.C. Jain), Bombay.

Shafi, M. (1967), Food Production Efficiency and Nutrition in India, *The Geographer,* 14, pp. 23-27.

Shafi, M. (1969), Can India Support Five Times Her Population, *Science Today,* 3., pp. 21-27.

Shafi, M. (1971), Measurement of Food Crop Productivity in India, *Studies in Applied and Regional Geography* (eds. M. Shafi and M. Raza), Aligarh, pp. 97-113.

Shafi, M. (1972), Measurement of Agricultural Productivity of the Great Indian Plains, *The Geographer,* 19 (11), pp. 4-13.

Shafi, M., (1984), *Agricultural Productivity and Regional Imbalances,* Concept Pub. Co. New Delhi.

Sharma, P.S. (1973), *Agricultural Regionalization of India,* New Delhi.

Shideler, J.H. (ed.) (1975), Agriculture in the Development of the Far East, *Agricultural History Centre,* University of California.

Siddiqi, M.F., (1967), Combinational Analysis – A Review of Methodology, *The Geographer,* 14, pp. 76-88.

Singh, D. et al., (1977), Crop-productivity Variation in India, *Journal of the Indian Society of Agricultural Statistics,* 29 (1), pp. 113-15.

Singh, H. (1966), Intensive Agricultural Approach to Agricultural Development, *Ind. Jour. of Agr. Eco.,* 21, pp. 141-49.

Singh, Jasbir (1972), Spatio-temporal Developments in Land use Efficiency in Haryana, *Geog. Rev. of India,* 1972.

Singh, Jasbir (1974), *Agricultural Atlas of India,* Vishal Publications, Kurukshetra.

Singh, Jasbir (1974), *The Green Revolution in India, How Green it is, Postscript to an Agricultural Atlas of India,* Vishal Publication, Kurukshetra.

Singh, Jasbir (1976), *Agricultural Geography of Haryana,* Vishal Pub., Kurukshetra.

Singh, T.P. (1977), *Drought-prone Areas of India,* People Pub. House, Delhi.

Singh, T.P. (1978), Bihar–A Study of Cropcombination Regions, *Indian Journal of Regional Science,* Vol. IX, No. 2, Kharagpur (W.B).

Sinha, B.N. (1968), Agricultural Efficiency in India, *The Geographer,* pp. 101-27.

Sivaraman, B. (1980), Approach to Higher Productivity of Crops, *Higher Productivity in Agriculture* (eds. D.K. Dasgupta and N.C. Chattopadhyay) Calcutta, pp. 4-12.

Sridharan, C.S. (1971), Role of Agricultural Machinery in Increasing Production, *Science and India's Food Problem*, New Delhi, pp. 271-74.

Stamp, L.D. (1940), Fertility, Productivity and Classification of Land in Britain, *The Geographical Journal*, 96, pp. 389-406.

Stamp, L.D. (1958), The Measurement of Land Resources, *The Geographical Review*, 48 (1).

Stout, T.T. & Ruttan, W. (1958), Regional Patterns of Technological Change in American Agriculture, *Journal of Farm Economics*, 40(2), pp. 196-207.

Streeter, C.P. (1970), *A Partnership to Improve Food Production in India*, New York.

Sukhatme, P.V. (1961), The World's Hunger and Future Needs in Food Supplies, *The Journal of the Royal Statistical Society*, Vol. 124, London.

Sukhatme, P.V. (1962), Food and Nutrition Situation in India, Pt II, *Indian Journal of Agricultural Economics*, Vol. 16.

Sukhatme, P.V. (1965), *Feeding India's Growing Millions*, Asia Publishing House, 1965.

Sukhatme, P.V. (1972), Protein Strategy and Agricultural Development, *31st Annual Conference of the Indian Society of Agricultural Economics*, Banaras Hindu University.

Swaminathan, M.S. (1968), Scientific Importance of HYV Programme, *Economic and Political Weekly*, 4 (1-2), pp. 67-75.

Swaminathan, M.S., (1983), *Science and the Conquest of Hunger*, Concept Pub. Co. New Delhi.

Tambad, S.B. (1965), Spatial and Temporal Variations in Agricultural Productivity in Mysore, *Indian Journal of Agricultural Economics*, 20, pp. 39-45.

Tambad, S.B. and Patel, K.V. (1970), Crop Yield Index as Measure of Productivity, *Eco. and Pol. Weekly*, 5 (25), June 20, pp. 878-79.

Taylor, M.C. (1966), *Foundation of Nutrition*, New York.

Teli, B.L. (1976), Irrigation and its Impact on Cropping Pattern, *Proceedings of Rajasthan Geographers Conference*, Kaladera.

Teli, B.L. (1977), Hydrological Regions of Rajasthan – An Analysis of Water Resource availability (M. Phil Dissertation), Regional Development, JNU, New Delhi.

Thingalaya, N.K. and Shetty, N.S. (1967), Measures of Farm Efficiency in Inter-regional Comparison, *Arth Vikas*, 3 (1), pp. 31-47.

Thorner, D. and Alice (1962), *Land and Labour in India*, Bombay.

Thorns, D.C., The Influence of Social Change upon the Farmer, *Fm. Economists*, 11.

U.N. Food and Agricultural Organisation, Fertilizers: An Annual Review of World Production, Consumption and Trade (1960–63).

U.S. Department of Agriculture and Economic Research Survey (1965), Agricultural Economic Report No. 23, Elasticity of Food Consumption Associated with Change in Income in Developing Countries, March, Washington, D.C.

United Nations, *Rural Progress Through Co-operatives,* New York, 1954.

United States Department of Agriculture, Changes in Farm Production and efficiency, *Statistical Bulletin* No. 233, 1961.

Valkenburg, S.V. (1950), The World Land use Survey, *Economic Geographer*, Vol. 26.

Van Den Noort, P.C. (1967), Agricultural Productivity in Western Europe, *Netherlands Journal of Agricultural Science*, 15 (2), pp. 115-126.

Venkateswaran, V. (1972), Failure of Crops in Maharashtra, *Hindu*, August 13.

Von Blankenberg, P. (1972), Who Leads Agricultural Modernization in India? – A Study of Some Progressive Farmers in Mysore and Punjab, *Eco. & Pol. Weekly*, Sept. 30.

Weaver, J.C. (1954), Crop-combination Regions in the Middle West, *Geographical Review,* 44, pp. 175-200.

Whetham, E.H. (1966), Diminishing Returns and Agriculture in Northern Nigeria, *Journal of Agricultural Economics*, 17.

Widdoson, E.M. (1954), Studies on the Nutritive Value of Bread and on the Effects of Variations in the Extraction Rate of Flour on the Growth of Undernourished Children, *Medical Research Council, Special Report Series*, No. 287 H.M.S.O., London.

Wortman, S. (1976), Food and Agriculture, *Scientific American*, Sept., pp. 3-11.

Wortman, S. (1980), World Food and Nutrition: The Scientific and Technological Base, *Science*, 209, (4452), 4 July, pp. 157-64.

Index